'This is a wonderful book, as wise and generous as it is
and compendious discussion of housing in all its comp
think more about how we live and how we build, and th(
Peter King, author of *The Principles of Housing* (Routledge, 2016)

'Flora Samuel's book – or manifesto – is both timely and essential reading in a political climate where dismay and quiet desperation is widespread. Samuel expresses the burning injustices in the UK's housing and explores its quality (or lack of) but also its delivery, ownership structures, and its binary model of adding value that is exclusively measured in terms of its financial benefits to private developers and landlords. Her sense of outrage that our housing is so poor is palpable and Samuel argues passionately for a different model of a housing system where value is measured in terms of health, happiness and wellbeing and a connection with the natural world. Samuel demonstrates what practical and political steps need be taken to achieve these alternative aims, covering policy, regulation, planning and also community empowerment via locally initiated models of development, concluding with a vision of a better world expressed via a truly democratic housing system might look like for the UK.'
Dr Piers Taylor, Architect, Invisible Studio

'There are few people as well-placed as Flora to talk on this subject. She does so with passion, rigour and empathy, creating one of the most comprehensive books I have read on how our built environment affects our health and wellbeing. Each chapter carefully unpicks a wide range of issues and offers solutions through well-researched, tangible examples.'
Professor Sadie Morgan OBE, dRMM Architects

Housing for Hope and Wellbeing

Housing and neighbourhoods have an important contribution to make to our wellbeing and our sense of our place in the world. This book, written for a lay audience (with policy makers firmly in mind) offers a useful and intelligible overview of our housing system and why it is in 'crisis' while acting as an important reminder of how housing contributes to social value, defined as community, health, self development and identity. It argues for a holistic digital map-based planning system that allows for the sensitive balancing of the triple bottom line of sustainability: social, environmental and economic value. It sets out a vision of what our housing system could look like if we really put the wellbeing of people and planet first, as well as a route map on how to get there.

Written primarily from the point of view of an architect, the account weaves across industry, practice and academia cross cutting disciplines to provide an integrated view of the field. The book focusses on the UK housing scene but draws on and provides lessons for housing cultures across the globe. Illustrated throughout with case studies, this is the go-to book for anyone who wants to look at housing in a holistic way.

Flora Samuel is Professor of Architecture at the University of Cambridge. She helped set up the new School of Architecture at the University of Reading and is former Head of the University of Sheffield School of Architecture and the first RIBA Vice President for Research. The author of *Why Architects Matter* (2018) she has spent the last decade researching the positive impact of good design on people. Her interests are now moving to land use and social justice, both key to addressing climate change. She is well known as industry advisor on the social value of the design of housing and places and a strong advocate of social value mapping. She is also known for her unorthodox writings on Le Corbusier, about whom she has published extensively. A mother of three daughters, she is based in Wales.

Housing for Hope and Wellbeing

FLORA SAMUEL

Routledge
Taylor & Francis Group
LONDON AND NEW YORK

Cover image: Marmalade Lane Cambridge, photo by Saul Golden

First published 2023
by Routledge
4 Park Square, Milton Park, Abingdon, Oxon OX14 4RN

and by Routledge
605 Third Avenue, New York, NY 10158

Routledge is an imprint of the Taylor & Francis Group, an informa business

© 2023 Flora Samuel

The right of Flora Samuel to be identified as author of this work has been asserted in accordance with sections 77 and 78 of the Copyright, Designs and Patents Act 1988.

All rights reserved. No part of this book may be reprinted or reproduced or utilised in any form or by any electronic, mechanical, or other means, now known or hereafter invented, including photocopying and recording, or in any information storage or retrieval system, without permission in writing from the publishers.

Trademark notice: Product or corporate names may be trademarks or registered trademarks, and are used only for identification and explanation without intent to infringe.

British Library Cataloguing-in-Publication Data
A catalogue record for this book is available from the British Library

ISBN: 978-0-367-46902-3 (hbk)
ISBN: 978-0-367-46903-0 (pbk)
ISBN: 978-1-003-03188-8 (ebk)

DOI: 10.4324/9781003031888

Typeset in Univers
by codeMantra

Printed in the United Kingdom
by Henry Ling Limited

One cannot live on bread alone...

Matthew 4:4

Contents

List of illustrations   xi
Acknowledgements   xiv

Introduction   1

Part I
The problem   11

  1   **Hopeless housing**   15

  2   **Who builds housing and how?**   29

  3   **Housing knowledge**   51

Part II
The impact of housing and neighbourhoods on hope and wellbeing   71

  4   **Measuring wellbeing and social value**   73

  5   **Connection**   83

  6   **Physical health**   98

  7   **Self actualisation**   113

  8   **Identity and belonging**   123

Part III
How to build a housing system for hope and wellbeing   135

  9   **A planning system for hope and wellbeing**   137

10	Policy for hope and wellbeing in housing and neighbourhoods	149
11	Rethinking local authorities around 20-minute communities	161
12	Professional knowledge and skills for building hope and wellbeing into housing and neighbourhoods	174
13	Common knowledge	191
14	Housing and neighbourhoods for hope and wellbeing	204
	Index	213

Illustrations

0.1	UK Green Building Council Defining social value diagram. Source: © UKGBC	4
1.1	Housing in Cardiff Bay, Wales. Source: © Flora Samuel	13
1.2	Housing Parc Derwen Wales. Source: © Flora Samuel	20
2.1	Custom-build housing at Heartlands, Camborne, Cornwall (2021). Source: © Flora Samuel	41
2.2	Custom-build site at Heartlands, Camborne, Cornwall (2021). Source: © Flora Samuel	41
4.1	Making maps with community for *Mapping Eco Social Assets* Project. Source: © Flora Samuel	77
4.2	Positive Emotions layer of community made map of an estate in Reading. Source: © Eli Hatleskog and Flora Samuel	78
4.3	Detail of community made map, part of *Mapping Eco Social Assets* Project, Reading. Source: © Eli Hatleskog and Flora Samuel	78
5.1	Understanding different types of social infrastructure. Source: © Connective Social Infrastructure, GLA, 2021	85
5.2	R-URBAN's L'Agrocité de Gennevilliers 2019. Source: © Atelier d'Architecture Autogérée	87
5.3	Rethinking Intergenerational Architecture. Source: © Matter Architecture	89
5.4	Castlemaine Court multigenerational housing by Archadia. Source: © Charlotte Wood	90
5.5	LILAC – Low Impact Living Affordable Community in Leeds. Source: © Magda Baborska-Narozny	91
5.6	Marmalade Lane, Cambridge. Source: © Saul Golden	92
6.1	Reconfigured access road at the Wintles. Source: © Bob Tomlinson and Village Makers	99
6.2	The pleasure of swimming in the harbour of Copenhagen for free. Source: © Flora Samuel	100
6.3	Spiel/Feld Marzahn is a CPUL urban agriculture project in the Berlin borough of Marzahn-Hellersdorf. Source: © Bohn & Viljoen Architects 2012	106

6.4	A CPUL project in Kokubunji, Japan, a city within the Tokyo metropolis. Source: © Bohn & Viljoen Architects, Laboratories for urban agriculture study 2019	106
6.5	Pollination Street, Incredible Edible, Todmorden. Source: © Incredible Edible Todmorden	107
6.6	Policeman with children, Incredible Edible, Todmorden. Source: © Incredible Edible Todmorden	107
7.1	Jung's Tower at Bollingen. Source: © Andrew Taylor	114
7.2	Designed with cleaning in mind. Stock Orchard Street by Sarah Wigglesworh Architects. Source: © Paul Smoothy	119
8.1	Behind the Byker Wall. Newcastle. Source: © Andrew Curtis (cc-by-sa/2.0)	124
8.2	Use of local materials at Nansledan, Cornwall. Source: © Adam Architecture/Duchy of Cormwall	125
8.3	East Quay, Watchet. Source: © Flora Samuel	126
8.4	Lock Down Library, Cardiff. Source: © Flora Samuel	129
8.5	Bozen's cottage. Source: © Adam Gibson	130
9.1	VeloCity Big Back Garden. Source: © VeloCity	140
9.2	Diagram showing layering of active and passive data to make social value maps. Source: © Stantec	142
9.3	*Community Consultation for Quality of Life* (CCQOL) Urban Room, Reading, 2022. Source: © Flora Samuel	143
9.4	Combining consultation with developing English language skills at CCQOL Urban Room, Reading. Source: © Flora Samuel	144
11.1	An illustration of a local social infrastructure system. Source: © Connective Social Infrastructure, GLA, 2021	163
11.2	Concept visual of the Ebbsfleet Health and Wellbeing Hub. Source by and in memory of Toby Carr, © Sarah Wigglesworth Architects. Thanks also to Ebbsfleet Development Corporation	165
11.3	Diagram exploring the delivery of intergenerational living in Ebbsfleet. Source by and in memory of Toby Carr, © Sarah Wigglesworth Architects. Thanks also to Ebbsfleet Development Corporation	165
11.4	Porters' Lodge, Sectie C, Eindhoven, Netherlands. Source: © Flora Samuel	166
12.1	Grangetown Pavilion, Cardiff. Source: © Flora Samuel	178
12.2	Pop Farm at Pop Brixton, Turner Works. Source: © Tim Crocker	180
12.3	Turner Works Hackney Bridge. Source: © Tim Crocker	181
12.4	Postcards expressing Weston wishes from the community. Turner Works, Super Weston. Source: © Tim Crocker	182
12.5	Play: Disrupt at work. Source: © Play Disrupt	183
12.6	The OWCH community. Source: © Joe Okpako	184
12.7	OWCH new ground housing. Source: © Galit Seligmann	185

12.8 Mass Bespoke housing under construction, Park Road, Doncaster.
Source: © Mass Bespoke   186
12.9 Mass Bespoke housing completed in Park Road, Doncaster
for Doncaster Central Development Trust. Source: © Mass Bespoke   186
13.1 A summer visit to Lammas Ecovillage. Source: © Flora Samuel   194
13.2 View out from home at Lammas Ecovillage. Source: © Flora Samuel 194
13.3 Black Mountain College proposal by Featherstone Young.
Source: © Featherstone Young   196

Acknowledgements

There are so many people to thank for all the conversations that have come together to make this book – all errors are of course entirely my own.

First I have to thank Peter King for being the first reader of this book and being so generous and insightful in his commentary. Nobody could have done it better. Special mention needs to be made of inspiring co-investigators on a series of funded research projects that I have worked on over the last few years. First of all Laura Coucill, Jonathan Rickard, Nick Rogers, David Birkbeck (Design for Homes), Fionn Stevenson, Fiona Mclachlan, Stephen Spier, Jon Sampson and David Rudlin (URBED), Robert Sakula and Cany Ash (Ash Sakula) who were my collaborators on the Arts and Humanities Research Council (AHRC) *Home Improvements* project. Jo Lintonbon, Carolyn Butterworth, Nishat Awan and Sophie Handler were collaborators on the AHRC *Cultural Value of Architects in Homes and Neighbourhoods* project. Rowena Hay was the researcher on my AHRC Leader Fellowship, *Evidencing and Communicating the Value of Architects* and also led the work on our review of post occupancy evaluation for the Architects Council of Europe. Leah de La Rosa was the Philippine base collaborator on our Newton Funded project *Mapping Eco Social Assets* on which Eli Hatleskog was researcher, a very fruitful collaboration. During this project Reading Borough Council housing Officer Ebony George gave me revelatory insight into her role. The *Better Places Toolkit* is a Knowledge Transfer Project developed with Stantec, a project that has brought me into a close collaboration with their remarkable visionary team Keith Mitchell, Jenny Hughes and Cara Mullholland. Carol MacAnally and Kimberley Steed German at the University of Reading Knowledge Transfer Centre are a force to be reckoned with and lovely people too. My friend and colleague Lorraine Farrelly at the University of Reading has been my partner in several of these projects. At the time of writing we are just embarking on the AHRC *Community Consultation for Quality of Life* Project, a collaboration with Sadie Morgan, Matt Morgan and Hani Salih at the Quality of Life Foundation, Mike Saunders, David Janner Klausner and Fatima Almawarni at Commonplace, Stephanie Edwards at Urban Symbiotics, Ruchit Purohit and Nisa Unis (Reading), Mhairi McVicar (Cardiff), Mymuna Soleman (Cardiff), John Brennan and Irina Tavera (Edinburgh), Saul Golden and Anna Skoura (Ulster) and Victoria Lawson (Sheffield). As a Trustee of the Quality of Life Foundation I have benefitted from many insightful conversations with colleagues for which I am grateful, though I should stress that opinions herein are my own.

I led the 'Place' strand within the UK Collaborative Centre for Housing Evidence led by Ken Gibb at the University of Glasgow and which includes one of my key mentors David Clapham who was kind enough to comment on parts of this text. During this period my close collaborators have been James White, Tom Kenny (formerly Royal Town Planning Institute), Bilge Serin (Glasgow), Gareth James (Glasgow), Chris Foye (Reading). The team assisted me in the development of a lengthy unpublished review of housing delivery, the underpinning of parts of this book, as are a series of interviews I undertook with policy makers and professionals on homes and neighbourhoods after the pandemic for another CaCHE report (on the impact of housing on people during the pandemic). I am also part of a large European Marie Curie Innovative Training Network RE-DWELL led by Leandro Madrazo Agudin, a consortium of housing experts from across Europe, all working to deliver truly affordable and sustainable housing. Early stage researchers Leonardo Ricaurte, Andreas Panagidis have had particular inputs into my work. Elanor Warwick of Clarion Housing has been superlatively generous and insightful across both of these projects. Her energy and enthusiasm takes some beating.

Elanor is also a member of the Edge. I have to mention Robin Nicholson and the Edge team who work indefatigably and hopefully on the improvement of our built environment. Robin who has been a particular source of inspiration and energy introduced me to his Cullinan Studio colleague Philip Graham. Working with Phil on his PhD has given access to some amazing conversations, first with supervisor Geoff Meen and then with valuation expert the late and deeply missed Sarah Sayce both of whom continued to deliver wisdom well into their 'retirement'. Sarah I so regret that we never got to deliver on the projects that we were cooking up together.

I owe a debt of thanks to the many students I have worked with over the years who have brought to my attention a steady flow of ideas and references that have enriched this book immeasurably. Notable 'PhD supervision' experiences include that of Piers Taylor of Invisible Studio and Gillian Horn of Penoyre and Prasad. 'Supervising' architectural practitioners can be very rewarding. I love writing about practitioner work as a form of co-creation so was very grateful to Mat Hinds of Taylor and Hinds architects in Tasmania when he asked me to write about Bozens Cottage which I did by interviewing his clients Doug and Ali Bridges and their building contractor Russell Chambers who reminded me of the role that good architecture plays in all this. Since 2016 I've been meeting with a group of leaders on research in practice, the Research Practice Leads, now led by Darryl Chen (Hawkins Brown), Mark Lumley (Architype) and Marilys Ramos (PRP). It was this group that set up and developed the *Social Value Toolkit for Architecture*, published by the RIBA, a turning point in my research. There were many practitioners involved in this journey but particular mention must be made of Felicie Kriekler at Assael Architecture, Riette Oosthuizen at HTA LLP and Kelly Watson at Hatch Regeneris (social value guru par excellence). On the subject of social value

I should mention Rob Wolfe (CHY Consultancy) who never ceases to amaze with his insight.

Rebecca Solnit writes 'underneath the task of writing a particular piece is the general one of making a self who can make the work you are meant to make' (2020, p. 122). I am very fortunate to live in a place where people talk to each other, celebrate together and help each other through the darkest of times. I thank our house that has stood here since 1903 and has been so much more than a roof for my family for the last 25 years. My gratitude to Alex, Alice, Oti and Emilia who have taught me the meaning of home knows no bounds. It takes some courage to write a book that is so unfashionably hopeful, but it is one that I feel compelled to write. Like Solnit 'what I'd wanted to offer is encouragement, a word that, though it carries the stigma of niceness, literally means to instil courage' (Solnit, 2020, p. 212).

Alice Ojeda and Michelle Gunn have been fellow travellers on the journey towards our Housing Co-Op Recommon. Please do sign up for our newsletter and get involved www.recommon.org.uk

Hopefully this book will give you as many ideas as these people have given me.

Introduction

To reimagine Britain we must thus reimagine housing.

(Welby, 2018, p. 139)

Our homes impact on our lives in so many ways, something that has become acutely apparent during lockdown. This is a book about making a housing system that foregrounds wellbeing as its most important outcome. I freely admit that it is a manifesto. It is written in the belief that returning to business as usual after the pandemic is not really an option.

My professional interest is in 'social value' (Samuel, 2020) a term which 'encompasses environmental, economic and social wellbeing' (UKGBC, 2021, p. 7), but leaves most people cold which is why use the term 'wellbeing' as a zip file for my concern with improving mental and physical health. Wellbeing isn't ideal either, as it is so complex and recent, and can translate poorly into other languages. There are many definitions of wellbeing or quality of life out there – if you want to get into the intricacies of this look no further than the *Journal of Happiness Studies*. I will admit in advance to some blurring between them. The one I am most interested in is 'eudaimonic wellbeing', the highest sort (Deci and Ryan, 2006) which relates to having a sense of purpose beyond yourself – in other words hope – one of the reasons why people with spiritual beliefs tend to be more happy. Empowerment plays an important role in this as without it a person or community will be unable to achieve its purpose. 'It holds that the key question to ask, when comparing societies and assessing them for their basic decency or justice, is, "What is each person able to do and to be"?' (Nussbaum, 2011, p. 18). This is the essence of the 'capabilities approach', an emergent theoretical framework for the study of wellbeing that loosely underpins the argument herein.

There is no denying that where you live impacts on what you do. Racialised white and identifying as female, this narrative will inevitably be coloured by, and sometimes illustrated with, by my own privileged but downwardly mobile 'housing pathway' (Clapham, 2005) that begins in a modernist house in North London, built by my father an architect (coupled with a colonising holiday house in Ireland), passing through student housing, and dismal private sector rental in London, to owning a small flat in London (filled with lodgers), escaping London (because we lived in the catchment area of the 'worst school in Britain') to damp and smelly rental accommodation in Sheffield, to our small first house in Plymouth as I tried to develop my career. It finishes in a small Victorian terrace house in inner city Cardiff, Wales (with allotment garden), where I have lived for almost 30 years. It cannot help being imbued with the rage and impotence I've experienced firsthand as representative of our community during numerous planning battles against the incursion of businesses into our quiet street. This account is also coloured by my husband's journey of helping his father build a constantly growing house in Lima, Peru (now filled with tenants to provide much needed income), living as a migrant on sofas in London flats, subletting council flats, squatting and private sector rental within Houses in Multiple Occupation (HMOs), before ending up with me. It is coloured by my brother's precarious life on disability benefits, living at home into his 30s and then moving into an isolated council maisonette in Tottenham. It is coloured by my mother's experience of living in a 'padded cell', a newly built, expensive and unsustainable assisted living scheme for the elderly and by my father spending the last two years of his life in a 15 m^2 room in a care home with one tiny window too high to see out of from the bed (£1,500 a week). It is coloured by my oldest daughter's experience of renting a damp, studio apartment with PVC windows clouded by internal condensation and mould regularly painted over by the landlord. It is also coloured by my experience of trying to set up co-operative housing with a group of young women and being thwarted by our inability to access suitable land to do it on. Why does the planning system make it so extremely hard for communities to help themselves? As a mother of three daughters and a teacher I am fully aware of the worries of the next generation about where they will end up living, so at odd with media presentations of a good or average life, and in many ways this book is written for them.

What I offer here is a speculation based on my intense professional immersion within the field of housing, as well as a series of funded research projects in this area. This book seeks to do the difficult task of bridging between lived experience and expert viewpoints, crossing a divide that has gender and class dimensions as well as one of race. I hope that all this contributes to making *Housing Hope and Wellbeing* a bit less dry and more inclusive than the average book on housing. Housing and neighbourhoods are generally made for 'default man' (Perry, 2014; Criado Perez, 2019). This book tries to highlight ways to do things differently.

My territory is what Ernest Boyer calls the 'scholarship of integration' and 'application', making connections across disciplines, 'placing specialities in larger context', often educating non-specialists too (Boyer, 1997, p. 18). Such diversity is challenging at a methodological level, requiring what Andrew Abbott calls the 'usual disclaimer a synthetic writer makes to area specialists' (Abott, 1988, p. xii). Further it is hard to set the limits of a poorly defined entity, housing, about which very little is known and 'to keep the coverage even', an academically desirable quality. Added to this is the fact that wellbeing and social value are mutable terms, changing in meaning according to context. Loretta Lees and Elanor Warwick's book *Defensible Space on the Move* offers a wonderful illustration of the way in which housing terminology shifts through use over time (Lees and Warwick, 2022).

According to research housing comprises four dimensions: physical structure, the home environment, the neighbourhood infrastructure and the community. All of these can have a direct or indirect effect on physical, social and mental health, and two or more dimensions combined may have a greater impact (Braubach, Jacobs and Ormandy, 2011). One of the biggest challenges of this book has been choosing the words to describe what needs to be done to make a housing system for wellbeing. This has to do with the history of the field, a process in which new words have regularly bubbled up to the surface usually at the behest of government. Professionals and local authorities scurry to align themselves with this new language if they want to get funded. Terminology tends to be tainted by ideology while being unintelligible to the public at large. Take, for example, 'place', the darling of New Labour at the start of this millennium through the conduit of CABE, the Commission for Architecture and the Built Environment a group of worthy people who were doing their best to get design onto the neoliberal government agenda, something they were quite successful at. 'Place' is currently writ quite large at the centre of planning policy, at least in the devolved authorities. 'Placemaking', although generally founded on good intentions, tends to be something that is done top-down by design professionals and others. Paternalistic (and gendered) terms from around this era includes: 'stakeholders', a definition that subtly prioritises businesses over locals; 'masterplan'; 'value management' and the truly dismal 'managing expectations'. Many more soul sapping examples will be encountered on this journey. As if this wasn't enough we have academics beavering away in the background 'problematising', in other words dismantling perhaps the only useful word we have to describe what this book is all about – community. Community is a useful catch all to talk about the people (and biodiversity) that lives in an area. Unfortunately though 'councils view communities as a homogenous lump' observed one community member we spoke with on a panel. 'Community remains a contested political space in many countries, but in both real and virtual worlds there is abundant evidence that the tide of individualism – epitomized by Margaret Thatcher's claim in the 1980s that "there is no such thing as society" – is receding' (McLaren and Agyeman, 2017, p. 38).

I have a geeky interest in quantitative measures that goes against the grain of my very being – feminists treat them with correct suspicion – as they are such powerful tools for communicating, and indeed solidifying, injustice. 'Reducing housing to quantities allows us to compartmentalise problems and posit easy solutions. But in doing so we actually forget what housing is for' (King, 2017, p. 1). Despite acknowledgement from the Ministry of Housing Communities and Local Government that 'A home is more than four walls and a roof – it is a symbol of security and a stake in our society' (MHCLG, 2020, p. 4) housing continues to be measured in numbers with little or no consideration of design or location. This seems all the more strange given the growing recognition of the impact of design on health and wellbeing (UKGBC, 2016; Design Council, 2018).

At the moment there is a 'cognitive dissonance' and a 'dangerous misalignment' between the way people want to live and the metrics used to measure success, usually money (Strickler, 2019, p. 12). As Mariana Mazzucato has illustrated so well in her book *The Value of Everything* economists have 'an intellectually impoverished idea of value' which is 'just taken as read' (2018, p. 8). I am going

Introduction

Figure 0.1
UK Green Building Council Defining social value diagram.
Source: © UKGBC.

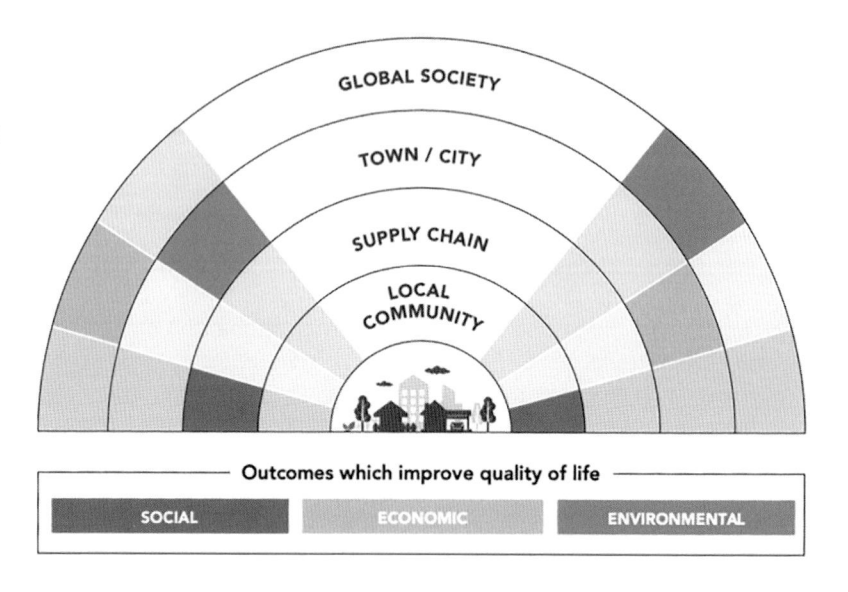

to argue for a more holistic understanding of value, one that encompasses social, environmental and economic value, the commonly known triple bottom line of sustainability. These are intrinsically linked, as this diagram by the UK Green Building Council makes clear (Figure 0.1), but I am going to try to prise social value away from its better known sisters to give it a temporary taste of fame. This means that urgent topics such as the climate emergency and the challenge of retrofitting the existing housing stock (Bergman and Foxon, 2020) will only be addressed in passing. A premise of this book is that climate change is fundamentally a social justice issue and that the collective action needed to tackle the climate change emergency won't happen unless it is made easy and intuitive for the majority of people.

Increasingly our homes are part of what Marshall McLuhan famously called the 'global village'. Communities are not the tight knit traditional local networks they are usually portrayed as. They are instead 'loosely bounded, sparsely knit networks of specialised ties' that cover wide geographic areas (Wellman, 2018). In this book I am going to be making the case for a rebalancing of the two, the local and the global, re-emphasising the unique nature of where we actually live in contributing to our happiness. I will make a distinction between the neoliberal term globalisation, the opening up of markets and the de-regulation of multinational corporations to enabling them to do their business across the globe, and what Teilhard de Chardin called 'planetisation', improved connectivity between one another and the planet (Samuel, 1999). New developments and discoveries are blurring the boundaries between ourselves, the digital, physical and biological. This, in turn, 'affects social and environmental ecologies as well as individual psychic and shared emotional landscapes' (Braidotti, 2019, p. 2). This has to be acknowledged in discussions of housing.

This book was written during the pandemic, a lively time for social and environmental change. My focus is on Britain, but includes ideas and examples relevant to the world over as access to 'adequate housing' is a basic human right (OHCHR, 2021). Within the UK housing is devolved to the four nations Wales, Northern Ireland, Scotland and England, each with different levels of funding dictated by the Westminster government. I live in Wales and work in England so the differences in policy are very evident to me. While design may have lost its hold on the government in Westminster it has gained strength in the devolved parliament of Scotland where it is now enshrined in the Scottish National Outcomes Framework (Scottish Government, 2011) against which the achievements of its government are measured. Scotland continues to pursue a place-based agenda (Scottish Government, 2013) with strong links made between the health service and planning. The Scottish Place Standard is one of the best tools we have for evaluating the quality of places (Place Standard Scotland, 2019). Meanwhile in Wales the predominantly Labour national assembly is developing a remarkable set of place-based policies, for example, *Planning Policy Wales* (Welsh Gov, 2018), which focusses on wellbeing, both now and in the future inspired by the visionary Wellbeing of Future Generations Act (Wales) 2015, one that may soon extend to the rest of the UK. Meanwhile the Northern Ireland Housing Executive is working hard, in difficult circumstances to make sure everyone has access to an 'affordable and decent home, appropriate to their needs, in a safe and attractive place' (NIHE, 2021). Even the most aspirational national governments are limited by the financial packages that are allocated to them by the centre. As community wellbeing is so high on the agenda in the devolved nations this book largely concentrates on England where policy tends to focus its gaze on a circle of high value land roughly 100 miles in radius around London.

I will argue that the creation of a housing system for health and happiness (and the planet) can never really be achieved under the prevailing discourse of neoliberalism, 'a collection of powerful, but loosely defined and contested ideas' (Clapham, 2019, p. 3). Neoliberalism is characterised by de-regulation, with governance left largely to the market, but this doesn't work in a system that is already sedimented with injustice. 'A truly free market would apply principles of zero hours or a gig economy between people who were equally powerful. Where there are asymmetries of power the market is never free' (Welby, 2018, p. 163).

Neoliberalism promotes unearned income and speculative wealth, things that bleed value out of the world around us, wealth extraction rather than wealth creation. An increasing amount of asset wealth is held in residential investment (Piketty, 2014). The impact of neoliberalism on housing has been in terms of privatisation, marketisation, commodification, financialisation and individualisation (Clapham, 2019, p. 4). In this situation housing ceases to be a place of shelter but becomes instead a means of wealth accumulation. As more housing is used as an investment, prices rise and less is available to the population at large.

Writing a book about a fixed housing system for the UK might seem very idealistic, but I have taken heart from a range of other writers and commentators who are putting themselves out there to say it doesn't need to be like this, not least our 'national treasure' veteran wildlife TV presenter David Attenborough whose documentary, *A Life on Our Planet* (2020), begins and ends in the now verdant city of Chernobyl, a potent symbol of nature's power to fight back against toxic technologies made by a species seemingly hell-bent on its own extinction. *Housing Hope and Wellbeing* is but one of a growing tide of work that anticipate a future beyond neoliberalism in politics (Monbiot, 2017), economics (Raworth, 2017), environmentalism (Webb, Hawkey and Tingey, 2016, p. 34), entrepreneurialism (Strickler, 2019), urban design (McLaren and Agyeman, 2017), planning (Aalbers, 2013), housing (Clapham, 2019), ageing population (Robinson, Green and Wilson, 2019) and values (Welby, 2018). In terms of race, Emma Dabiri argues that artificial classifications of blackness and whiteness have their roots in capitalism, the stirring up of trouble between racial groups being used as a smokescreen to distract disempowered people of every sort from tackling the true source of their ills, inequality, together. She proposes, as do I, a rebuilding of the commons to give opportunity to all (Dabiri, 2021). For this to happen we have to accept 'enough' in housing (King, 2008). This requires a rather different world view.

Oddly enough, in my opinion, it is Archbishop of Canterbury, Justin Welby's *Reimaging Britain* (revised in 2021) that addresses the issue of housing in the most comprehensive and visionary way perhaps because he looks at the situation from the perspective of 'of what is good in absolute and permanent terms' (Welby, 2018, p. 16). That society is moving in a positive direction, though it might not always look that way, is endorsed by the scientific work of Steven Pinker (2012). I have personally been fortunate enough to see radical improvements in the treatment of women in my own lifetime, this being one subset of inequality more widely. Like Rebecca Solnit I see hopefulness as a form of resistance to the powerlessness pedalled to us through the media (Solnit, 2020).

Much of the discourse of housing and urban design neatly sidesteps the issue of faith. While what Welby calls 'privatised religion' and its internal power plays may be distasteful, to exclude spirituality from the account completely is to exclude the experiences of many people (in the last census around 75% identified with a religion) including the many 'non white ethnic minority immigrant populations' who tend to be far more religious than the white population (Crockett and Voas, 2006). We also have to pay attention to what Jay Griffiths calls the 'economy of the imagination' (Griffiths, 2013, p. 347) and the narratives that make us human. I will argue that the arts and humanities play a vital role in enabling us to process our responsibilities to ourselves, our families and our neighbours (Bazalgette, 2017). These are so often left out of the story of housing but will try to bring them into the fold here.

Although housing is a very political subject, and I will refer to many left leaning thinkers, it will be seen that concerns with community and housing supply tend to transcend partisan lines. Indeed the brain behind the Social Value Act 2012 (England) that underpins much of my argument was Conservative. Conceived out of a growing unease about the way public money was being used on goods and services its aim was to cause a cultural change within the procurement system. In this book I make the case for 'community wealth building', a 'people-centred approach to local economic development, which redirects wealth back into the local economy, and places control and benefits into the hands of local people' (CLES, 2019). Part of this has to come through a rethinking of our welfare state – social security, health, education and housing – set up in more public spirited times to provide a safety net for all but which is being dismantled piece by piece before our very eyes (Kemeny, 2001). A fundamental problem of the welfare state, as Hilary Cottam illustrates so beautifully in her book *Radical Help* (2018), is that it is so top-down. It fails to capitalise on the potential of citizens to contribute to the making of society, neighbourhoods and indeed homes. A system is needed that balances a need for individual autonomy with collective good.

Housing Hope and Wellbeing is in three parts. The first sets out the current housing scene, the people responsible for housing delivery and the knowledge that underpins the process. The second part looks at the way in which housing contributes to wellbeing (social value), the reasons why it is so important to get it right both at the scale of the town or city and at the scale of the home. It begins with a discussion of connectivity between people and with nature before moving onto issues of health. This is closely linked to mental health and the way in which homes impact on individual self development and the ways in which neighbourhoods impact on collective identity and belonging. One issue that spans across them all is the importance of empowerment, as well as the need for connection with the natural world. The third part sets out a vision for a housing system built on knowledge of what works, gathered spatially through maps. It begins with policy and regulation and its impact on local authorities and planning. The discussion then moves to the knowledge and skills needed to make this vision happen. This includes harnessing the voice of people in the co-creation of their environments. The book finishes with what I hope is an enticing vision of what a housing system for hope and wellbeing might actually look like.

Note
Justin Welby quotes, © Justin Welby, 2018, *Reimagining Britain*, Bloomsbury Continuum, an imprint of Bloomsbury Publishing Plc.

References
Aalbers, M.L. (2013) 'Neoliberalism is dead…long live neoliberalism', *International Journal of Urban and Regional Research*, 37(3), pp. 1083–1090.

Abott, A. (1988) *The System of Professions*. Chicago: University of Chicago Press.

Bazalgette, P. (2017) *The Empathy Instinct: How to Create a More Civil Society*. London: John Murray.

Bergman, N. and Foxon, T.J. (2020) 'Reframing policy for the energy efficiency challenge: insights from housing retrofits in the UK', *Energy Research and Social Science*, 63, 101386.

Boyer, E. (1997) *Scholarship Reconsidered: Priorities of the Professoriate*. London: John Wiley & Sons.

Braidotti, R. (2019) *Posthuman Knowledge*. Cambridge: Polity Press.

Braubach, M., Jacobs, D.E. and Ormandy, D. (2011) *Environmental Burden of Disease*. Europe: World Health Organization. Available at: http://www.euro.who.int/__data/assets/pdf_file/0003/142077/e95004.pdf.

Clapham, D. (2005) *The Meaning of Housing: A Pathways Approach*. Policy Press.

Clapham, D. (2019) *Remaking Housing Policy: An International Study*. London: Routledge.

CLES. (2019) *What is Community Wealth Building?*, The National Organisation for Local Economies. Available at: https://cles.org.uk/community-wealth-building/what-is-community-wealth-building/.

Cottam, H. (2018) *Radical Help*. London: Virago.

Criado Perez, D. (2019) *Invisible Women*. London: Chato and Windus.

Crockett, A. and Voas, D. (2006) 'Generations of decline: religious change in 20th century Britain', *Journal for the Scientific Study of Religion*, 45(4), pp. 567–584.

Dabiri, E. (2021) *What White People Can Do Next: From Allyship to Coalition*. London: Penguin.

Deci, E.L. and Ryan, R.M. (2006) 'Hedonia, eudaimonia and well-being: an introduction', *Journal of Happiness Studies*, 9, pp. 1–11.

Design Council. (2018) *Healthy Placemaking*. London: Design Council/Social Change UK. Available at: https://www.designcouncil.org.uk/sites/default/files/asset/document/Healthy_Placemaking_Report.pdf.

Gray, C. and Woodfine, L. (2018) *Adverse Childhood Experiences (ACESs) and Housing Vulnerability - Report and Evaluation of ACE-informed Training for Housing*. Public Health Wales. Available at: http://www.wales.nhs.uk/sitesplus/documents/888/5%20ACE%20Informed%20Training%20for%20Housing.pdf.

Griffiths, J. (2013) *Kith: The Riddle of the Childscape*. London: Penguin.

Kemeny, J. (2001) 'Comparative housing and welfare: theorising the relationship', *Journal of Housing in the Built Environment*, 16, pp. 53–70.

Lees, L. and Warwick, E. (2022) *Defensible Space on the Move*. London: Wiley.

McLaren, D. and Agyeman, J. (2017) *Sharing Cities: A Case for Truly Smart and Sustainable Cities*. Cambridge MA: MIT.

MHCLG. (2020) *Planning for the Future*. Available at: https://assets.publishing.service.gov.uk/government/uploads/system/uploads/attachment_data/file/872091/Planning_for_the_Future.pdf.

Monbiot, G. (2017) *Out of the Wreckage: A New Politics for an Age of Crisis*. London: Verso.

NIHE. (2021) *Our Vision for Housing in Northern Ireland*. Available at: https://nihe.gov.uk/About-Us/Our-Mission-Vision/Our-vision.

Nussbaum, M. (2011) *Creating Capabilities*. Cambridge MA: Harvard University Press.

OHCHR. (2021) *The Right to Adequate Housing Toolkit*. Available at: https://www.ohchr.org/EN/Issues/Housing/toolkit/Pages/RighttoAdequateHousingToolkit.aspx.

Perry, G. (2014) 'The Rise and Fall of Default Man', *New Statesman*. Available at: https://www.newstatesman.com/long-reads/2014/10/grayson-perry-rise-and-fall-default-man.

Piketty, T. (2014) *Capital in the Twenty First Century*. Cambridge, MA: Harvard University Press.

Pinker, S. (2012) *The Better Angels of Our Nature: A History of Violence and Humanity*. London: Penguin.

Place Standard Scotland. (2019) *Place Standard: How Good is Our Place?* Available at: https://www.placestandard.scot/.

Raworth, K. (2017) *Doughnut Economics: Seven Ways to Think Like a 21st Century Economist*. London: Random House.

Robinson, D., Green, S. and Wilson, I. (2019) 'Housing options for older people in a reimagined housing system: a case study from England', *International Journal of Housing Policy* [Preprint]. doi:10.1080/19491247.2019.1644020.

Samuel, F. (1999) 'Le Corbusier, Teilhard de Chardin and the Planetisation of Mankind', *Journal of Architecture*, 4, pp. 149–165.

Samuel, F. (2020) *Social Value Toolkit for Architecture*. London: RIBA. Available at: https://www.architecture.com/knowledge-and-resources/resources-landing-page/social-value-toolkit-for-architecture.

Scottish Government. (2013) *Creating Places: A policy statement on architecture and place for Scotland*. Available at: https://www2.gov.scot/Publications/2013/06/9811.

Scottish Government, S.A.H. (2011) *National Outcomes*. Available at: http://www.scotland.gov.uk/About/Performance/scotPerforms/outcome (Accessed: 16 April 2014).

Solnit, R. (2020) *Recollections of My Non-Existence*. London: Granta.

Strickler, Y. (2019) *This Could Be Our Future: A Manifesto for a More Generous World*. London: Penguin.

UKGBC. (2016) *Health and Wellbeing in Homes*. Available at: https://media.prp-co.uk/web/reports/PRP_UKGBC-HealthyHomesReport.pdf.

Webb, J., Hawkey, D. and Tingey, M. (2016) 'Governing cities for sustainable energy: The UK case', *Cities*, 54, pp. 28–35.

Welby, J. (2018) *Reimagining Britain*. London: Bloomsbury.

Wellman, B. (ed.) (2018) *Networks in the Global Village: Life in Contemporary Communities*. New York: Routledge.

Welsh Gov. (2018) *Planning Policy Wales*. Available at: https://gov.wales/planning-policy-wales.

Part I
The problem

60

Figure 1.1
Housing in Cardiff Bay, Wales. Source: © Flora Samuel.

Chapter 1

Hopeless housing

We can focus on policies and on quantities; we can argue over white papers, policies and population projections, but what matters is how housing is used by those currently occupying it.

(King, 2017, p. 1).

Housing isn't just about providing four affordable walls and a leakproof roof, Housing has to be conceived as a foundation from which to build individual and community hope and wellbeing (Figure. 1.1). Instead, for many, it has become a pervasive source of worry (McKee and Soaita, 2018).

Roughly 65% of homes in England are owner-occupied, meaning that 35% of people are renting (DLUHC, 2021). We deduce from this that the 65% that own are likely to be fairly satisfied with their accommodation. However, even if contented with their own home – and people always tend to want more (Foye, 2017) – they are likely to be concerned about where their children are going to live. This chapter, describing the limited offerings of the current housing situation in Britain, focuses on the 35% who rent – 19% in the private sector and the rest in the public sector (DLUHC, 2021), and of course with the homeless. These are the people most constrained by lack of choice.

I start by providing some context about where we live and who owns our homes before moving on to its impact on wellbeing. From here I move on to reductions in the provision of social infrastructure and the way it impacts, in particular, on the most vulnerable contributing to an epidemic of loneliness and mental health issues. This agenda finishes with a discussion of social infrastructure and the way its poor distribution is contributing to the terrible inequalities that we see in Britain today. None of this is helped by crime and reports of crime, a subject too big for me to enter into here (ONS, 2017). Please feel free to skip this bleak but necessary context chapter if you are already familiar with the terrain.

Where do we live?
Housing comes in all shapes and sizes. The majority of the 24 million homes in England are houses 19% of households live in the private rental sector, 17% in social rented housing and the rest on owner occupied homes (DLUHC, 2021).

About 40% of homes were built prior to 1939 (Sunnikka-Blank and Galvin, 2016, p. 97). Since 1991 levels of construction have only amounted to about 0.5% of the existing stock per year, with amounts of demolition even less (Lowe and Lai Fong, 2020). This means that a great many houses are old and leaky. The Committee on Climate Change has identified a Government spend of £15 billion needed each year to reduce carbon emissions from domestic housing (NFB, 2019, p. 7).

Sixty per cent of homes have three or more bedrooms, rising to 74% for owner-occupied homes; and 41% of households are families, compared with 28% one-person households and 28% couples (DCLG, 2014). Single occupation homes are inherently less sustainable (Ivanova, 2021), yet the number of people living alone increased by 8.3% over the years 2011–2021 (ONS, 2022). It is therefore no surprise that an increasing number of homes are being divided into Houses in Multiple Occupation (HMOs) (DCLG, 2017).

In the UK 80% of households live in houses, with 20% in flats most of which are in blocks of three storeys or less. Most owner occupied homes take the form of houses, while social and private sector homes are more likely to take the form of flats (DLUHC, 2021). High rise housing can have negative psychological and social impacts, on people, particularly those in low income groups (Kalantari and Shepley, 2021). Minority groups and young people are the most likely to live in rented flats (MHCLG, 2018, p. 5), a situation which is commonly associated with poor physical and mental health (Gray and Woodfine, 2018; Bimpson and Preece, 2019), with the situation being particularly bad for families (Young Foundation, 2019). Tenants categorised as Black, Asian and disabled are more likely to suffer from housing discrimination (Butler, 2021). While the rental sector does offer some good quality accommodation and professional facilities management 'poor quality property is most prevalent and poor management practices unacceptably frequent' (Marsh and Gibb, 2019, p. 6), with implications for health (Barton and Kenny, 2018). 'Not only do home owners benefit financially, through state-led tax breaks, at the expense of renters; they also benefit from having higher status than renters, and from 'being normal'' (Foye, Clapham and Gabrieli, 2018, p. 1303).

Home ownership

In the UK recent government rhetoric and policy strongly favours home ownership. 'This government believes in supporting people who are working hard to own their home' (MHCLG, 2020, p. 4). There is a moral element here that suggests homes owners are less lazy when research suggests that the opposite might in fact the case (Blanden and Machin, 2017). Interestingly there is no clear cut relationship between housing tenure and voting patterns (Swift, 2021). That lack of access to decent housing is an issue that crosses party lines can be seen from an article on 'Conservative Home' website.

> I've never really wanted to write about or research housing. I have no idea what a good planning policy would be. I'm just someone who thought as a child they would grow up and live in a nice house. I feel lied to in a way, as

I expect many other people my age do, when we were told that 'hard work pays off' at school. Actually, it just goes towards landlords.

(Gill, 2021).

The fact that many young people don't have the same access to owner-occupation as their parents is an intergenerational inequity that is getting worse due to the house price inflation that continues to widen the gap between owners and renters. Young people are now having to rent housing long term, an idea that sits awkwardly with societal norms and aspirations (McKee et al., 2017). What can be seen here is a very neoliberal shift to the private sector. Margaret Thatcher's Conservative Government came into power in 1979 bringing it with it the Right to Buy legislation (Disney and Luo, 2015) and the radical reduction of state-funded, social rented housing and housing departments (Boughton, 2018) that has been so destructive to the public provision of housing ever since (Murie, 2016). In Wales 90% of social housing was sold through Right to Buy, 40% of it is now for rent with the Private Rental Sector (Dicks, 2020).

Public spending on housing has lagged behind expenditure on other public services over the past 20 years, with the focus of spending being increasingly on housing benefits rather than investment in new social or affordable housing (Capital Economics, 2019, p. 2). This means that a considerable amount of public money is funnelling through benefits into the pockets of the private sector landlords. The number of households living in the private sector has steeply increased to 4.5 million in 2017 (ONS, 2019), with the number of people living in social rented housing reducing 4.5 million (ONS, 2019). Liam Halligan's book *Home Truths* provides some very useful historical context for this situation (2019).

Over recent years home sales have plummeted. The people who do tend to move generally have mortgages already (Hudson and Green, 2017, p. 8), this despite government efforts to assist people to get onto the housing ladder, for example, the government's Help to Buy scheme. I was once in a meeting where a volume house builder had one word to describe this kind of policy from his perspective – 'kerrching!'. This is because the resultant scrabble to buy leads to inflation in price, ultimately making it harder for people to own their own homes, particularly since household incomes have remained roughly static (Anacker, 2019).

The UK government defines affordability as being below market rent (Pickerill, 2019, p. 77), meaning that so called 'affordable' housing is out of reach of most people. The waiting list for social rented housing is therefore predicted to double to 2 million with evictions in the aftermath of the pandemic (Savage, 2020). The shortfall in social rented housing means that numbers of households are forced to live in temporary accommodation at enormous expense to the public purse. The grim reality of this situation and its impact on children in particular is well portrayed in Jacqueline Wilson's book *The Bed and Breakfast Star* (2006). People on housing lists are put into a very difficult position as some of the permanent accommodation they are offered may well be of a terrible standard or be located miles away from jobs, family and friends. If they don't accept the first place they are offered they have to accept the second or they will be removed from the housing list altogether. The situation is so bad in Wales that night shelters are being used as 'interim accommodation'. If an applicant turns down 'interim accommodation' in a squalid Bed and Breakfast they forfeit the long-term right to accommodation. A cynical council might use this to their advantage.

Although we are constantly told there isn't enough housing the irony is that there is now more housing space per person than ever (Dorling, 2014). A review of 'low use' domestic property in England and Wales suggests that its value is £123 billion and (Bourne, 2019). It seems that over 11,000 in England and Wales have sat empty for over ten years (Mason, 2018) while very few Local Authorities are taking advantage of Empty Dwelling Management Orders (EDMOs) to buy disused property for social housing purposes (Mason, 2018). London, in particular, has been seen as a good place to invest through the acquisition of domestic property. This can cause local inflation of house prices that trickles down to less expensive properties (Bourne, 2019). Airbnb can mean that properties that would normally be rented out long term are being taken off the long-term rental market with the increased income and demand for houses in particular areas triggering gentrification (Marsh, 2020). Cornwall has a particular issue with this (Letcher, 2021). Second home ownership in desirable touristic areas is extremely problematic for the people who live nearby (Bourne, 2019). All this contributes to oppressive buzz of injustice felt by many in the UK today. The Welsh were known for burning down holiday homes in the 1980s, the feeling is similarly high today.

Homelessness

The blight of homelessness will not be solved without sorting out the general 'housing regime' (Clapham, 2019, p. 10). Homeless people suffer from a complete inability to exclude others from their personal space (King, 2004), this powerlessness having major ramifications for wellbeing. Homelessness comes in various forms: 'roofless' sleeping rough; 'houseless' people in homeless shelters; 'insecure' people in temporary accommodation or under threat in some way and lastly people living in 'inadequate' accommodation (ETHOS, 2017). England's recent record on universal homelessness prevention is 'dismal', with the situation being particularly bad in London and the South East (Fitzpatrick, Mackie and Wood, 2019, p. 3). In ignoring the terrible plight of people living on the street, with many suffering from trauma and self medicated through addictions, we are living under a cloud of collective shame that does nobody any good.

There are a range of emergency housing options that are offered to homeless people including: hostels; refuges; supported accommodation and less supported forms of temporary accommodation such as Bed and Breakfast hotels, private hotels and other shared forms of private housing. Many of these solutions can be scary and inappropriate options for people who might be feeling particularly vulnerable, the situation being worse for refugee and asylum-seeking women and children who have no recourse to public funds. Gender strongly impacts on the experience of homelessness (Hastings, Mackenzie and Earley, 2021) – a pervasive feeling of vulnerability, reinforced by the media, can make women's experience of public space very different from that of men (Solnit, 2020).

Those who are homeless are doubly dispossessed. Homelessness is a curse both from its physical dimensions and also for the role that homemaking plays in self actualisation and identity formation. Carin Tunåker illustrates this with her remarkable anthropological study of LGBT youth in Kent. 'To these young people, the "house" and "home" become a source of confusion and precariousness', with their own state of homelessness referring to a perceived position outside of societal norms (2015, p. 253). Further individuals with 'lifetime homelessness' (having ever experienced homelessness lasting more than one month) have been seen to have experienced higher rates of all Adverse Childhood Experiences (ACEs) than individuals without lifetime homelessness (Roos *et al.*, 2013) and are therefore prone to all manner of health issues.

Health and housing design

Even if people do have a roof to call their own, poorly designed and constructed homes are not delivering the healthy environments that we might expect. Although environmental conditions are not the focus of this book they need to be briefly mentioned because of their impact on wellbeing. According to Building Research Establishment (BRE) calculations poor housing costs the National Health service (NHS) £1.4 billion a year (Nicol and Garrett, 2019, p. 6). Whatever you think of their methodology – which to me looks quite conservative – the number is high. In a temperate country like the UK design can achieve good levels of comfort without the need for any energy input in all but the most extreme weather conditions, yet we regularly hear accounts of vulnerable people suffering and even dying in their homes because of overheating and cold (as well as fuel poverty), with the situation is only getting worse as extreme weather conditions prevail and the cost of living rises.

At the same time the air quality within our homes is impacting on our health through things like toxic household products, off gassing from fire retardants in our furniture, poor ventilation and mould (NICE, 2020). A fugged up, poorly ventilated, centrally heated life poisoned by a cocktail of toxic cleaning fluids, chemicals in our clothes and furniture, charged up by Wi-Fi and electronic gizmos – with a soupçon of mould thrown in – and lacking the zing of morning light to ensure our circadian rhythms stay on track. These are no good thing for our bodies or our minds. So toxic are our interior environments that concentrations of pollution are likely to be worse inside the home than outside (Sharpe *et al.*, 2018). That is saying something given the terrible quality of air in the UK, caused in the main by transport pollution.

Transport infrastructure

Walkability, and cycling are simple, democratic and healthy ways to get about but other types of transportation, the ones that need expensive infrastructure, have been consistently prioritised over forms of active travel (Urban Transport Group, 2016). Local authorities often waive basic active travel requirements for new homes such is the pressure on them to deliver their targets (FIT, 2018, p. 5). Standard volume house builder developments include around 35 units per hectare – a loose fit approach that favours car usage and works against transport provision. One example is Parc Derwen, a new housing development outside Bridgend which has no public transport links because the route is not viable for

Figure 1.2
Housing Parc Derwen Wales.
Source: © **Flora Samuel.**

private sector bus operators. Here the public realm is dominated by cars (Figure 1.2). The privatisation of transportation in the UK, resulting in prohibitively expensive costs to commuters and a lack of infrastructure investment and others has been identified as a human rights issue (Alston, Khawaja and Riddell, 2021).

Green space

The vital role that balconies, gardens, urban parks, national parks and foot paths play in physical and mental health and happiness for every generation has never been more obvious than during the pandemic, particularly for those poor souls living in over-crowded conditions with no windows (as sometimes happens with office to rental converted accommodation). Supply does not however meet demand (Boulton, Dedekorkut-Howes and Byrne, 2018). There is no statutory requirement for cash strapped local authorities to provide or look after parks, one reason why many are loathe to adopt green space in new developments (White *et al*., 2020).

We are fortunate in Britain to have a hard-won network of public foot paths that provide connection, exercise and pleasure. However the vast majority of our land has been rendered inaccessible by private landlords (Shrubsole, 2019). The advent of factory farming, the destruction of hedgerows and the liberal application of pesticides and fertilisers have made some parts of the landscape inhospitable and indeed dangerous to humans, and wildlife alike. The ecosystems of the UK are now extremely meagre compared to those over the Channel in Europe and are now generally recognised as being pale shadow of what they once were.

> For statistics and columns of figures do not begin to express the effects of the changes at a personal and interior level. For some people agricultural intensification has triggered and emotionally charged, even visceral response, at the root of which is a baffling confrontation with local extinction and loss of meaning. The effect is powerful enough to alter an individual's personality and their entire view of life. It amounts to a persistent low-level heartache, a background melancholia, for which there is little remedy short of emigration.
>
> (Cocker, 2018, p. 195)

An unpleasant new development is the 'Fortress Farm' (Smith, 2019), a rural future that we need to avert at all costs. Feeling their way of life is under threat farmers – 85% of which are male, 40% over the age of 65 (DEFRA, 2016) – are in a difficult place at the moment. They need support to transition to more environmental, social and indeed economic ways of working. Food security is set to be an enormous issue in the coming years as more and more agricultural land is flooded. Britain imports 45% of its food (DEFRA, 2019), statistics that are used in a highly political way to increase the market share and power of agribusinesses (Tomlinson, 2013), with impacts on our wildlife and landscapes that are there for all to see.

Social cohesion and loneliness

Social cohesion – 'the belief – held by citizens in a given nation state – that they share a moral community that enables them to trust one another' grew in Sweden and Denmark during the latter part of the 20th century while is shrank in the UK and the US (Albrekt Larsen, 2013), these being the most undemocratic of 'democratic' countries (Monbiot, 2017). A dismal 11% of the UK population will borrow things and exchange favours with neighbours, a number that is steadily decreasing (UKGov, 2019). So, as well has having to duplicate a lot of the stuff in our possession, we have a 'loneliness epidemic' (ONS, 2018) all this despite our unprecedented levels of digital connectivity.

Although loneliness is highly subjective there is a 'substantial research literature' with a 'significant historical pedigree' on loneliness in the UK (Yang and Victor, 2011). Loneliness is a 'subjective, unwelcome feeling of lack or loss of companionship. It happens when we have a mismatch between the quantity and quality of social relationships that we have, and those that we want' (Perlman and Peplau, 1981). It is a major cause of depression and poor health for all age groups (Victor and Yang, 2011). That feelings of loneliness are bad for health outcomes, including dementia, is widely recognised (Holwerda *et al.*, 2014). Interestingly young people thrive on lots of social contact while for older people it is the quality of the relationship that is more important (Victor and Yang, 2011). Although there is great emphasis on loneliness among old people (over 65), it is actually the young (under 25) that are most lonely (Yang and Victor, 2011), particularly those categorised as disabled (Emerson *et al.*, 2021).

Children

A recent UNICEF report revealed that wellbeing for children and young people in the UK is extremely low compared with 20 other OECD countries (third from bottom). Here 'compulsive acquisition and protective, symbolic brand purchases among time poor parents' is the norm (IPSOS Mori, 2011, p. 3). One of the few places that children (and parents) can hang out safely is the local shopping centre something that obviously plays into the hands of consumerism and feelings of inequality. A lack of appropriate places to go and (free) things to do outside, a sense of personal danger, poor air quality, dangerous roads and lack of safe bicycling routes all work against children leading active healthy lifestyles and playing out. A 'shocking' lack of physical activity among girls is a real concern (Youth Sport Trust, 2017). Across the UK youth club closures by local authorities are having major impacts on young people (Booth, 2019). In the UK poorer children tend to spend more time at home in front of screens while more affluent children have access to a range of outdoor activities (IPSOS Mori, 2011, p. 4). Teenagers loitering around in groups, particular males, are seen as anti-social which, in turn, becomes a kind of self-fulfilling prophecy (Neary *et al.*, 2012). They are an easy target for drug dealers and gangs.

No wonder mental health services in the UK are so stretched. In the words of Public Health England 'Childhood obesity and excess weight are significant health issues for children and their families (PHE, 2020). A recent UK study found that 70% of children in the UK eat while watching TV, an activity that was associated with the consumption of 'ultra processed foods'. The researchers observe therefore that ' interventions designed to promote healthy eating habits should include aspects related to the context of meals' (Martines *et al.*, 2019). Seemingly house builders and landlords are not helping the situation by building flats that are so small that they cannot accommodate a dining table or indeed anywhere to eat apart from in front of the TV. Further, due to the way our cities are planned, some parts of the UK, for example, Reading, are 'food deserts', areas with limited access to affordable and nutritious food (Geofutures, 2021).

Living and ageing in the community

The cost of poor housing to the National Health Service (NHS) is estimated at £1.4 billion per year, of which almost half is attributed to unfit housing for older people (Ibid). That older people are happier ageing in place is widely recognised (Life Changes Trust, 2017), but their needs are not being well met by current provisions (Age UK, 2019). Currently care happens at multiple scales but is unevenly distributed, and often exploitative, using migrant workers (often female) to deliver services that we ourselves are not prepared to deliver (Trogal, 2017). 'In the varying imports of care there are nevertheless moral boundaries and physical limits to how much emotional labour can be outsourced before the relations themselves and the people involved, are damaged' (Trogal, 2019, p.193). Unpaid care work falls disproportionately on the shoulders of women (Criado Perez, 2019) and is ignored in performance measures of gross domestic product yet it is the thing that holds our society together and is a key ingredient of social value. Around one-third of households in England are headed by someone aged over 65 and this is set to grow by 54% by 2041 (Age UK, 2019, p. 5). If we can get through the climate change emergency, housing and caring for an ageing population that lacks a cushion of adequate pension provision will be the next 'crisis' on the list.

Conclusion

This chapter has set out a range of ills in our current housing system, one that is failing to offer even the most basic provision to a very large swathe of society and is characterised by a lack of choice. People are constrained by their homes and neighbourhoods. They are preventing them from living their best lives. Despite our unprecedented ability to connect through digital media, loneliness is reaching epidemic proportions. Growing and eating food together in a convivial manner is a central part of what it means to be human however in our world of long hours, poorly paid jobs, junk food and TV dinners are spawning a health crisis. The people who are suffering most are the most vulnerable, young and old. Beneath the scratch card of neoliberal society is a layer of addiction, criminality, poverty and homelessness. This is our bequest to the next generation.

Note

Justin Welby quotes, © Justin Welby, 2018, *Reimagining Britain*, Bloomsbury Continuum, an imprint of Bloomsbury Publishing Plc.

References

Age UK. (2019) *Later Life in the United Kingdom 2019*. Age UK. Available at: https://www.ageuk.org.uk/globalassets/age-uk/documents/reports-and-publications/later_life_uk_factsheet.pdf.

Albrekt Larsen, C. (2013) *The Rise and Fall of Social Cohesion*. Oxford: Oxford University Press.

Alston, P., Khawaja, B. and Riddell, R. (2021) *Public Transport, Private Profit*. Centre for Human Rights and Global Justice. Available at: https://chrgj.org/wp-content/uploads/2021/07/Report-Public-Transport-Private-Profit.pdf.

Anacker, K.B. (2019) 'Introduction: housing affordability and affordable housing', *International Journal of Housing Policy*, 19(1), pp. 1–16.

Barton, C. and Kenny, C. (2018) *Health in Private-Rented Housing*. Available at: https://researchbriefings.parliament.uk/ResearchBriefing/Summary/POST-PN-0573#fullreport.

Bimpson, E. and Preece, J. (2019) *Housing Insecurity and Mental Health*. CACHE. Available at: https://housingevidence.ac.uk/wp-content/uploads/2019/03/Housing-insecurity-and-mental-health-Policy-Briefing.pdf.

Blanden, J. and Machin, S. (2017) 'Home ownership and social mobility', *LSE Research Online* [Preprint]. Available at: http://eprints.lse.ac.uk/83596/.

Booth, R. (2019) 'Youth club closures put young people at risk of violence, warn MPs', *The Guardian*. 7 May. Available at: https://www.theguardian.com/society/2019/may/07/youth-club-closures-young-people-risk-violence-mps.

Boughton, J. (2018) *Municipal Dreams: The Rise and Fall of Council Housing*. London: Verso.

Boulton, C., Dedekorkut-Howes, A. and Byrne, J. (2018) 'Factors shaping urban greenspace provision: A systematic review of the literature', *Landscape and Urban Planning*, 178, pp. 82–101.

Bourne, J. (2019) 'Empty homes: mapping the extent and value of low-se domestic property in England and Wales', *Palgrave Communications*, 5(9). Available at: https://www.nature.com/articles/s41599-019-0216-y.

Butler, P. (2021) 'Black, Asian and disabled tenants 'more likely to face housing descrimination', *The Guardian*. 26 May. Available at: https://www.theguardian.com/society/2021/may/26/black-asian-disabled-tenants-more-likely-face-housing-discrimination.

Capital Economics. (2019) *Increasing Investment in Social Housing*. London: Shelter England.

Clapham, D. (2019) *Remaking Housing Policy: An International Study*. London: Routledge.

Cocker, M. (2018) *Our Place: Can We Save Britian's Wildlife Before It Is Too Late*. London: Jonathan Cape.

Criado Perez, C. (2019) *Invisible Women*. London: Chatto and Windus.

DCLG. (2017) *Houses in Multiple Occupancy and Residential Property Licensing Reforms*. UK Gov. Available at: https://assets.publishing.service.gov.uk/government/uploads/system/uploads/attachment_data/file/670536/HMO_licensing_reforms_response.pdf.

DEFRA. (2016) *Agricultural Labour in England and the UK*. Available at: https://assets.publishing.service.gov.uk/government/uploads/system/uploads/attachment_data/file/771494/FSS2013-labour-statsnotice-17jan19.pdf.

DEFRA. (2019) *Food Statisticz in Your Pocket: Global and UK Supply*. Department for Environment Food and Rural Affairs. Available at: https://www.gov.uk/government/publications/food-statistics-pocketbook/food-statistics-in-your-pocket-global-and-uk-supply.

Dicks, M. (2020) 'CIH Cymru', in. *Wiserd 2020*, Cardiff University.

Disney, R. and Luo, G. (2015) *The Right to Buy Public Housing in Britain: A Welfare Analysis*. Institute of Fiscal Studies. Available at: https://ifs.org.uk/uploads/publications/wps/WP201505.pdf.

DLUHC. (2021) *English Housing Survey Headline Report*. Available at: https://assets.publishing.service.gov.uk/government/uploads/system/uploads/attachment_data/file/1060141/2020-21_EHS_Headline_Report_revised.pdf.

Dorling, D. (2014) *All Thay Is Solid: The Great Housing Disaster*. London: Penguin.

Emerson, E. (2021) 'Loneliness, social support, social isolation and wellbeing among working age adults with and without disability: Cross-sectional study', *Disability and Health Journal*, 14(1), 100965.

ETHOS. (2017) *European Typology of Homelessness and Housing Exclusion*. European Federation of National Associations Working with the Homeless AISBL. Available at: https://www.feantsa.org/download/en-16822651433655843804.pdf.

FIT. (2018) *Transport for New Homes: Summary and Recommendations*. Foundation for Integrated Transport. Available at: https://www.transportfornewhomes.org.uk/wp-content/uploads/2018/07/transport-for-new-homes-summary-web.pdf.

Fitzpatrick, S., Mackie, P. and Wood, J. (2019) *Homelessness Prevention in the UK*. UK Collaborative Centre for Housing Evidence. Available at: https://housingevidence.ac.uk/publications/homelessness-prevention-in-the-uk/.

Foye, C. (2017) 'The relationship between size of living space and subjective well-being', *Journal of Happiness Studies*, 18(2), pp. 427–461. Available at: https://timetable.reading.ac.uk/CMISGo/Web/Timetable.

Foye, C., Clapham, D. and Gabrieli, T. (2018) 'Home-ownership as a social norm and positional good: subjective wellbeing evidence from panel data', 55(6), pp. 1290–1312.

Geofutures. (2021) *The Geofutures Food Map*. Available at: https://www.geofutures.com/food/where-are-the-uk-food-deserts/.

Gill, C. (2021) *I Love My New Flat. But I'm Also Sick of Moving. We Renters Need a Greta Thunberg of the Housing Crisis. Conservative Home*. Available at: https://www.conservativehome.com/thetorydiary/2021/04/i-love-my-new-flat-but-im-also-sick-of-moving-we-renters-need-a-greta-thunberg-of-the-housing-crisis.html.

Gray, C. and Woodfine, L. (2018) *Adverse Childhood Experiences (ACESs) and Housing Vulnerability - Report and Evaluation of ACE-informed Training for Housing*. Public Health Wales. Available at: http://www.wales.nhs.uk/sitesplus/documents/888/5%20ACE%20Informed%20Training%20for%20Housing.pdf.

Halligan, L. (2019) *Home Truths: The UK's Chronnic Housing Shortage*. London: Biteback.

Hastings, A., Mackenzie, M. and Earley, A. (2021) *Domestic Abuse and Housing*. Available at: https://housingevidence.ac.uk/wp-content/uploads/2021/02/DA-Covid-19-report-FINAL.pdf.

Holwerda, T.J. et al. (2014) 'Feelings of loneliness, but not social isolation predict dementia onset: results from the Amsterdam Study of the Elderly (AMSTEL)', *Journal of Neurology, Neurosurgery & Psychiatry*, 85(2), pp. 135–142.

Hudson, N. and Green. (2017) *Missing Movers: A Long Term Decline in Housing Transactions*. Council of Mortgage Lenders. Last accessed on November 2021: file:///Users/vw911381/Downloads/cml-missing-movers-research-report%20(2).pdf.

IPSOS Mori. (2011) *Children's Well-being in UK, Sweden and Spain: The Role of Inequality and Materialism*. UNICEF. Available at: https://www.unicef.org.uk/wp-content/uploads/2011/09/IPSOS_UNICEF_ChildWellBeingreport.pdf.

Ivanova, D. (2021) 'The Sustainability Implications of Single Occupancy Households', *Buildings and Cities*, February 9. Available at: https://www.buildingsandcities.org/insights/commentaries/sustainability-single-households.html.

Kalantari, S. and Shepley, M. (2021) 'Psychological and social impacts of high-rise buildings: a review of the post-occupancy evaluation literature', *Housing Studies*, 36(8), pp. 1147–1176.

King, P. (2004) *Private Dwelling*. London: Routledge.

King, P. (2017) *Living Alone, Living Together*. Bingley: Emerald Publishing.

Letcher, L. (2021) 'Cornwall has 10, 000 Airbnbs but only 69 homes available to rent', *Cornwall Live*. 3 June. Available at: https://www.cornwalllive.com/news/cornwall-news/cornwall-10000-airbnbs-only-69-5486028?utm_source=twitter.com&utm_medium=social&utm_campaign=sharebar.

Life Changes Trust. (2017) *Being Home*. University of West of Scotland. Available at: https://www.lifechangestrust.org.uk/publications/being-home-full-report.

Lowe, R. and Lai Fong, C. (2020) 'Innovation in deep housing retrofit in the United Kingdom: The role of situated creativity in transforming practice', *Energy Research and Social Science*, 63, 101391.

Marsh, A. (2020) 'Raising standards in the UK Private Sector', in. *Wiserd 2020*, Cardiff University.

Marsh, A. and Gibb, K. (2019) *The Private Rented Sector in the UK: An Overview of the Policy and Regulatory Landscape*. CACHE. Available at: https://housingevidence.ac.uk/wp-content/uploads/2019/07/TDS-Overview-paper_final.pdf.

Martines, R. *et al.* (2019) 'Association between watching TV whilst eating and children's consumption of ultra processed foods in United Kingdom', *Maternal and Child Nutrition*, 15(4). Available at: https://onlinelibrary.wiley.com/doi/full/10.1111/mcn.12819.

Mason, R. (2018) 'Over 11,000 homes have stood empty for at least 10 years, data shows', *The Guardian*. Available at: https://www.theguardian.com/society/2018/jan/01/over-11000-homes-have-stood-empty-for-at-least-10-years-data-shows.

McKee, K. and Soaita, A (2018) *The 'frustrated' housing aspirations of generation rent,* UK Collaborative Centre for Housing Evidence, https://housingevidence.ac.uk/wp-content/uploads/2018/08/R2018_06_01_Frustrated_Housing_Aspirations_of_Gen_Rent.pdf

McKee, K. *et al.* (2017) '"Generation rent" and the fallacy of choice', *International Journal of Urban and Regional Research*, 41(2).

MHCLG. (2018) *English Housing Survey: Households Report, 2017–2018*. Available at: https://assets.publishing.service.gov.uk/government/uploads/system/uploads/attachment_data/file/817286/EHS_2017-18_Households_Report.pdf.

MHCLG. (2020) *Planning for the Future*. Available at: https://assets.publishing.service.gov.uk/government/uploads/system/uploads/attachment_data/file/872091/Planning_for_the_Future.pdf.

Monbiot, G. (2017) *Out of the Wreckage: A New Politics for an Age of Crisis*. London: Verso.

Murie, A. (2016) *The Right to Buy: Selling Off Public and Social Housing*. Cambridge: Policy Press.

Neary, J. *et al.* (2012) 'Damned if they do, damned if they don't: negotiating the tricky context of anti-social behaviour and keeping safe in disadvantaged urban neighbourhoods', *Journal of Youth Studies*, 16(1), pp. 118–134.

NFB (2019) *Transforming Construction for a Low Carbon Future*. National Federation of Builders.

NICE. (2020) *Indoor Air Quality at Home, National Institute for Health and Care Excellence*. Available at: https://www.nice.org.uk/guidance/ng149/chapter/Recommendations.

Nicol, S. and Garrett, H. (2019) *The Full Cost of Poor Housing in Wales*. BRE/Trust/NHS Cymru. Available at: https://www.bregroup.com/bretrust/wp-content/uploads/sites/12/2019/05/The-Cost-of-Poor-Housing-in-Wales-2017.002.pdf.

ONS. (2017) *Public perceptions of crime in England and Wales: year ending March 2016*. Office for National Statistics.

ONS. (2018) *Loneliness*. Available at: https://www.ons.gov.uk/aboutus/transparencyandgovernance/freedomofinformationfoi/loneliness.

ONS. (2019) *UK private rented sector: 2018*. Office for National Statistics. Available at: https://www.ons.gov.uk/economy/inflationandpriceindices/articles/ukprivaterentedsector/2018#things-you-need-to-know.

ONS. (2022) *Families and Households in the UK 2021*. Office for National Statistics. Available at: https://www.ons.gov.uk/peoplepopulationandcommunity/birthsdeathsandmarriages/families/bulletins/familiesandhouseholds/2021.

Orford, S. (2018) 'The capitalisation of school choice into property prices: A case study of grammar and all ability state schools in Buckinghamshire, UK', *Geoforum*, 97, pp. 231–241.

Perlman, D. and Peplau, L.A. (1981) 'Toward a social psychology of loneliness', in Gilmour, R. and Duck, S. (eds) *Personal Relationships in Disorder*, pp. 31–56. London: Academic Press.

PHE. (2020) *Childhood Obesity: Applying All Our Health*. Public Health England. Available at: https://www.gov.uk/government/publications/childhood-obesity-applying-all-our-health/childhood-obesity-applying-all-our-health.

Pickerill, J. (2019) 'Building eco-homes for all', in Trogal, K. (ed.) *Architecture and Resilience*. London: Routledge, pp. 76–87.

Roos, L. *et al.* (2013) 'Relationship between adverse childhood experiences and homelessness', *American Journal of Public Health*, 103(Supplement 2), pp. S275–S281.

Savage, M. (2020) 'Waiting list of council homes in England "will double to 2 million"', *The Guardian*. 14 November. Available at: https://www.theguardian.com/society/2020/nov/14/waiting-list-for-council-homes-in-england-will-double-to-2-million.

Sharpe, R.A. *et al.* (2018) 'Making the case for "whole system" approaches: integrating public health and housing', *International Journal of Environmental Research and Public Health*, 15, p. 2345.

Shrubsole, G. (2019) *Who Owns England?* London: William Collins.

Smith, R. (2019) 'The "fortress farm": articulating a new approach to redesigning "defensible space" in a rural context', *Crime Prevention & Community Safety*, 21(3), pp. 215–230.

Solnit, R. (2020) *Recollections of My Non-Existence*. London: Granta.

Sunnikka-Blank, M. and Galvin, R. (2016) 'Irrational homeowners? How aesthetics adn heritage values influence thermal retrofit decisions in the United Kingdom', *Energy Research and Social Science*, 11, pp. 97–108.

Swift, D. (2021) 'The left is wrong about housing', *Unherd*. Available at: https://unherd.com/2021/11/labour-is-wrong-about-housing/.

Tomlinson, I. (2013) 'Doubling food production to feed the 9 billion: A critical perspective on a key discourse of food security in the UK', *Journal of Rural Studies*, 29, pp. 81–90.

Trogal, K. (2017) 'Caring: making commons, making connections', in Petrescu, D. and Trogal, K. (eds) *The Social (Re)production of Architecture*. London: Routledge.

Trogal, K. (2019) 'Resilience as interdependence', in Trogal, K., Bauman, I., Lawrence, R., and Petrescu, D. (eds), *Architecture and Resilience*. London: Routledge, pp.190–203.

Tunaker, C. (2015) '"No place like home?" Locating homeless LGBT youth', *Home Cultures*, 12(2), pp. 241–259.

Urban Transport Group. (2016) *The Case for Active Travel: How Walking an Cycling Can Support More Vibrant Urban Economies*. Available at: https://www.urbantransportgroup.org/system/files/general-docs/The%20Case%20for%20Active%20Travel_0.pdf.

Victor, C. and Yang, K. (2011) 'The prevalence of loneliness among adults: a case study of the United Kingdom', *The Journal of Psychology*, 146(1–2), pp. 85–104.

White, J. et al. (2020) *Delivering Design Value: Housebuilding and the Design Quality Conundrum*. UK Collaborative Centre for Housing Evidence.

Yang, K. and Victor, C. (2011) 'Age and loneliness in 25 European nations', *Ageing & Society*, 31(8), pp. 1368–1388. Available at: https://www.cambridge.org/core/journals/ageing-and-society/article/abs/age-and-loneliness-in-25-european-nations/CB2D91D8793AA3522286EAD7203FA492.

Young Foundation. (2019) *New Perspectives on Housing*. Young Foundation. Available at: https://youngfoundation.org/wp-content/uploads/2019/04/New-Perspectives-Final-Report-SMALL-2.pdf.

Youth Sport Trust. (2017) *Survey Shows Large Gender Gap in Attitudes to Physical Activity for Teenagers*. Available at: https://www.youthsporttrust.org/news/survey-shows-large-gender-gap-attitudes-physical-activity-teenagers.

Chapter 2

Who builds housing and how?

So who are the key protagonists in the drama of 21st-century housing 'delivery' in the UK? How are they contributing to hope and wellbeing? The picture painted here is one of a neoliberal world of short-termism and complex, wasteful, messy and indeed dangerous interfaces between the public and private sector, often resulting in monoculture of housing that is 'overwhelmingly mediocre or poor' (Place Alliance, 2019). The 2017 Grenfell Tragedy in which 72 people died in the burning housing block, leaving many more deeply traumatised and homeless was because of failures across professional teams. Learned helplessness prevails – somehow our systems have been set up to make perfectly reasonable and pleasant people feel comfortable about making destructive business decisions. Value, social, environmental and indeed economic (depending on how you measure it) appears to drain out of the process at almost every stage (White *et al.*, 2020). Developers do not carry the long-term cost of bad design but local authorities, health, education and police services do (CABE, 2006, p. 12).

'Tinkering with speculative housebuilding, which has been the approach of successive governments for decades, will not deliver the homes we need' (Jefferys and Lloyd, 2017, p. 2). In the 2017 White Paper, *Fixing our broken housing market,* the Ministry of Housing Communities and Local Government (England) acknowledged the extent of the mess we are in. Notice the emphasis on 'market' – we're not talking about making homes here. One problem seems to be lack of long-term thinking. Despite the fact that housing is a domestic priority we have had 18 housing ministers since 1997, the highest rate of churn of any ministerial position. Knowing their days are numbered these politicians tend to focus on short-term high media impact wins and numerical outcomes (Lewis, 2019), but housing is too important to be treated as a numbers game. Only 6% of UK land is built on (Rae, 2017), yet access to land is always cited as the main blockage to housing delivery so this account begins with a discussion of access to land before moving onto the activities of the private sector client teams, house builders and, lastly the local authorities and self builders who are attempting to truly affordable homes.

Land acquisition

Land can be understood both as 'locational space and its use over time' and as a form of 'capital' (Clapham, 2019, p. 43) but, as this book argues, it is so much more than that. Our land has been colonised, subdivided, held ransom and parcelled off resulting in the enclosure of land for private benefit and the rentier economy, a system with cruel historic origins (Linebaugh, 2014), exemplified by the word 'landlord'. Beginning around the 15th century land enclosures and the dismantling of the commons (and with it the right to a subsistence existence) meant that many rural workers lost vital income generated through things like grazing and were reliant on landlords or the parish for welfare support. Not only did they lose the right to use the land, they also lost any say over what happened on that land even when it impacts on the communities around. Ancient estates were often built on the pain, blood and sweat of others. The Centre for Studies of British Slavery enables a quick search of the association of some large estates (and some high profile people) with this evil trade (UCL, 2021) as well as a vast financial bailout on its abolition (Manning, 2013).

Landowners are defined as those with the highest form of property right, the freehold, and are therefore extremely powerful (for a useful introduction to this complex area, see Adams and Tiesdell, 2012). Half of England is owned by 1% of the population (Evans, 2019), with most of this being owned and controlled by a relatively small number of owners, in particular the traditional landed aristocracy and gentry. An example is the Buccleuch family which owns almost 217,000 acres of rural Britain (Buccleuch, 2021). A great deal of land in Britain is owned by very few rich, sometimes overseas, landlords, a situation that is assisted by our current tax and farming subsidy system. Whether this land is really being managed for public good is highly questionable. George Monbiot, for example, illustrates the waste and destruction caused by keeping large areas of the Scottish Highlands for the sporadic hunting activities of the privileged (2013), when that same land could be used for other much more environmentally, socially and economically productive purposes. There is, as Mark Cocker observes, a need to 'challenge the vested interests who would wish us not to be aware or to understand the uses and abuses of our countryside' (Cocker, 2018, p. 298).

Land ownership plays no small role in the maintenance of the UK's divisive class structure (Munton, 2009). Women weren't allowed to inherit property until the 1870 Married Women's Property Act and have been catching up ever since. Further the rule of male primogeniture, handing down property (and power) through the male line – which came in with William the Conqueror – has historically consolidated women's place as second class citizens in society. In 2016 the inheritance of the £9.9 billion Grosvenor estate bypassed the daughters of the family landing squarely on the youthful shoulders of Hugh Grosvenor, then the richest person in the world under the age of 30. Clever trust planning meant that he was also able to avoid some £4 billion in inheritance tax (Da Costa, 2018).

Rural landowners enjoy tax emptions on business rates as well as on their land. It seems to be no accident that what Cocker calls the 'land secrecy' of the landed dovetails so nicely with policy and with the 'land blindness' of society as a whole (2018, p. 297). Despite recent moves towards increasing the coverage of the Land Registry there is considerable 'secrecy' within the field of land ownership (Shrubsole, 2019). Evidence is growing that UK property has 'become a safe haven for corrupt capital stolen from around the world, facilitated by the laws which allow UK property to be owned by secret offshore companies' (Transparency International, 2015).

The development of brownfield (a term often used interchangeably with Previously Developed Land) sites is being encouraged through planning policy (MHCLG, 2020, p. 5) to reduce inroads into 'green' space. The use of brownfield sites can be important for the regeneration and the preservation of heritage assets but they present developers with considerable risk in terms of unknown hazards and increased development costs (Leger *et al.*, 2016). They can also be havens for wildlife, more so than blank tracts of agricultural land blasted with chemicals. Terms like brownfield and green belt are very blunt instruments when sites are characterised by a whole range of types of potential.

Some 10% of the British landmass went from the public sector to private ownership between 1979 and 2018 with the effects seen most profoundly in housing. 'Of all the recent privatisations in England, the most valuable, and yet least recorded, is of land'. (Layard, 2019, p. 151). Local authorities try to earmark land for such high social value developments as Community Land Trusts, Self Build and Cohousing but this is difficult when there is pressure to sell to the highest bidder (Wainwright, 2020). 'Viability assessments and the dark arts of accounting' have become 'all-powerful' in the shaping of our places (Wainwright, 2015). Land speculation in a particular area can overheat the market, raising landowner expectations of the value of their land. Without readily available data on past sales it is very hard to value 'unimproved' land in a rigorous way (Hughes *et al.*, 2020, p. 5). The situation is made worse by having an incomplete Land Registry. 'Not knowing who truly controls a piece of land makes it difficult for local and combined authorities to plan effectively, for new entrants to enter into the development sector, and for land to be accurately valued' (Banks, 2016, p.7).

Two methods tend to be used for the valuation of development land based on the Royal Institute of Chartered Surveyors (RICS) *Red Book* (2020). According to the 'residual valuation method' projected income minus costs (including profit) are used to calculate the residual land value. This can be a barrier to delivering a high-quality outcome as it is all about financial profit. The other more commonly used approach is 'discounted cash flow'. Expenditure is set out according to a programme plan, meaning that it is possible to work out the net present cashflow value of a project at any stage. This is more accurate as it takes time into account, including the amount of interest that needs to be paid on borrowed money. It also enables other kinds of value to be built into projections (RICS, 2019, p. 17).

As developers generally need to borrow as much money as possible from funders they tend to provide optimistic valuations for the finished houses based on the best possible market performance. When it looks like targets are unlikely to be achieved design quality (and potential social value) tends to be reduced in order to save money and maximise profit. Often developers go back to local authorities using financial arguments as an excuse not to deliver the promised affordable housing or to provide the quality of work specified in the planning application (White *et al.*, 2020). Local Authorities tend to be so desperate to fulfil their housing quotas, the number of houses they have promised the government they will deliver, that they offer little resistance.

Even if a landowner tries to sell land to an organisation that they believe to be responsible it is often 'flipped', in other words sold on, to another potentially less salubrious organisation. Housebuilders may take over other housebuilders in order to get access to their 'land bank' and there are quite a lot of inter firm transactions (Adams, Croudace and Tiesdell, 2012). Sometimes land is 'banked' because housebuilders don't want to flood the market with new homes, reducing prices in the process. Fenced off, vacant and derelict land can have major negative impacts on communities (Stantec, 2019) but can be a haven for wildlife. Anecdotally some housebuilders regularly raze their land to ensure that no protected species get too established.

Enter stage right the 'land promoters' who assemble packages of land to be sold on to developers, often once the likelihood of securing planning permission has been negotiated with local authorities (local authorities themselves can act as land promoters). The Land Promoters and Developers Federation claims on their website that 41% of sites above 1,000 homes involved a specialist land promoter, a higher proportion than housebuilders or public sector bodies (LDPF, 2019). There is very little literature on land agents and land promoters (Fraser, 2017) despite their large and growing role in assembling housing sites. Ultimately, land promoters are able to operate on a 'no win, no fee' basis, which is highly tempting to landowners, especially those who don't have confidence in engaging with the planning system. The Council for the Protection of Rural England is highly critical of land promoters arguing that they are driven by speculation and profit causing them to challenge local policy in ways that are unhelpful for the community (CPRE, 2017).

When the government announces major infrastructure investment in a particular area the private sector investors buy up or seek options in tracts of land in that area, benefitting from the likely value uplift to come. Homes England, a government body, offers incentives to oil the process. In this way considerable value that could go into community wealth is lost from the system and public investment results in private gain. It is isn't very surprising that property reform and transparency is so slow in coming when so many in power have such a vested interest in its perpetuation (Shrubsole, 2019, p. 132).

The New Economics Foundation did an analysis of ten tranches of public land that were put up for sale in 2017. They argue that there would have been benefit savings of £230 million over the subsequent 30 years if that land had been retained for public housing (Martin, 2017). There are various ways to try to capture land value uplift but they are messy and inconsistent. 'Planning Gain' mechanisms such as Community Infrastructure Levies (CIL) and Section 106 agreements (in England) exist to claw back money from developers – for example, through the throwing in of a school into the proposal – but they seem to be implemented in a very random and subjective manner with little, if any, input from the community.

Planning

Bullied and undermined, planning authorities have been left castrated and toothless, stripped of the skills and power they need to regulate, and sapped of the spatial imagination to actually plan places.

(Wainwright, 2014)

The planning of housing, communities, health and wellbeing are intertwined issues that are being kept artificially separate by the way government and local authorities work – in the words of one Local Authority Planner I interviewed:

I've given various presentations where, for example, in Wales you have the Public Service Boards? So, you'll have key people from the fire service, police, social services, the NHS, all sorts. And you'll give a presentation on the benefits of good public open space, and how it can reduce the NHS's bill by you know, basic stuff, keeping people fit, et cetera, et cetera. And then, if you try to turn the conversation to the NHS, and say, look, why don't you help contribute towards some of this green infrastructure? Boom. You've lost them. . .

(2020)

Another expert I spoke with cited (with figures) the financial waste caused to the National Health Service (NHS) for GP appointments to provide medicalised solutions for social isolation which could potentially be alleviated through the outcomes of good planning. 'And that could be anything from just nice friendly neighbours around the corner with a cup of tea . . . or good housing'. Planning needs to be holistic, involving the entire public service team.

Planning cannot be assumed to be making good communities, particularly in the current situation in which the total expenditure on planning by local planning authorities is now just £900 million a year across England. More than half of this is recouped in income (mostly fees), meaning that the total net investment in planning is now just £400 million, or £1.2 million per local authority. This is 50 times less than local authority spending on housing welfare, and 20 times less than estimates of the additional uplift in land values which could be captured for the public during development (RTPI, 2019, p. 3).

Lack of investment means that planners and the teams that they consult with (highways, ecologists and others) are overworked and struggling with their basic caseloads with little time or opportunity for professional development or engagement with data (Uandl, 2021) or meaningful dialogue with communities (Harrison, Galland and Tewdwr Jones, 2021). This impacts on the speed at which decisions are made can be very slow, a well-known barrier to development (see, for example, Payne, 2016) and indeed on the quality of decisions made. In some councils developers can pay extra to have a dedicated team of planners work on their team to get the project processed in a timely manner, effectively privatisation by the back door. Several of the planners that I spoke with were loath to stand up for making better communities as they felt that their decisions were likely to be overturned at appeal. Dealing with highways departments provided a further constraint. One planning consultant I spoke with observed that although highways are supposed to be consultants it sometimes looks as though they have the upper hand over planning officers. 'Cars and bins should not be determining how developments are designed but in some cases projects look as if housing has become the residual design element'. Highways departments are supposed to be thinking about how to make better streets and places (WSP, 2007), but a strong message coming through the interviews I undertook for the CaCHE Delivering Design Value Project is that highways can take a very conservative approach to design so fearful are they about being held liable for accidents.

There is still a great deal of subjectivity in planning, particularly with regard to aesthetics. This means that predicting what planners are going to say can be quite difficult, something that adds risk to every development journey. The planners I interviewed freely admitted their lack of design training and were aware that this was an issue. When only 25% of local authorities have access to architectural expertise (Hopkirk, 2021) it is unsurprising that design is so low on the agenda. Some local authorities use a design review process to try to push up quality but these panels tend to be behind closed doors and lack diversity (Public Practice, 2020). Anyway emphasis on aesthetic design isn't always a good thing as Victoria Lawson's forensic study of the acclaimed Liverpool One development has shown, 'design led schemes can be socially regressive. The promise of high quality can be used to mask less democratic design processes and thus make a scheme more acceptable' (2018, p. 256).

The National Planning Policy Framework (NPPF, 2021) in England requires local planning authorities (LPAs) to identify a supply of development sites sufficient to meet five years' worth of local housing need. The purpose of this is to provide and indication of whether there are sufficient sites available to meet the housing requirement set out in a local authority's adopted strategic policies for the next five years (UK Gov, 2019). When – as was fairly common over the last decade – 'the most relevant Local Plan policies for determining a planning application are out of date (or the Local Plan is silent on a matter), the application should be approved unless it is in a protected area (as defined by the NPPF) or the harms caused by the application significantly outweigh its benefits'. This policy, known as 'the tilted balance' has skewed the probability of getting planning permission onto the side of the developer (Savills, 2021).

The government offers guidance on 'Housing and Economic Needs Assessment' (UK Gov, 2015) including 'household growth projections' and techniques for assessing affordable housing need (Dunning et al., 2020). Despite this the assessment of housing need is poorly defined. It is usually based on calculations of existing stock compared to households and future need (based on net immigration, mortality and the formation of new households). Young people move out to set up their own homes based on the availability of housing (Clapham, 2019) so there is slight chicken and egg air to this which should make us sceptical about these calculations. The forecasting demand for homes in local authorities, often commissioned from private sector organisations, is done at a very blunt level, flats versus houses, two beds versus three beds. It fails to take into account the 'other' kinds of multi-adult households that are set to grow (Adam, 2015, p. 7).

Given the profiling capability of industries like retail we could do so much more to make sophisticated projections of housing need that take lifestyle into account.

Planning is also urgently in need of a technological makeover. As Harrison and Tewdwr-Jones argue the era of regional planning based on fixed fast outdated plans is drawing swiftly to a close (2021). Every five years or so a local authority will produce a local (development) plan which sets out what can be built and where in the intervening years. These plans tend to be done by a very small group of people who are working at speed to fulfil targets on a minimum budget. Local Plans are based on economic and sustainability assessments with minimal consideration of social value. In marketable areas land promoters and developers cluster round local authorities these teams like bees on a honeypot. Promoters know that having a 'Red Line' drawn around their site, usually cheap agricultural land, earmarking it for housing in a local development plan can result in huge windfall of cash. Local authorities keen to deliver housing targets seem to merrily go along with them. It isn't just about housing, local authorities will be lobbied by all sorts of big business (see, for example, KFC, 2018) to promote their own interests. A valuation expert I spoke to observed that the loose nature of Local Development Plans 'allow speculators to dance in the spaces'.

When so much of the focus of planning is on trying to generate economic value consultation with the public becomes a time consuming nuisance – 'stakeholder management' as opposed to 'stakeholder engagement'. Our system of consultation has its origins in the post-war era when speed of reconstruction was prioritised over community voice. It has changed little since, with opportunities for consultation being brief, disjointed, poorly publicised, confusing, exclusionary and seemingly pointless (Lawson *et al.*, 2022). There are no regulations to ensure basic standards of inclusion in participation are met so consultation can be a very perfunctory thing. In England Local Planning Authorities fail to see their local communities as a useful decision making resource and Statements of Community Involvement which talk about the way the local authority will engage with its local community are poorly utilised (Parker, Dobson and Lynn, 2021).

'Community consultation' tends to be driven by regulation while 'engagement' is about a much more long-term approach to working with communities. As one planner I spoke with observed 'as community groups so rarely engage in the Local Plan process, their involvement comes as reactors to applications which is too late'. It is very difficult to get community input into proposals often because the ideas presented seem so abstract and unrelated to day-to-day life. Try, as a citizen, to get involved in influencing your Local Plan and you will see what I mean – it is pretty much a full-time job and can be expensive. This has become very apparent to me at a personal level while fighting with our community to stop the encroachment of restaurants and beer gardens onto our quiet, diverse, inner city street. We've had to fight some ten planning applications and each time we have lost because of the Local Plan into which we had no meaningful input. This process has not been helped by the fact that 70% of planning decisions in Cardiff are done through 'delegated responsibility', in other words the planners decide what the community should want (Lawson *et al.*, 2022). '71% of UK adults say they have no or not much control over important decisions that affect their neighbourhood and local community' (Cares Family & Power to Change, 2022, p. 28). Guidance exists on who among the public should be consulted with but authorities 'have discretion' on how they inform the public of proposals (DLUHC, 2021), meaning that this guidance is fairly toothless. The only way to get a slot to present the community voice in the planning meeting, quite an unpleasant and humiliating experience for those brave enough enter what feels like a lair of jaded 'experts' with their eyes on the clock, has been to get a petition of 50 names from neighbours. We've done this on a few occasions now – it was particularly challenging during the pandemic (but lovely to reconnect with neighbours) – and the only time we had any traction in the planning meeting was when we (the street) paid to employ a planning consultant who could talk in the language of planning law. The process is entirely disempowering and does nothing for one's faith in democratic processes. Planning Aid is available for such situations but we couldn't find it when we needed it.

In a recent survey by the developer Grosvenor, only 2% of respondents trusted developers and only 7% trusted local councils to make decisions in the best interests of their area. 66% per cent of people who shared their view with the council about a specific project had a negative experience, and 62% of people who went to a consultation meeting about a specific project had a negative experience (Grosvenor, 2019). A code of conduct for truly inclusive community consultation is urgently needed.

At the local level it is elected councillors that carry a good deal of weight in making decisions about planning though all those that I interviewed expressed a feeling of extreme powerlessness in the face of planning officer's recommendations, a sentiment echoed by the councillors in my own area. Councillors have to mediate between an inhumane planning system and distraught, and sometimes aggressive, residents. No wonder this job is so unpopular (MacFadyen, 2020). Their remuneration is very low and their conditions of employment are poor – there is, for example, no provision for maternity leave (Criado Perez, 2019). The average age of local government councillors is 59.4 (45% are retired), 94% identify as white and 63% identify as male (LGA, 2018). Councillors, depending on their expertise and level of engagement, can play an important role in alerting the public to planning applications in their area and in translating drawings and proposals to their constituents. Generally though there is a high level of non-engagement.

Clients, procurement and the construction team
Taking the cue from their funding bodies – banks, investors and so on – clients set the tone for a development, enshrining project priorities through its brief. The client will assemble a professional team and consultants and decide on the best route for procurement. Some clients will have a vested interest in the project after completion, others will take the money and run. The Victorians built to last centuries – the terrace house is a case in point so what are we doing nowadays in this area? Designing Buildings Wiki tells me that buildings should last a mere 50 years (2021), but one valuation expert I know told me the shortest design life/

build life she had encountered in her career was seven years. Twenty-five years seem to be a rough average. Seen in this light most housing is temporary. Client representatives know that their buildings won't last but, given the high levels of churn in their organisations, they know that this they will be long gone before the problem comes to light.

A potentially negative influence on the housing sector's ability to innovate are 'framework agreements' made by local authorities and others to streamline their processes. Here a select corpus of businesses are vetted long in advance, ready to jump at the opportunity to assist in building a new project. To get onto the framework businesses are often required to have high levels of experience and insurance to cover any eventuality. This can rule out the employment of new and small organisations. One way to get round this is to develop frameworks for different scales of projects. Peabody's small projects panel provides a good example (Peabody Trust, 2014)).

Although perhaps a dry subject it is important to recognise the radical impact of building contracts on the final outcome. Ever since the 1980s, as part of the construction 'improvement' agenda characterised by the Egan Report – *Rethinking Construction* (1998) 'Design and Build' contracts have become more widespread. Indeed by 2012 50% of private contracts and 40% of public contracts were procured this way (RIBA and Colander, 2014). Here the architect is novated by the employer to the contractor – with the agreement of the contractor and the architect. The contractor then holds overall responsibility for the quality of the outputs, theoretically making things more straightforward for the client but the result has been an abdication of responsibility on all sides (Curtis, 2020).

At the same time, as a result of the construction 'improvement' agenda, construction companies have been 'hollowed out', shedding in house operatives to whom they have a long-term commitment for development and training (Green, 2011). This means that very few main contractors carry their own trades and most work happens through the subcontracting process. As a result there is a further abdication of responsibility around training, employee wellbeing, and the building of knowledge.

'All this before one starts to consider modern methods of construction (MMC)' sighed one industry expert I spoke with. MMC includes off site construction of modules, digitally printed components, components that arrive on site already enclosing space in three dimensions modules, and panel systems assembled to enclose space. MMC is currently used to supply less than 5% of all new dwellings in the UK, but this is estimated to rise to at least 20% of all new homes by 2030 (McCarthy, 2020). China is shooting ahead in the modular construction field by investing in vast factories capable of delivering to the world (Fortune, 2020), sometimes working with local suppliers. The insurance company Legal & General has laid down the gauntlet in the UK by building a large modular construction facility in Leeds, its aim being to facilitate the 'pipeline' of new homes, for all ages, social groups and housing tenures (L & G, 2020) and the Off Site Homes Alliance is working to align the work of multiple housing providers but so much more work in this area is needed.

Housing delivery has been slowed by escalation of construction material costs and supply chain difficulties in the wake of Brexit (and the pandemic). The UK construction sector is dogged by a large trade deficit caused by the erosion of UK manufacturing (Kelly *et al.*, 2002) impacting on its ability to innovate. Problems in innovation, upskilling and digital manufacturing are particularly acute for SME and micro building contractors. Neoliberalism has made the construction of homes, once one of the most satisfying and collegial of activities, into a miserable husk of its former self – high suicide rates, an aggressive culture and even modern day slavery being indicators of its ills.

House building

It stands to reason that a housing sector that involves a healthy and diverse ecology of builders is likely to be more resilient to shifts in the system, yet housing construction has become big business. Small housebuilders – those who produce less than 100 homes a year – provide the backbone of the system constructing a steady drip feed of homes that are generally better. designed for their context than that of volume house builders. Small housebuilders have the advantage when it comes to tackling small, difficult and bespoke sites (Sinnett *et al.*, 2014) and, being local, they are more accountable to their local communities. Despite all their virtues small housebuilders are an endangered species, something that puts the whole system at risk. The number of homes developed by smaller housebuilders has declined steeply in recent decades (Federation of Master Builders, 2018, p. 6). The reasons behind this are cited as availability of land, bureaucracy, planning and finance as well as difficulties in engaging with highways departments (HBF, 2017). My neighbourhood used to be a small housebuilder but he has since given up for exactly these reasons.

Volume housebuilders (VHBs) generally have one simple focus on the production of housing units and the maximising of profit. They provide a one stop shop for home buyers and also for registered providers of housing (also known as housing associations) that sometimes buy their products in bulk. In the words of one of the experts I interviewed 'the template for housing provision has been shaped by the VHBs. In 2016, over 60% of new private housing (which equates to over 80,000 homes (MHCLG, 2019) was built by the top 10 volume housebuilders (VHBs) and the top five accounted for 38% of the output (Building, 2017; Rhodes, 2018). If the Government housing targets of 300,000 homes per year are met and the present patterns of volume housebuilder dominance continues over 1 million new houses will be built over the next five years, the majority by just a handful of volume housebuilders (Barton et al., 2022). In Cardiff, for example, thousands of new houses will be promoted by just four organisations – Kier Living, Bellway, Persimmon and Redrow – each with its own limited range of housing typologies. The impact on our landscape in terms of homogeneity (and wellbeing) is profound. This is without any consideration of the relatively poor environmental performance of most volume house builder products.

Volume housebuilders are, in the main Public Limited Companies. They have a heavy dependence on external debt and equity funding meaning that they have to report quarterly on profits to shareholders, something that works against long-term thinking (Walker, 2021). The financial models used by volume housebuilders rely on the use of standard house types that are reconfigured to suit the target constituency – young professionals and families with little in between (Adams and Tiesdell, 2012). While the appearance of VHB homes may have stayed roughly the same for many years, much innovation has gone into improving efficiencies at many levels (NHBC, 2019).

Mixed development, generally a good thing for people, adds to complexity, risk and cost. It therefore sits poorly within VHB business models which tend to be quite rigid (Payne, 2020). Some VHBs are better than others. Persimmon, a company that has reputational issues bravely put itself through a revealing apparently independent review (Barwise, 2019). This didn't stop the company more recently apparently building a block of flats the wrong way round with its windows 'facing backwards' (Munbodh, 2021) and its chief Dean Finch from receiving an annual pay and bonus package of £2.6 million in 2021 (Koellewe, 2022).

The system as it stands is set up to incentivises land-banking – holding onto land, keeping it undeveloped for reasons of profit. Large housebuilders are among the biggest corporate landowners in Britain. Land Registry data suggests that Taylor Wimpey owned nearly 15,000 acres in 2015 but research suggests that this figure should be a great deal higher if subsidiaries are taken into account (Powell-Smith and Shrubsole, 2017). Guy Shrubsole notes that, despite the fact that housebuilders regularly bemoan the lack of housing to build on, Persimmon's founder, Duncan Davidson, himself owns a 26,000 acre farm and grouse moor in Northumberland (Shrubsole, 2019, p. 131).

Social rented housing

Such is the complexity of the private public interface that it is difficult to separate 'social' or 'public rented' housing produced by local authorities out from other kinds of housing, particularly 'affordable' housing delivered by housing associations and providers (Shelter, 2015). Housing associations receive much of their funding from government (Clapham, 2019) and are in the business of supplying affordable housing, but this can involve developing a mixed portfolio including market homes (including the acquisition of volume house builder homes). The private sector has taken over the delivery of public sector homes. Over recent years however the pursuit of economies of scale have resulted in a series of mergers resulting in a reduction of diversity both in terms of what is delivered and choice (see Adams, Tiesdell and White, 2013). As housing associations end up managing the properties, they theoretically have a long-term stake in the quality achieved, with some taking a quasi social services type role in caring for their residents (Samuel, 2020). In the opinion of Justin Welby the primary purpose of housing associations has to be 'to build bridges towards both personal and community health, using housing as their key asset to deliver this' (Welby, 2018, p. 142). These functions are too important to be left to quasi private sector organisations who may or may not deliver.

Historically the majority of homes built by local authorities were intended to be council-owned social rented housing. However, very few of these have been built since 1990, and the continued commitment to Right to Buy in England (now scrapped in Wales and Scotland) means that local authorities are under pressure to sell on their assets thus reducing social housing provision (Stone, 2017; Welsh Gov, 2018). Nottingham has built 600 affordable homes over three years but loses 400 per year through Right to Buy (Clifford, 2020).

The motivation for local authorities to deliver new homes include: diversifying the housing market, improving stock for private renting, producing tenure neutral new homes, and directly improving design and sustainability (Hackett, 2017). Local authorities traditionally built new 'council housing' for social rent, through their Housing Revenue Account (HRA) and with grant funding from central government, an element of which was debt repayment. However, grants from central government have all but disappeared and many local authorities no longer have an HRA, normally because they transferred all of their housing stock to housing associations. Local authorities have very little money to play with (Fitzgerald and Lupton, 2015). Despite all this councils are experimenting with delivering housing through other means, including semi-independent housing companies (Morphet and Clifford, 2017, 2019) and partnerships with the private sector (see White, 2020). These council-owned companies had, until 2018, been given little attention by government as a way of driving up supply (Hackett, 2017, p. 4). However, they are now beginning to produce significant numbers of new homes, which are likely to exhibit both high design quality and to be policy compliant (Morphet and Clifford, 2019). 95% are building on their own land. The 2019 Stirling Prize Winning development Goldsmith Street in Norwich designed by Mikhail Riches shows what is possible in this area. The 105 homes at Goldsmith Street were funded through a mixture of borrowing, council reserves and funds from Right to Buy (for a useful introduction to local authority borrowing see Lees and Warwick, 2022, p. 212).

Self build & community led housing

Local communities can determine their needs far better than state planning which, of necessity, resorts to standardised models (Turner, 1976). According to Jenny Pickerill around 34% of a cost of a house is labour (Pickerill, 2019, p. 77), so it makes a lot of sense to do it yourself yet UK rates of self build are very low in comparison to other European countries (Wilson, 2017). The mission of the National Custom and Self Build Association is to mainstream self build (NaCSBA, 2019), housing conceived by the residents for the residents (Lloyd, Peel and Janssen-Jansen, 2015). Self build housing can take a variety of forms, ranging literally from building and designing a home yourself, through employing an architect or contractor to assist with the process, to buying a kit house or customising a house from a kit of parts – custom-build – usually on a site with a Local Development Order (LDO), an agreed set of planning rules for that site. As long as the building fits into the rules of the LDO getting planning permission should be swift and simple.

New models, for example, the Igloo 'custom build' systems proposed for their experimental site in Camborne in Cornwall (Waite 2014), offer self builders

Figure 2.1
Custom-build housing at Heartlands, Camborne, Cornwall (2021).
Source: © **Flora Samuel.**

Figure 2.2
Custom-build site at Heartlands, Camborne, Cornwall (2021).
Source: © **Flora Samuel.**

greater choice (Figure 2.1). A local resident I spoke to at Heartlands in Camborne, seemingly a very successful regeneration of an old mining site, told me she'd love to live in one of the custom-build houses if she 'won the lottery'. It is hard to tell whether it is the cost of the plot (circa £50K) or the perceived complexity of the process that is making the development slow going (Figure 2.2).

Community-led developments, for example, Community Land Trusts, housing Co-Ops and cohousing (Scanlon and Fernandez Arrigoitia, 2015) are a small part of the market, but may play a larger role in the future. There has been a major growth in Community Land Trusts since their birth in the 1980s and it is something that the government is supposed to be encouraging. Over 17,000 people are members of CLTs and over 5,000 homes are now in the pipeline (CLT, 2019). An example is Atmos Totnes which had a plan to develop a former Dairy Crest creamery site outside Totnes into 99 homes, including 62 truly affordable houses and 37 ring-fenced homes for older people, as well as a range of other community benefits. To do this the team went through an amazingly convoluted process to take advantage of the new Community Right to Build (Atmos Totnes, 2021). Despite all this the land was sold from beneath them leading George Monbiot to describe the Community Right to Build Laws in England as 'tokenistic and feeble' (2021).

Diversity in housing delivery

One thing that needs to be mentioned before I wrap up this chapter on the people and organisations that play a central role in the delivery of housing is lack of diversity the delivery teams and how this might impact on lack of choice in housing. One survey of housing organisations suggests that only 4% of its executives are racialised black or minority ethnic and 25% identify as women (Inside Housing, 2016), with other surveys backing up this data, a situation doesn't seem to be improving. The statistics in the architecture profession are very similar, and slightly worse in construction (Threlfall, 2019). Fifteen per cent of Royal Institute of Chartered Surveyors (RICS) are women, with only 1% being racialised BAME. This, as RICS admits, is impacting on their ability to attract talent into the field (Clack, 2019). It feels like there must be historical links for all this back to the time, less than 150 years ago, when women weren't allowed to inherit property in the UK. Rather than owning property they *were* property.

One Jamaican smallholding and B & B owner I spoke to told me of the disbelief and tears of joy of a guest, a young woman, racialised black, when she discovered that the owner of the land was Jamaican. The idea of women owning considerable property in their own right, let alone a woman racialised black, still feels shocking. The exclusion of minority groups from the British countryside has to be a direct corollary of the situation described above.

Conclusion

In the UK since 1991 levels of housing construction have only amounted to about 0.5% of the existing stock per year, with amounts of demolition even less (Lowe and Lai Fong, 2020). In 2018 housebuilding reached its highest level in more than 20 years and the UK government has set a target of 300,000 homes constructed per year by the mid-2020s (McKinsey, 2019, p. 11), but this still falls way short of what is needed. If the industry continues to rely on traditional construction methods reaching this goal will require a 40% increase in the current construction workforce headcount with major improvements in productivity. In short, the government can't reach its target if the industry continues to operate the way it has for decades (McKinsey, 2019, p. 11). This chapter has introduced some of the key players in housing delivery in the UK starting with landowners, ranging across the murky world of public/private sector delivery and finishing in the high social value world of self-build and community led development. The issue across the board is gaining access to land which has to be distributed in ways that valorise other kinds of value than money. Not only does housing delivery reflect the societal inequalities we see around us in UK society, but it also reflects historical iniquities around property ownership that continue remorselessly to this day. One result is that housing is not being conceived to accommodate different ways of life but is instead being built on stereotypical assumptions of behaviour and needs (Darke, 1983; Criado Perez, 2019), typified by the current crude emphasis on numbers rather than holistic value.

References

Adam. (2015) *Tomorrow's Home: Emerging Social Trends and Their Impact on the Built Environment*. Adam Architecture. Available at: https://adamarchitecture.com/wp-content/uploads/2019/04/Tomorrows-Home-SUMMARY-report-ADAM-Urbanism-Grainger-plc.pdf.

Adams, D., Croudace, R. and Tiesdell, S. (2012) 'Exploring the "Notional Property Developer" as a policy construct', *Urban Studies*, 49(12), pp. 2577–2596.

Adams, D. and Tiesdell, S. (2012) *Shaping Places, Urban Planning, Design and Development*. London: Routledge.

Adams, D., Tiesdell, S. and White, J. (2013) 'Smart parcelisation: reconciling development and design priorities', *Journal of Urban Design*, 18(4), pp. 459–477.

Atmos Totnes. (2021) *Totnes Community Development Society*. Available at: http://totnescommunity.org.uk/atmos-totnes/.

Banks, C. (2016) *Briefing: The Case for Greater Land Market Transparency*. Shelter. Available at: https://england.shelter.org.uk/professional_resources/policy_and_research/policy_library/briefing_the_case_for_greater_land_market_transparency.

Barton, C., Booth, L. and Wilson, W. (2022) 'Tackling the under-supply of housing in England', *House of Commons Library Research Briefing*. Available at: https://commonslibrary.parliament.uk/research-briefings/cbp-7671/.

Barwise, S. (2019) *Persimmon Homes: Findings of the Independent Review*. Persimmon. Available at: https://www.persimmonhomes.com/corporate/media/397416/findings-of-the-independent-review.pdf.

Buccleuch. (2021) *Buccleuch: Delivering More*. Available at: https://www.buccleuch.com/.

Building. (2017) *Top 20 Housebuilders 2017*, *Building*. Available at: https://www.building.co.uk/data/top-20-housebuilders-2017/5088919.article (Accessed: 15 March 2018).

CABE. (2006) *The Cost of Bad Design*. Available at: http://webarchive.nationalarchives.gov.uk/20110118095356/http://www.cabe.org.uk/files/the-cost-of-bad-design.pdf.

Cares Family & Power to Change. (2022) *Building Our Social Infrastructure*. The Cares Family and Power to Change. Available at: https://files.thecaresfamily.org.uk/thecaresfamily/images/Building-our-social-infrastructure-Final.pdf.

Clack, A. (2019) *Why Diversity and Inclusion Is Crucial to The Built Environment Sector*, *RICS*. Available at: https://www.rics.org/uk/news-insight/future-of-surveying/talent-and-skills/why-diversity-and-inclusion-is-crucial-in-the-built-environment-sector/.

Clapham, D. (2019) *Remaking Housing Policy: An International Study*. London: Routledge.

Clifford, B. (2020) 'Update for RIBA Housing Group'. *Housing Group*, RIBA, London, 25 February.

CLT. (2019) *Community Land Trusts*. Available at: http://www.community-landtrusts.org.uk/what-is-a-clt/about-clts.

Cocker, M. (2018) *Our Place: Can We Save Britian's Wildlife Before It is Too Late*. London: Jonathan Cape.

CPRE. (2017) *CPRE Briefing - How 'Land Promoters' Exploit Legal Loopholes at the Expense of Communities and the Countryside*. Campaign for the Protection of Rural England. Available at: https://www.google.com/url?sa=t&rct=j&q=&esrc=s&source=web&cd=2&ved=2ahUKEwi749Hm6N7iAhVZRxUIHdJJCKEQFjABegQIEBAE&url=https%3A%2F%2Fwww.cpre.org.uk%2Fresources%2Fhousing-and-planning%2Fplanning%2Fitem%2Fdownload%2F5314&usg=AOvVaw2ShYeFAxXk-ReaCWLvmv1A.

Criado Perez, C. (2019) *Invisible Women*. London: Chatto and Windus.

Curtis, R. (2020) 'Grenfell enquiry has exposed design and built as our dirty little secret', *Architect's Journal*. Available at: https://www.architectsjournal.co.uk/opinion/grenfell-inquiry-has-exposed-design-and-build-as-our-dirty-little-secret/10046391.article.

Da Costa, N. (2018) *How Britain's Richest Duke Saved £4billion in Inheritance Tax*, *Linked In*. Available at: https://www.linkedin.com/pulse/how-britains-richest-duke-saved-4-billion-inheritance-neil-da-costa/.

Darke, J. (1983) *The Design of Public Housing: Architects' Intentions and Users' Reaction*. University of Sheffield: Sheffield.

Designing Buildings Wiki. (2021) *Design Life*. Available at: https://www.designing-buildings.co.uk/wiki/Design_life.

Dixon, T. (2006) 'Integrating sustainability into brownfield regeneration: rhetoric or reality? - An analysis of the UK development industry', *Journal of Property Research*, 23(3), pp. 237–267.

DLUHC. (2021) *Consutation and Pre-Decision Matters, Guidance and Support*. Available at: https://www.gov.uk/guidance/consultation-and-pre-decision-matters#Statutory-consultees-on-applications.

Dunning, R. *et al.* (2020) *Affordable Housing Need in Scotland Post 2021*. Available at: https://www.sfha.co.uk/mediaLibrary/other/english/62960.pdf.

Egan, J. (1998) *Rethinking Construction*. Construction Task Force. Available at: http://www.constructingexcellence.org.uk/pdf/rethinking%20construction/rethinking_construction_report.pdf (Accessed: 27 January 2014).

Evans, R. (2019) 'Half of England is owned by less than 1% of the population', *The Guardian*. Available at: https://www.theguardian.com/money/2019/apr/17/who-owns-england-thousand-secret-landowners-author.

Federation of Master Builders. (2018) *FMB House Builders' Survey*. Available at: https://www.fmb.org.uk/media/41090/18-09-05-house-builders-27-survey-2018-final.pdf?utm_source=Report&utm_medium=pdf&utm_campaign=Housebuilderssurvey.

Fitzgerald, A. and Lupton, R. (2015) 'The limits to resilience? The impact of local government spending cuts in London', *Local Government Studies*, 41(4), pp. 582–600.

Fortune. (2020) *Modular Construction, Fortune Business Insights*. Available at: https://www.fortunebusinessinsights.com/industry-reports/modular-construction-market-101662.

Fraser, I. (2017) 'The modern-day barons: inside the murky underbelly of land promotion', *Telegraph.co.uk*. 5 August. Available at: https://www.telegraph.co.uk/business/2017/08/05/modern-day-barons-inside-murky-underbelly-land-promotion/.

Green, S. (2011) *Making Sense of Construction Improvement*. Wiley.

Grosvenor. (2019) *Rebuilding Trust*. Available at: https://www.grosvenor.com/Grosvenor/files/a2/a222517e-e270-4a5c-ab9f-7a7b4d99b1f3.pdf.

Hackett, P. (2017) *Delivering the Renaissance in Council-Built Homes: The Rise of Local Housing Companies*. Ths Smith Institute. Available at: http://www.smith-institute.org.uk/wp-content/uploads/2017/10/The-rise-of-local-housing-companies.pdf.

Harrison, J., Galland, D. and Tewdwr Jones, M. (2021) 'Regional planning is dead: long live planning regional futures', *Regional Studies*, 55(1), pp. 6–18.

HBF. (2017) *Reversing the Decline of Small Housebuilders*. House Builders Federation. Available at: https://www.hbf.co.uk/documents/6879/HBF_SME_Report_2017_Web.pdf.

Hopkirk, E. (2021) '75% of planning authorities have no access to architectural advice', *Building Design*. Available at: https://www.bdonline.co.uk/news/75-of-planning-authorities-have-no-access-to-architectural-advice/5112931.article.

Hughes, C. et al. (2020) 'Implementing a land value tax: Consdieration on moving from theory to practice', *Land Use Policy*, 94, pp. 104–494.

Inside Housing. (2016) 'Diversity focus: Race at the top', *Inside Housing*. Available at: https://jobs.insidehousing.co.uk/article/diversity-focus-race-at-the-top/.

Jefferys, P. and Lloyd, T. (2017) *New Civic Housebuilding: Rediscovering Our Tradiion of Building Beautiful and Affordable Homes*. Shelter England. Available at: https://england.shelter.org.uk/__data/assets/pdf_file/0005/1348223/2017_03_02_New_Civic_Housebuilding_Policy_Report.pdf.

Kelly, J. et al. (2002) *Best Value in Construction*. Oxford; Malden, MA: Blackwell Science.

KFC. (2018) *Kentucky Fried Chicken Limited Response to London Draft Plan*. Available at: https://www.london.gov.uk/sites/default/files/Kentucky%20Fried%20Chicken%20%28KFC%29%20%282723%29.pdf.

King, P. (2017) *Living Alone, Living Together*. Bingley: Emerald Publishing.

Koellewe, J. (2022) 'UK's biggest housebuilders hand top bossess bumber bonuses', *The Guardian*. 26 March. Available at: https://www.theguardian.com/business/2022/mar/26/uk-biggest-housebuilders-persimmon-taylor-wimpey-bumper-bonuses?CMP=Share_iOSApp_Other.

Lawson, V. (2018) *Can a Design-Led Approach to Redevelopment Deliver City Centre Regeneration? A Liverpool Case Study of the Design Dimension of Planning and Development Processes*. University of Manchester. Available at: https://www.research.manchester.ac.uk/portal/en/theses/can-a-designled-approach-to-redevelopment-deliver-city-centre-regeneration-a-liverpool-case-study-of-the-design-dimension-of-planning-and-development-processes(f9cf1b8f-6c7e-4b3b-a854-14122270bfe1).html.

Lawson, V., Purohit, R., Samuel, F., Brennan, J., Farrelly, L., Golden, S., McVicar, M.(2022) *Public Participation in Planning*. CaCHE. https://housingevidence.ac.uk/wp-content/uploads/2022/04/220406-Public-participation-in-planning-in-the-UK_v3.pdf

Layard, A. (2019) 'Privatising land in England', *Journal of Property, Planning and Environmental Law*, 11(2), pp. 151–168.

Leger, C., Balch, C. and Essex, S. (2016) 'Understanding the Planning Challenges of Brownfield Development in Coastal Urban Areas of England', *Planning Practice and Research*, 31(2), pp. 119–131.

Lewis, N. (2019) 'No wonder nothings ever joined up! Housing minister role has highest ministerial churn'. Available at: https://thenegotiator.co.uk/housing-minister-church/.

LGA. (2018) *National Census of Local Authority Councillors 2018*. Local Government Association. Available at: https://www.local.gov.uk/sites/default/files/documents/Councillors%27%20Census%202018%20-%20report%20FINAL.pdf.

Linebaugh, P. (2014) *Stop, Thief!: The Commons, Enclosures, and Resistance*. San Francisco, CA: PM Press/Spectre.

Lloyd, M.G., Peel, D. and Janssen-Jansen, L.B. (2015) 'Self-build in the UK and Netherlands: mainstreaming self-development to address housing shortages?', *Urban, Planning and Transport Research*, 3(1), pp. 19–31.

Lowe, R. and Lai Fong, C. (2020) 'Innovation in deep housing retrofit in the United Kingdom: the role of situated creativity in transforming practice', *Energy Research and Social Science*, 63(May), p. 101391.

MacFadyen, P. (2020) *Flatpack Democracy 2.0*. Bath: Eco-logic Books.

Manning, S. (2013) 'Britain's colonial shame: slave-owners given huge payouts after abolition', *The Independent*. 24 February. Available at: https://www.independent.co.uk/news/uk/home-news/britain-s-colonial-shame-slave-owners-given-huge-payouts-after-abolition-8508358.html.

Martin, A. (2017) *Making the Case for Affordable Housing on Public Land: We Must Use Public Land in the Public Interest*. New Economics Foundation. Available at: https://neweconomics.org/2017/07/affordable-housing-public-land/.

McCarthy, S. (2020) 'MMC set to benefit from the post-Covid housing delivery push', *Property Week*. 18 June. Available at: https://www.propertyweek.com/residential-and-development/mmc-set-to-benefit-from-the-post-covid-housing-delivery-push/5108466.article.

MCCB. (2015) Motivating *Collective Custom Build*. https://shura.shu.ac.uk/21838/1/Motivating_Collective_Custom_Build_%282013%29_-_Full_Report.pdf

McKinsey. (2019) *Scaling Modulor Construction*. Global Infrastructure Initiative. Available at: https://www.mckinsey.com/~/media/McKinsey/Industries/Capital%20Projects%20and%20Infrastructure/Our%20Insights/Voices%20 on%20Infrastructure%20Scaling%20modular%20construction/GII-Voices-Sept-2019.ashx.

MHCLG. (2017) *Fixing Our Broken Housing Market*. Available at: https://www.gov.uk/government/publications/fixing-our-broken-housing-market.

MHCLG. (2019) 'Live tables on housing: New Build Dwellings. Table 241: permanent dwellings completed, by tenure, United Kingdom, historical calendar year series'. https://www.gov.uk/government/statistical-data-sets/live-tables-on-house-building

MHCLG. (2020) *Planning for the Future*. Available at: https://assets.publishing.service.gov.uk/government/uploads/system/uploads/attachment_data/file/872091/Planning_for_the_Future.pdf.

Monbiot, G. (2013) *Feral*. London: Penguin.

Monbiot, G. (2021) 'England's right-to-build laws are tokenistic and feeble - just ask the people of Totnes'. Available at: https://www.theguardian.com/commentisfree/2021/sep/15/england-right-to-build-laws-totnes-devon-housing.

Munbodh, E. (2021) 'Persimmon builds block of flats wrong way round with windows facing backwards', *Daily Mirror*, 14 October. Available at: https://www.mirror.co.uk/money/persimmon-builds-entire-block-flats-25211166?utm_source=twitter.com&utm_medium=social&utm_campaign=sharebar.

Munton, R. (2009) 'Rural land ownership in the United Kingdom: Cahnging patterns and future possibilities for land use', *Land Use Policy*, 26(Supplement 1), pp. 554–561.

NaCSBA. (2019) *NaCSBA, National Custom and Self Build Association*. Available at: https://nacsba.org.uk/.

NHBC. (2019) *Housebuilding: A Century of Innovation*. NHBC Foundation. https://www.nhbcfoundation.org/publication/house-building-a-century-of-innovation/

Parker, G., Dobson, M. and Lynn, T. (2021) *'Paper Tigers': A critical review of statements of community involvement in England*. Civic Voice. Available at: http://www.civicvoice.org.uk/uploads/files/SCI_Research_Final_Report_Oct21.pdf?dm_i=5ZTJ, CNCU, 329J3Y, 1J3UU, 1.

Payne, S. (2016) *Examining housebuilder behaviour in a recovering housing market: recommendations for improving Britain's housing supply*. Available at: https://www.researchgate.net/publication/292139418_Examining_Housebuilder_Behaviour_in_a_Recovering_Housing_Market_Recommendations_for_Improving_Britain%27s_Housing_Supply?channel=doi&linkId=56a9d70e08ae2df821656a37&showFulltext=true.

Payne, S. (2020) 'Advancing understandings of housing supply constraints: housing market recovery and institutional transitions in speculative housebuilding', *Housing Studies*, 35(2), pp. 266–289.

Peabody Trust, *Peabody announces small projects panel*. (2014) *Peabody*. Available at: https://www.peabody.org.uk/news-views/2014/feb/peabody-announces-small-projects-panel.

Pickerill, J. (2019) 'Building eco-homes for all', in Trogal, K., Bauman, I., Lawrence, R., and Petrescu, D. (eds.) *Architecture and Resilience*. London: Routledge, pp. 76–87.

Place Alliance. (2019) *National Housing Design Audit*. Available at: https://placealliance.us9.list-manage.com/track/click?u=281b97ce7de7511e7312f2003&id=b9cd026769&e=7699dd745e.

Powell-Smith, A. and Shrubsole, G. (2017) *What Land Is Owned by Housing Developers, Who Owns England?* Available at: https://whoownsengland.org/2017/11/22/what-land-is-owned-by-housing-developers/.

Public Practice. (2020) *Diversifying Planning: How Can We Make Sure Design Review Panels Represent the Diversity of the Communities They Serve*. Available at: https://publicpractice.org.uk/resources/how-can-we-make-sure-design-review-panels-represent-the-diversity-of-the-communities-they-serve.

Rae, A. (2017) *A Land Cover Atlas of the UK*. University of Sheffield. Available at: https://figshare.com/articles/journal_contribution/A_Land_Cover_Atlas_of_the_United_Kingdom_Document_/5266495.

Rhodes, C. (2018) *Briefing Paper: Construction Industry: Statistics and Policy*. Briefing Paper 01432. House of Commons Library.

RIBA and Colander. (2014) *RIBA Business Benchmarking Report 2013/14*. London: RIBA.

RICS. (2019) *Revalue Synoptic Report*. Available at: https://revalue-project.eu/wp-content/uploads/2019/08/D4.4-Synoptic-Report.pdf.

RTPI. (2019) *Resourcing Public Planning*. RoyalTown Planning Institute. Available at: https://www.rtpi.org.uk/media/3415870/ResourcingPublicPlanning2019.pdf.

Samuel, F. (2020) *Impact of Housing Design and Placemaking on Social Value and Wellbeing in the Pandemic Interim Report*. UK Collaborative Centre for Housing Evidence (CaCHE). https://housingevidence.ac.uk/publications/impact-of-housing-design-and-placemaking-on-social-value-and-wellbeing-in-the-pandemic-interim-report/

Savills. (2021) *In Plain English: The Tilted Balance*. Available at: https://www.savills.co.uk/blog/article/312988/residential-property/in-plain-english--the-tilted-balance.aspx.

Scanlon, K. and Fernandez Arrigoitia, M. (2015) 'Development of new cohousing: lessons from a London scheme for the over-50s', *Urban Research and Practice*, 8(1), pp. 106–121.

Shelter. (2015) *Housing Supply*. Available at: http://england.shelter.org.uk/campaigns_/why_we_campaign/housing_facts_and_figures/subsection?section=housing_supply#hf_4.

Shrubsole, G. (2019) *Who Owns England?* London: William Collins.

Sinnett, D. et al. (2014) *From Wasted Space to Living Spaces: The Availability of Brownfield Land for Housing Development in England*. Council for the Protection of Rural England. Available at: https://www.cpre.org.uk/wp-content/uploads/2021/05/From_Wasted_Space_to_Living_Spaces_CPRE-report-Nov-2014.pdf.

Stantec. (2019) *Vacant and Derelict Land in Scotland*. Scottish Land Commission. Available at: https://www.landcommission.gov.scot/downloads/5dd7d4dfa39b6_VDL%20in%20Scotland%20Final%20Report%2020191008.pdf.

Stone, J. (2017) 'New Government plan to extend Right to Buy "to hit affordable housebuilding"', *Independent*. 19 February. Available at: https://www.independent.co.uk/news/uk/politics/right-to-buy-housing-crisis-housebuilding-corporations-companies-john-healey-a7582336.html.

Threlfall, R. (2019) 'Construction must admit it has a problem with diversity', *Building*. Available at: https://www.building.co.uk/comment/construction-must-admit-it-has-a-problem-with-diversity/5098743.article.

Transparency International. (2015) *UK property gives global corrupt a home*. Available at: https://www.transparency.org/en/press/uk-property-gives-global-corrupt-a-home#.

Turner, J. (1976) *Housing by People: Towards Autonomy in Building Environments*. London: Marion Boyars.

Uandl. (2021) *Data and the Planning System*. London: U and I plc. Available at: https://www.uandiplc.com/media/2914/uandi_ppp-datareport_05.pdf.

UCL. (2021) *Centre for the Study of the Legacies of British Slavery*. University College London. Available at: https://www.ucl.ac.uk/lbs/.

UK Gov. (2015) *Housing and Economic Needs Assessment*.

UK Gov. (2019) *Housing Supply and Delivery*. Available at: https://www.gov.uk/guidance/housing-supply-and-delivery.

Wainwright, O. (2014) 'The truth about property developers: how they are exploiting planning authorities and ruining our cities', *The Guardian*. 17 September. Available at: https://www.theguardian.com/cities/2014/sep/17/truth-property-developers-builders-exploit-planning-cities.

Wainwright, O. (2015) 'Revealed: how developers exploit flawed planning system to minimise affordable housing'. Available at: https://www.theguardian.com/cities/2015/jun/25/london-developers-viability-planning-affordable-social-housing-regeneration-oliver-wainwright.

Wainwright, O. (2020) '"This is the Everest of zero carbon" - indisde York's green home revolution', *The Guardian*. 4 October. Available at: https://www.theguardian.com/artanddesign/2020/oct/04/everest-zero-carbon-inside-yorks-green-home-revolution.

Waite, R. (2014) 'Carillion Igloo unveils designs for pioneering custom-build scheme', *Architects Journal*. Available at: https://www.architectsjournal.co.uk/news/carillion-igloo-unveils-designs-for-pioneering-custom-build-scheme/8673238.article (Accessed: 7 February 2017).

Walker, R. (2021) *Green Grocer*. London: Dorling Kindersley.

Welby, J. (2018) *Reimagining Britain*. London: Bloomsbury.

Welsh Gov. (2018) *Abolition of the Right to Buy and Associated Rights (Wales) Act 2018*. Available at: https://gov.wales/topics/housing-and-regeneration/legislation/abolition-of-right-to-buy-and-associated-rights/?lang=en.

White, J. *et al*. (2020) *Delivering Design Value: Housebuilding and the Design Quality Conundrum*. UK Collaborative Centre for Housing Evidence (CaCHE). https://housingevidence.ac.uk/publications/delivering-design-value-the-housing-design-quality-conundrum/

Wilson, W. (2017) *Self-Build and Custom Build Housing*. Available at: https://commonslibrary.parliament.uk/research-briefings/sn06784/.

WSP. (2007) *Manual for Streets*. Thomas Telford Publishing. Available at: https://assets.publishing.service.gov.uk/government/uploads/system/uploads/attachment_data/file/341513/pdfmanforstreets.pdf.

Chapter 3

Housing knowledge

Can we properly examine the lack of something without fully appreciating what that something is and does? But this is precisely what the field of academic research known as 'housing studies does'.

(King, 2022, p. 5)

We lack any solid knowledge of what actually works in housing, let alone what might make people happy, so it is hard to make the case for doing things differently. I begin this chapter with a reflection on the UK research agenda and the way it plays out in universities, before moving onto a discussion of housing research and some of its silos. This account builds on a more in-depth discussion of 'knowledge' development in the construction industry set out in my book *Why Architects Matter* (2018) and is skewed towards a discussion of architectural knowledge. It should however be noted that architecture, according to the Department of Culture Media and Sport definitions, includes planning (DCMS, 2014). It finishes with a reflection on the paucity of reliable information available to the general public.

What is research?
Research is a process of systematic and original investigation undertaken in order to gain knowledge and understanding and to also to de-risk innovation. Ideally research is disseminated in a way that enables others to learn from it. The ultimate aim of much research, as it has developed over the years through generations of scholars, is to predict the future and to gain advantage therein.

While the research process may be systematic it takes judgement and creativity to come up with the right question. Recently there has been greater acknowledgement of the creative element within science (Sheldrake, 2020), while conversely the systematic 'scientific' nature of art practice is acquiring more credence (Leski, 2015, p. xx). The boundaries between art and science are not really that clear cut (Latour, 1998) with the complex and diverse subject of housing sitting very uncomfortably in their murky interstices.

Systematic research has been around for a very long time. I have no inclination to go back into the spaces of early Western modernism, which in philosophical terms was somewhere in the 17th century, or into the origins of 'scientific' methods, about which a great deal has been written (see, for example, Buchli, 2013). Suffice to say this was a time when natural processes were artificially separated out from spiritual experience and became constructs formulated to help explain phenomena (Ray, 2008, p. 21). The 'enlightenment' excluded forms of knowledge that didn't fit the mould, notably that of the many women who were burnt at the stake for apparently knowing too much. It sought to limit what counts as knowledge to that which can be felt through our physical senses. Not only did this deny any sense of the spiritual but undermined the importance of subjective experiences that cannot be independently verified. It 'gave us modernity, yet it also bequeathed us a splintered world in which we struggle to find ourselves' (Steel, 2020, p. 244). It became still more complex with advent of postmodernism in the 1960s which shattered modernist conceptions of totalising truth (that there is one way of seeing the world) by recognising the validity of a multiplicity of different viewpoints or subjectivities, most notably those of under-represented peoples. Since then it has been widely acknowledged that distributed consciousnesses of all kinds, whether in creatures, plants or people, matter (Braidotti, 2019, p. 54). As a result reflexivity, acknowledging the limitations of one's own approach, has become a key element of high-quality research, even 'hard' science. It is also vital for sharing expert knowledge and risk with society (Beck, 1986; Nowotny, Scott and Gibbons, 2001).

Research is always highly political. Nowhere is this more clear than in the way in which it is funded, the allocation of research resource being an important tool for delivering government agendas. Research cultures vary considerably across the world as does investment in research with the UK lagging behind, even before Brexit. In 2015 South Korea invested 4.23% of gross domestic product in research, Germany 2.93%, China 2.07% and the UK 1.71% (Visual Capitalist, 2017; UNESCO, 2020). The results are there for all to see in the things in our homes. Researchers and their teams apply for funding from a variety of national bodies – in the UK the research councils, charities and sometimes industry – or international bodies such the European Research Council. STEM (Science Technology Engineering Mathematics) subjects historically receive favourable treatment over arts and humanities, at least financially. A good deal of early stage research is publicly funded with the private sector moving in to provide investment only when the process has largely been de-risked (Mazzucato, 2018). In this way community wealth is continually drained from the system.

Within Britain itself Research and Development (R & D) investments is unfairly spread, expressing itself as two distinct economies firstly London and the South-East and secondly the rest of the UK. 'The UK's unbalanced R & D landscape is reflected in its unbalanced economic performance, and we've chosen it to be this way' (Forth and Jones, 2020, p. 1). 'If the government were to spend at the same intensity in the rest of the country as it does in the wider South East of England, it would spend £4 billion more' (Forth and Jones, 2020, p. 5).

Research knowledge is disseminated through the publication of refereed journal papers. The knowledge in them is supposedly of the highest quality as it has been vetted by other experts through a refereeing process. Until recently refereed journals were expensive and difficult to access for people in industry –

universities pay for licences that make access free to academics and students. An outcry about publishers cashing in on research paid for by the UK taxpayer means that publicly funded research has to be open access. This means that a great deal more research is freely available to the housing research community than before, but those in industry have acclimatised themselves to doing without, one result being a tendency to constantly re-invent the wheel (Samuel, 2018).

Government data collection

> *Why isn't land and location taught or seen as important in modern economics or integrated into national accounting?*
> *(Ryan-Collins, Lloyd and Macfarlane, 2017, p. 2)*

According to the scientific rationalist world view decision making is based on evidence produced by scientists, however it isn't always possible to slice the world up into evidenced outcomes and any claims by government that policy is evidence based are hollow (Lees and Warwick, 2022). In reality governments take a pick and mix approach to evidence, trying things out to see how well it goes down with the key interest groups that they are trying to impress (Clapham, 2019, p. 15). 'With poor data housing policy and practice remain inordinately reliant, respectively, on polemic and fashion' (Maclennan and More, 1999, p. 23). That policies fail on a regular basis, and why, is rarely discussed (Temenos, Lauermann, 2020). You might think that governments would be looking at what other governments are doing to see what works in terms of policy but there is a paucity of research into comparative approaches (Stephens, 2011). It seems that international policy transfer is a difficult subject.

It has come as a surprise to me to discover how rarely the government is cross correlating datasets. The 'Administrative data', the information we all give out routinely – for example, at Accident & Emergency departments in hospitals is only now being correlated with homelessness data to understand who, and where, services are being used. This is being done by academic researchers and not by the government (Browne-Gott, 2019). It is also worth noting that there are no agreed measures for important things like digital exclusion and housing density (Harper, 2013) making data gathering in this area very difficult. Lees and Warwick note the presence of 'policy blind spots on data', for example on the location of high rise council housing and who lives in them (Lees and Warwick, 2022, p. 108). None of this helps.

In terms of the data that is regularly collected about the UK the UK Statistics Authority 'promotes and safeguards the production and publication of statistics that serve the public good' (Statistics Authority, 2021). Much of this is collected by the Office of National Statistics (ONS), the recognised national statistical institute of the UK, responsible for collating and publishing statistics related to the economy, population and society at national, regional and local levels. Interestingly the ONS has very little data on the activities of the very wealthy which remain shrouded in mystery (Dorling, 2014). The British Household Panel Survey has been going since 1991 and is a particularly important dataset about housing (British Household Panel Survey, 2018), but the questions that it asks tell us little about the specific impacts of types of housing on quality of life. Census data is available in map form from the digital platform Digimap alongside a range of other fascinating information but the cost of licensing impacts on the ability of people and organisations to use it. Data still tends to be collected on a periodic basis and is 'focussed on economic rather than social pursuits' (Batty, 2017, p.800), but all this is set to change.

The UK government has signed up to the idea of 'Open Government Data (OGD)', a sub-set of open data, that is open to all to support the purposes of democracy however only a very small amount of OGD data is actually intelligible to the public (Wang and Shepherd, 2020). A recent report by the UK Geospatial Commission found that improved communication was needed if people were going to feel comfortable about sharing their data and to help them make more informed choices (Cabinet Office, 2021). The Open Data institute has been working with government and others to open up the Land Registry for public perusal as this is so key to the planning and delivery of houses in the right places. A complete Land Registry can help us make important cross-correlations of data such as links between health and fast food outlets, access to green space and so on (Shrubsole, 2019, p. 193).

Guy Shrubsole's excellent book *Who Owns England* make clear just how very little is known about land ownership, particularly in England. Knowledge of land ownership is vital for transparency and taxation but also to make sure that people are accountable for the way that they use their land. According to Shrubsole around 17% of England and Wales remains unregistered, with their likely owners being the aristocracy. Having an incomplete Land Registry means that it is very difficult to do systematic holistic data gathering and planning. Often we can only find out what is happening on private estates when the landowner deposits an estate map with a local authority with the aim of making sure nobody makes claims to rights of way across their estate. These maps are 'buried' in local authority websites and 'gathering dust' in council offices with only a very few digitising them and making them available to the public (Shrubsole, 2019, p. 39). Landowners have been quick to cash in on the benefits available to them, the late Queen and James Dyson being leaders in this field (Ibid), so data on farm subsidies can also provide a useful means to establish ultimate ownership.

Research in universities

UK Research and Innovation, the organisation that sets the tone for research both in industry and academia is waking up to the urgent need to join the dots through data (UKRI, 2020) but the university sector is poorly placed to respond. Working for a university is now very different to how it was when I began teaching in 1996. The replacement of the university grants system with punitive fees is disincentivising people from undertaking higher education while universities themselves are being starved of cash as the value of UK fees and research income dwindles. Universities look to overseas students to fill the hole but UK universities recently suffered their worst performance in history in world rankings (Hall, 2020) meaning that the likelihood that students will still want to come to our universities is set to diminish. Not only will the UK's status as a knowledge leader dwindle, but local authorities will be wondering what to do about all the empty student accommodation and losses in jobs caused by their departure.

As funding sources move more towards measurable impact and cross disciplinary work housing ought to be attracting more funding but it is a messy and complex area that fails to lend itself to the disaggregation into soluble parts, easy comparisons or established methodological approaches that are so necessary for getting past funding council reviewers. Further university promotions tend to favour numbers of publications in refereed journals and access to grant funding over real world impact as it is less easy to quantify. This makes working with industry and communities an unattractive prospect for early career researchers who are simultaneously overwhelmed by teaching load and precarious contracts.

There is at the same time a decline in housing education which remains a low status and unattractive subject, despite its impact on our lives, evidenced perhaps by the fact that there are almost no dedicated housing masters programmes to be found in the UK. One expert that I spoke with observed that when he did his Chartered Institute of Housing professional qualification it was a three year course roughly at degree level. The current diploma is just 60 credits at level 5. It is now easier to become professionally qualified as an expert in housing, but the level of knowledge expected has decreased dramatically.

Public sector research

Arguably the pinnacle of housing research funding happened after the Second World War (Darke and Darke, 1979, p. 134) when it 'enjoyed widespread and uncritical support' (Lansley, 1997, p. 320). At this time there was a major push on Codes of Practice, standardisation and non-traditional forms of construction resulting in the creation of New Directorates of Post-War Building, and Building Materials within the portfolio of the Minister of Works – a dedicated ministry being indicative of the support given to construction and infrastructure at that time. Research in the 1950s was focussed largely on the improving the functional relationship between space and activities as well as the improved development of environment control. 'Each study was securely financed to its conclusion, and the pressures of the design/build process were taken off in the interests of careful testing of the proposed solutions' (Musgrove et al., 1975, p. 41). Nearly all of this research took place in the public sector. The idea that government action should flow from scientific evidence became popular building on from Labour Prime Minister Harold Wilson's 'White Heat of Technology Speech' of 1963 (Sharr and Thornton, 2013; Cocker, 2018).

The situation was to deteriorate as the policies of the Conservative government kicked in in the early 1980s and the local authority housing departments were closed down, together with their considerable efforts at housing research. Market economies are wasteful in terms of innovation because of the amount of duplication and spillover that happens in different organisations (Bloom, Van Reenen and Williams, 2019), an issue that underpins this book. Research needs clear leadership.

There has been a minor renaissance in local authority research of late. An interesting example is the Proptech Engagement Fund pilots recently proffered by Department of Levelling Up, Housing and Communities (DLUHC) to encourage the digital transformation of local authority planning (Say, 2021). These bids tend to rely on a fast turnaround of activity meaning that local authorities need to have bidding teams set with 'oven ready' proposals if they are to have any chance of success, something that is quite challenging in the current context, particularly in public sector organisations. This may be why the government tends to rely on the private sector to undertake its research. An example is that that the government's Geospatial Commission has recently appointed Atkins to deliver a digital map of underground pipes and cables throughout the UK (Hakimian, 2021). This is a vitally necessary undertaking and Atkins is full of clever and responsible people, including former students of mine, but why is it outsourced?

Universities too are very often sidelined from the process. Hamstrung by arcane processes they are largely unable to work at the pace necessary government and industry collaboration. My personal experience of tendering for government research jobs is unfathomable contractual obligation and a deadline of three weeks, something that is completely impossible when it takes a minimum of three months to employ a research assistant in every university context I have encountered. I'd say I have had to spend as much time ploughing through systems to make new things possible as I've actually been able to spend actually doing research. This is not accounted for in any 'workload model' and another reason why universities are losing out.

Housing research in industry and practice

That public faith in professionals is on the wane is not helped by the fact that so many professionals are working on the basis of second rate knowledge (Samuel, 2018). This has much to do with the activities of certain professional institutions which have been more concerned with raising revenue through increased membership, than with the safeguarding of standards.

Since the demise of public sector research the private sector has shown itself to be woefully unprepared to shoulder the responsibility of housing research (Samuel, 2018). There are, for example, a number of major hindrances to the development of research in architecture practice, including a hostility to the word 'research' with its overly academic associations (Dye, 2014), lack of research training in architecture schools, lack of investment in research (Lu and Sexton, 2009), lack of support from the academic community, as well as a 'papyrophobic' reluctance to commit experiments to paper in a systematic manner in the written word (Groak, 1992, p. 170). Further diffident attitudes to data have resulted in a 'skills gap in the ability to develop robust business cases using accurate and up to date evidence' (CDBB, 2021, p. 10). Despite this 'Research performed by practitioners has an important role to play in the development of the field' (Kirk Hamilton and Watkins, 2009, p. 39). It is also the research that practitioners value the most (Samuel et al., 2013).

In architecture the act of returning to a building to find out how it is performing is generally referred to as Post Occupancy Evaluation or POE (Stevenson, 2019). It is something that rarely, if ever, happens – POE only accounted for 1% of practice income in the Royal Institute of British Architects (RIBA) 2017 Business Benchmarking survey – partly because of nervousness about the results and partly because nobody wants to pay for it. There are a variety of POE systems in place, with considerable overlap between them. It tends to focus on things that are relatively easy to measure like energy use, not on less tangible but extremely important things such as impact of housing on wellbeing, the focus of this book (Hay *et al.*, 2017). Measures to express the relationship between housing and health are, as a result, crude and mechanistic (Baker *et al.*, 2017) and there is dearth of knowledge on what works.

The Creative Industries are taking over from Financial Services as the biggest generator of UK GDP (Innovate UK, 2015). If only we could use some of that creative industries sparkle to bring life to our moribund housing and construction industries. Architecture ought to act as a conduit between construction and other parts of the creative industries, for example, software & computer games, visual arts and museums, but is largely failing to do this because of its own underdeveloped research culture.

There are pockets of housing research happening within the digital industries. Discussions of smart homes remain almost exclusively within electrical engineering, information technology, computer science, gerontology, biomedicine and robotics (Marikyan et al., 2019. These are the people introducing frictionless experiences into our homes using algorithms often gendered male (Criado Perez, 2019). There is a 'knowledge gap between the disciplines of computing, architecture and healthcare meaning causing a delay in the uptake of smart home technologies. 'Architecture and town planning have been much less involved with smart house technologies, although they will be the professional group that will be responsible for designing and implementing smart homes and the future smart city' (Bitterman and Schach-Pinsly, 2015, p. 266).

The historic adoption of digital technologies by different industry sectors is a barrier to joined up thinking on housing. The architecture and construction industries have been encouraged by some government initiatives like Digital Built Britain (2015) to move to Building Information Modelling (BIM) using software such as Revit in which layers can be tagged with information. This tends to start with the building and move down to the ground, perhaps encompassing things like car parks. People working in infrastructure, often engineers, have come through the Computer-Aided Design (CAD) route of starting with the ground. At the same time groups such as geographers who work on the systems of things have mobilised Geographic Information Systems (GIS) to make models and maps of places. Neither tend to work with the gaming engines that are so effective in bringing places to life in the imaginations of people. These ways of working and tools are in urgent need of alignment. The Centre for Digital Built Britain has been tasked with integration through the 'National Digital Twin', but it feels like a long way off.

Little research has been undertaken into the connection between housing, housing and food production despite the intimate connections between them.

There is, for example, an urgent need to collect examples of 'effective governance instruments and experiences' in order to' better identify successful approaches for integrating city-based food production into urban sector policies and urban land use planning instruments, and to facilitate the development of safe and sustainable urban agriculture' (Russo *et al.*, 2017, p. 62). This also has to be a concern of housing. In general 'Urban planning, both research and practice, has a lot of catching up to do' (Wilson and Tewdwr-Jones, 2022, p.16).

Academic housing research

'What is being studied in the field of housing studies is not housing as such. Rather it is the study of the failure of policy' (King, 2022, p. 6). Peter King calls this approach 'policy thinking', setting it in opposition to the lived experience of 'dwelling', the literature of which has 'not been written yet' (King, 2009, p. 50). In my experience 'housing studies' focusses on economics, though this is rarely said outright. That housing research is such a vaguely constituted field of academic research – not a discipline – doesn't help (Kemeny, 1991; Ruonavaara, 2017). Whether housing studies should be a field of its own or the common denominator or multiple fields is highly contested (Maclennan and Bannister, 1995, p. 1581). Hani Ruonavaara describes it 'as a multidisciplinary field of research comprised of research in sociology, psychology, economics, anthropology, history, planning, architecture, philosophy and other academic and professional disciplines' (Ruonavaara, 2017, p. 180). Each of these fields is itself in a constant state of flux (Maclennan and Bannister, 1995).

> An approximation of what is housing-related could be something like this: a topic of research is housing-related if its description entails a reference to housing or housing as well as environments in which these are embedded. According to this definition housing choice, home-making, homelessness, the history and organization of social housing, housing equity release, residential segregation, squatting, self-building, privatization of public rental stock, housing policy, neighbouring, neighbourhood community, et cetera are all housing-related topics.
>
> (Ruonavaara, 2017, p. 172)

This definition is unusually inclusive as design and construction are rarely included in academic housing research a field characterised by silos. One casualty of all this is a lack of agreement on the lived experience of housing and how best to evaluate housing outcomes, in other words, what makes good housing (Foye, 2021).

Housing research in architecture

Architects have actually been writing about the lived experience of dwelling for millennia but, because architects have been so unclear about whether they are artists or scientists and the specific methodologies that they bring to the table their work tends to be disregarded (Samuel, 2019). Within the field of architecture evidence-based design emerged in the second half of the 20th century as 'a process for the conscious, explicit, and judicious use of current best evidence from research and practice in making critical decisions, together with an informed client, about the design of each individual and unique project' (Kirk Hamilton and Watkins, 2009, p. 9). Important protagonists of evidence-based and systems thinking (the clustering of data to inform decision making) were Leslie Martin and Lionel March at Cambridge University and Richard Llewelyn Davis at University College London, instigators of the 1958 Oxford Conference on Education, an attempt to place architecture within the academy of science-based research. It was at this point that experiments in ecological building began to take off. Martin's principles were absorbed into a wide range of initiatives still extant, for example, the National Building Specification, defining and setting standards for construction. Such design guides were seen as 'generative rules' ripe with programming potential by early computing researchers (Sprunt, 1975, p. 15).

The systems thinkers who worked steadily on the development of architectural computing and computer-aided design throughout the 1970s and 1980s (Samuel, 2014) laid the platform for digital design through the evolution of generative rules, in particular parametric design, through which data is seemingly translated into form through three dimensional modelling software. They also laid the platform for the code based planning system that is likely to be our future. The knowledge generated by evidence-based approaches is often characterised as being overly simplistic and functionalist (Fraser, 2013), but an examination of its history and conversations with its advocates reveals that this was not the intention.

The late 1960s and early 1970s were a heyday of collaborative research between evidence-based architects, planners and social scientists on the impact of new housing models. There was a particular hunger for knowledge about how well these experimental buildings were working for people (Gutman, 1972, p. 179; Reizenstein, 1975, p. 28), but only it seemed if the results showed architects in a positive light (Broady, 1972, p. 179). It was at this time that architects were accused of 'determinism', for exaggerating their impact (see, for example, Broady, 1968, pp. 7–14) – a claim that caused great damage to the research culture of the profession, stunting its emergent knowledge base on the relationship between people and the environment (Macmillan, 2006, p. 258). During this period, despite the fact that the built environment has a very obvious impact on quality of life (Halpern, 1995), architects dropped the thread of environment-behaviour research leaving it largely to environmental psychologists and others to unravel (Gifford, 1997), concerning themselves instead with the more aesthetic side of buildings (Samuel, 2018).

Important, but often ignored, impetus for evidence-based design came from a growing band of feminist architects who were outraged at the way in which the built environment failed to address the problems of the disadvantaged, particularly women (Matrix, 1984). Researchers in the 1960s became increasingly aware that architects were developing designs based on stereotype conceptions of the council tenants who they were to house (Morris and Mogey, 1965, p. 9).

When interviewing the architects of six social rented (council) housing schemes in London designed during the mid-to late 1960s and completed in the early 1970s Jane Darke found that architects made little if any 'attempt to evaluate the accuracy of their images of the users' (Darke, 1984a, p. 389). Although they had little direct knowledge of council tenants they never questioned the adequacy of their knowledge as a basis for design (Darke, 1984b, p. 405). 'For all the lip service paid to the occupiers' desire to personalise their homes, actual scope for doing so was limited to conventional opportunities to choose furnishings' (Darke, 1984a, p. 393). Research continues to be a characteristic of feminist design practice. Fionn Stevenson's book *Housing Fit Purpose*, which promotes the use of evidence in housing design and is one of the best resources we have on how to make sustainable housing (Stevenson, 2019), comes out of this stable.

The architectural design process, based on a design studio teaching model is 'unique to architectural education and possibly our major contribution' (Ray, 2008, p. 19). Design studio is a collective method of working in which multiple parties negotiate solutions through constant adjustment of 'artefacts of knowing' (Ewenstein and Whyte, 2007; Latour, 1986). These can take the form of drawings, models and diagrams, but can also be networks, processes and strategies. The 'boundary objects' are to work as tools of negotiation they need to 'represent, learn about and transform knowledge' (Carlile, 2002). Architects have the useful skill of making imaginaries of buildings and places that can change and evolve with input from others, but they have been very bad at making this known.

Academic housing research in the social sciences

In line with the neoliberal fixation on financial analysis economists have 'colonised' areas previously owned by other disciplines, notably housing which, as Bill Jordan argues, has provided further justification for governments to look at the world through the lens of money (2008). Believing problems can be solved through fiscal policy alone economists have discouraged other kinds of government intervention in housing (Whitehead, 2014). Economists have been known to use 'social discounting rates' to calculate the impact of what is done now on the next generation, in this way causing what Roman Krzarnic calls the 'enslavement' of our descendants (2020, p. 76). It is important to note that economics comprises a very wide range of approaches and political persuasions (Gibb, 2014) and there is potential within 'behavioural economics' for more engagement with the needs and wants of 'actors'. There is however a danger that they are stylised into variants of 'economic man' with little or no variation to account for cultural or physical differences.

Most housing studies people can be found in planning schools which tend to sit firmly in the social sciences. This is probably why books like *The Sage Handbook of Housing* are almost entirely social science based, with the boundaries between social science disciplines being increasingly blurred. In an effort to identify themselves with standards of rigour required of university research (and to avoid the cost of expensive construction laboratories), construction, project management and real estate have nearly all aligned themselves with the social sciences with a focus on the study and enhancement of processes. You are more likely to find the messy business of making buildings happening in engineering or product design schools than construction schools.

What the social science based housing studies field may have lacked in multidisciplinary innovation it has made up for in a cohesiveness that enabled it to take leadership of the field. Interestingly Chris Allen has argued that social science based 'housing studies' as a field is 'wounded' because of its lack of interest in 'the conceptualisations of ordinary people' (Allen, 2009). Examples include the omission of discussions of nostalgia (Jarvis and Bonnett, 2013) and taste (Horn, 2019). Engagement with issues of race is a key issue. Building on the early work of John Rex and Robert Moore, *Race, Community and Conflict* (1969) and Jeff Henderson and Valerie Karn's *Race, Class and State Housing* (1987) studies around ethnicity and class inequality and class are gaining more traction in the field. Social scientists are finding themselves increasingly drawn into the urgent action oriented movements such as Black Lives Matter and the Climate Change Emergency. Hilary Cottam, trained as a social scientist, describes the radically different mindset that she has had to develop on her route to becoming a designer who could actually make new things happen (2018). Increasingly 'an interdisciplinary housing studies that moves beyond the limits of positivism and is built around the relationship between humans and the material house' (Clapham, 2009) is becoming an exciting possibility.

Housing research in the arts

If architects are marginal to housing research the situation has to be even worse for the arts and humanities which, largely unable to deliver measurable impact, have an increasingly precarious role in neoliberal universities, despite being the crucible of creativity and innovation (Edmondson, 2020). 'For many years, artists have contributed to the design and organization of structures of living together, often with ambivalent effect' (Phillips and Erdemici, 2012, p. 16). Here is one example:

> . . . SKOR curator Nils van Beek describes an action organized by a group of Amsterdam-based volunteers in collaboration with the Yes Men, to directly intervene in the process of a housing regulation change, and how this resulted in questions being asked in parliament. A direct form of politics, concludes van Beek, but was it necessary to call it art?
> (Phillips and Erdemici, 2012, p. 19)

Not only do artists (and writers) depict homes and housing in their works (Rachel Whiteread's Turner Prize Winning, *House,* 1993, is a case in point), they produce art for homes and neighbourhoods, including performative art events that draw attention to different forms of inhabitation (Super Slow Way, 2020). They can also be part of developer teams, playing a role in visioning and consultation on placemaking (Lennon, 2020), yet somehow their artistic ways of knowing are very largely excluded from mainstream housing debate or production. 'Arts-activism' is however playing an important role in helping people to rethink their homes and places (Renold *et al.*, 2020). That the arts and crafts, performance, music, dance, film and so provide glue for the making of communities, the formation of identity and critically the way that we are collectively addressing global challenges is unequivocal but unfortunately there isn't much research to prove it. The point here is that neighbourhoods and housing have to be looked at in an interdisciplinary way (Moulaert *et al.*, 2010) and that has to include 'the arts' which have an uncanny ability to shift entrenched positions by appealing to the emotional self (Madgin and Lesh, 2021). There is a major job to do here in winning hearts and minds when people's ideas about housing are set in stone with the mortar of media misinformation.

Public information limited

In theory we are already part of a system that embraces the viewpoints of citizens through the processes, of representative and deliberative democracy but the public is lacking a trustworthy baseline of evidence-based knowledge from which to make informed decisions about what they want from their housing and places. Despite efforts by some local authorities (see, for example, Nottinghamshire County Council, 2021) knowledge can be hard to access or it is communicated in language that includes so much jargon that it can only be understood by experts or presented in a highly unengaging manner. Not only that but it lacks the editorial touch so urgently needed for busy people to read. I received a recent tweet from Wendy Blyth of the Federation of Cambridge Residents' Associations:

> Community consultation? Try wading through the 10,000pp of Gter Cambs Planning Service's Local Plan focused on employment growth. So many growth arcs impacting Cambridge. Not just #OxCamArc. You cite 'process' of consultation? Where is the public in this?
>
> 15 October 2021

In a further tweet she makes the cogent point that the Director of Greater Cambridge Planning Service's job title is 'Director of Planning and Economic Development', further evidence of the common collusion between the two fields.

The way in which the public are asked to participate in a process can impact strongly on the preferences that they express. 'Community surveys and participatory mapping generated more accurate and representative community information compared to the formal public participation process which was characterised by lower participation and vulnerability to special interest manipulation' (Brown and Eckold, 2020, p. 85). Sherry Arnstein's eight stage 'Ladder of Participation' is a well-known tool for delineating the different stages of the participation process starting with 'Manipulation', moving through 'Therapy', 'Informing', 'Consultation', 'Placation' – all forms of 'tokenism' – through to 'Partnership', 'Delegated Power' and 'Citizen Control', the culmination of the process (Arnstein, 1969). Seen in this way we in Britain seem to be stuck in the throes of tokenistic engagement but it is hard to judge when there is a general lack of 'systematic empirical studies on how public participation is practiced' (Uittenbroek *et al.*, 2019) and ways to improve social learning (Jarvis, 2019, p. 65).

In the business world there is much talk of brain drains and the need to capitalise on the knowledge economy. If only there was similar talk about lived experience of non-experts. That people lack the language or ambition to articulate what they really want or need in terms of their housing (Samuel, 2008) clearly has its origins in our education system which is, in turn, based on the dysfunctional system described above. Perhaps unsurprisingly the subject of housing is poorly represented within UK schools. Housing has great affinity with Geography, a subject that is stripped of meaning and importance within the strictures of the national curriculum in England and is being blown about according to political whim. This is partly because of a lack of clarity about what is key Geographical knowledge at the scale of society and at the scale of schools (Rawling, 2020). Criticisms of the National Curriculum for England, a mechanistic form of education preparing people for a mechanistic way of life, are widespread. Alarmingly curriculum design is 'controlled by non-specialist civil servants operating within government departments' (Rawling, 2020, p. 74). The creation of dictatorial lists of what must be learnt the National Curriculum limits teacher creativity and disaggregates subjects into contextless chunks.

Learning how to be good citizens in our homes, our workplaces and our schools has taken a back seat when there are measurable deliverables to be reached, yet this is the first stage in learning how to be an active and useful member of our community. In schools the teaching of citizenship focusses on the processes of government and volunteering, worthy subjects which need to be discussed in the context of community building and digital literacy (Polizzi, 2020). Unsurprisingly the built environment receives little mention (Parnell, 2010). I should say that the recently instigated Welsh Baccalaureate has bucked this trend – my teenage daughter has, for example, recently been tasked to write an essay on housing supply. Research shows that 'civic education' for young people is likely to result in greater political engagement later on (Nelsen, 2021). Maybe this is why it is so low on the neoliberal education agenda.

Conclusion

Given that homes and housing have been around forever it is astonishing how little evidence based knowledge is available about making the best kind of housing for most people and how little we know about people's experience of dwelling. This is in part because of the recent domination of the field by economists who have sought to address issues through the sticking plaster of financial strategy alone. In the words of Christine Whitehead the financialisation of housing is a 'failure of theory as well as practice' (2014, p. 123). It is also a failure in leadership. We have a hazy understanding of housing knowledge for a range of complex reasons including government policy; large gaps in government data sets and a paucity of cross fertilisation of knowledge between disciplines and industries, universities and practice. Our inability to communicate what works in housing has ramifications for democracy too. The public cannot make sensible decisions about their homes and neighbourhoods with the information currently available to them. No wonder trust in local authorities, developers and professionals is so low (Grosvenor, 2019).

References

Allen, C. (2009) 'The fallacy of "housing studies": philosophical problems of knowledge and understanding in housing research', *Housing Theory and Society*, 26(1), pp. 53–79.

Arnstein, S. (1969) 'A ladder of citizen participation', *Journal of the American Institute of Planners*, 35(2), pp. 216–224. Available at: https://www.tandfonline.com/doi/pdf/10.1080/01944366908977225?needAccess=true.

Baker, E. et al. (2017) 'Is housing a health insult?', *Internations Journal of Environmental Research and Public Health*, 14(6), p. 567.

Batty, M. (2017) 'The Digital Future', *Environment and Planning B*, 44(5), pp. 799–801.

Beck, U. (1986) *Risk Society: Towards a New Modernity*. London: Sage.

Bitterman, N. and Schach-Pinsly, D. (2015) 'Smart home - a challenge for architects and designers', *Architectural Science Review*, 3, pp. 226–274.

Bloom, N., Van Reenen, J. and Williams, H. (2019) 'A toolkit of policies to promote innovation', *Journal of Economic Perspectives*, 33(3), pp. 163–184.

Braidotti, R. (2019) *Posthuman Knowledge*. Cambridge: Polity Press.

British Household Panel Survey (2018) *British Household Panel Survey*. Available at: https://www.iser.essex.ac.uk/bhps.

Broady, M. (1968) *Planning for People*. London: National Council for Social Service.

Broady, M. (1972) 'Social theory in architectural design', in Gutman, R. (ed.) *People and Buildings*. New York: Basic Books, p. 179.

Brown, G. and Eckold, H. (2020) 'Local environment', *The International Journal of Justice and Sustainability*, 25(2), pp. 85–100.

Browne-Gott, H. (2019) 'Using administrative data to understand the service interactions of people experiencing homelessness', *International Journal of Population Data Science*, 4(3), p. 169. Available at: https://ijpds.org/article/view/1333/2463.

Buchli, V. (2013) *An Anthropology of Architecture*. London; New York: Berg Publishers.

Cabinet Office. (2021) *Public Dialogue on Location Data Ethics*. Available at: https://www.gov.uk/government/publications/public-dialogue-on-location-data-ethics.

Carlile, P.R. (2002) 'a pragmatic view of knowledge and boundaries: boundary objects in new product development', *Organization Science*, 13(4), pp. 442–455.

CDBB. (2021) *Skills and Competency Framework*. Centre for Digital Built Britain. Available at: https://www.cdbb.cam.ac.uk/files/010321cdbb_skills_capability_framework_vfinal.pdf.

Clapham, D. (2009) 'Introduction to the special issue - a theory of housing: problems and potential', 26(1), pp. 1–9. Available at: https://www.tandfonline.com/doi/pdf/10.1080/14036090802704445.

Clapham, D. (2019) *Remaking Housing Policy: An International Study*. London: Routledge.

Cocker, M. (2018) *Our Place: Can We Save Britian's Wildlife Before It is Too Late*. London: Jonathan Cape.

Cottam, H. (2018) *Radical Help*. London: Virago.

Criado Perez, C. (2019) *Invisible Women*. London: Chatto and Windus.

Darke, J. (1984a) 'Architects and user requirements in public-sector housing: 1. Architects' assumptions about the users", *Environment and Planning B: Planning and Design*, 11(4), pp. 398–404.

Darke, J. (1984b) '"Architects and user requirements in public-sector housing: 2. The sources for architects" assumptions, Environment and Planning B: Planning and Design', *Environment and Planning B*, 11, pp. 405–16.

Darke, J. and Darke, R. (1979) *Who Needs Housing?* London: Macmillan.

DCMS. (2014) *Creative Industries Focus on Employment*. UK Gov. Available at: https://www.gov.uk/government/publications/creative-industries-economic-estimates-january-2015/creative-industries-economic-estimates-january-2015-key-findings.

Dorling, D. (2014) *Inequality and the 1%*. London: Verso.

Dye, A. (2014) *Architects and Research Based Knowledge*. London: RIBA. Available at: http://www.architecture.com/Files/RIBAProfessionalServices/ResearchAndDevelopment/Publications/ArchitectsandResearch-BasedKnowledgeALiteratureReview.pdf.

Edmondson, J. (2020) 'Teaching Intangibles: Uncertainty and Imperfection and the Institutional Challenge of the Unmeasurable', in Formica, P. and Edmondson, J. (eds.) *Innovation and the Arts: The Value of Humanities Studies for Business*. Bingley: Emerald Publishing, pp. 59–71.

Ewenstein, B. and Whyte, J. (2007) 'Visual representations as "artefacts of knowing"', *Building Research & Information*, 35(1), pp. 81–89.

Forth, T. and Jones, R. (2020) *The Missing £4 Billion*. NESTA. Available at: https://www.nesta.org.uk/report/the-missing-4-billion/.

Foye, C. (2021) 'Ethically -speaking, what is the most reasonable way of evaluating housing outcomes', *Housing, Theory and Society*, 38(1), pp. 115–131.

Fraser, M. (2013) *Design Research in Architecture*. London: Ashgate.

Gibb, K. (2014) 'Institutional Economics', in Clapham, D., Clark, W., and Gibb, K. (eds.) *Sage Handbook of Housing*. London: Sage, p. 131.

Gifford, R. (1997) *Environmental Psychology: Principles and Practice*. Boston, MA: Allyn & Bacon.

Groak, S. (1992) *The Idea of Building: Thought and Action in the Design and Production of Buildings*. Oxford: Taylor and Francis.

Grosvenor (2019), *Rebuilding Trust in Developers*, https://www.grosvenor.com/property/property-uk/community-success/building-trust

Gutman, R. (1972) 'The questions architects ask', in Gutman, R. (ed.), *People and Buildings*. New York: Basic Books, p. 179.

Hakimian, R. (2021) *Atkins to Deliver UK-Wide Digital Map of Underground Utilities*. New Civil Engineer. Available at: https://www.newcivilengineer.com/latest/atkins-to-deliver-uk-wide-digital-map-of-underground-utilities-16-10-2021/.

Hall, R. (2020) 'UK universities suffer worst-ever rankings in world league table', *The Guardian*. 10 June. Available at: https://www.theguardian.com/education/2020/jun/10/uk-universities-suffer-worst-ever-rankings-in-world-league-table.

Halpern, D. (1995) *Mental Health and the Built Environment: More Than Bricks and Mortar?* London; Bristol: Taylor & Francis.

Harper, C. (2013) *Compaction, Scale and Proximity: An Investigation into the Spatial Implications of Density for the Design of New Urban Housing*. University of Westminster. Available at: https://westminsterresearch.westminster.ac.uk/item/8yzz9/compaction-scale-and-proximity-an-investigation-into-the-spatial-implications-of-density-for-the-design-of-new-urban-housing.

Hay, R. et al. (2017) 'Post-occupancy evaluation in architecture: experiences and perspectives from UK practice', *Building Research & Information*, pp. 1–13. doi:10.1080/09613218.2017.1314692.

Henderson, J. and Karn, V. (1987) *Race, Class and State Housing*. Aldershot: Gower.

Horn, G. (2019) *Unpopular Taste: Formulating a Framework for Discussing Taste with Reference to English Volume-Built Housing and the Schism in Taste Between the Lay Public and the Architectural Elite*. PhD thesis, University of Sheffield. https://etheses.whiterose.ac.uk/view/iau/Sheffield=2EARC/2019.html.

Jarvis, H. (2019) 'Age-friendly community resilience', in Trogal, K., Bauman, I., Lawrence, R., and Petrescu, D. (eds.) *Architecture and Resilience*. London: Routledge, pp. 61–73.

Jarvis, H. and Bonnett, A. (2013) 'Progressive nostalgia in novel living arrangements: a counterpoint to neo-traditional new urbanism?', *Urban Studies*, 50(11), pp. 2349–2370.

Jordan, B. (2008) *Welfare and Wellbeing: Social Value in Public Policy*. Bristol: Policy Press.

Kemeny, J. (1991) *Housing and Social Theory*. London: Routledge.

King, P. (2008) 'Memory and exile: time and place in Tarkovsky's mirror', *Housing Theory and Society*, 25(1), pp. 66–78.

King, P. (2009) 'Using theory or making theory: can there be theories of housing?', *Housing Theory and Society*, 26(1), pp. 41–52.

King, P. (2022) *Speculations on the Question: What Is Housing?* London: Routledge.

Kirk Hamilton, D. and Watkins, D.H. (2009) *Evidence Based Design for Multiple Building Types*. New York: Wiley and Son.

Krznaric, R. (2020) *The Good Ancestor: How to Think Long Term in a Short Term World*. London: WH Allen.

Lansley, P.R. (1997) 'The impact of BRE's commercialization on the research community', *Building Research & Information*, 25(5), pp. 301–312.

Latour, B. (1986) 'Visualisation and cognition: thinking with eyes and hands', *Knowledge and Society: Studies in the Sociology of Culture PAS and Present*, 6, pp. 1–40.

Latour, B. (1998) 'From the world of science to the world of research?', *Science*, 280, pp. 208–9.

Lee, T. (1971) 'Psychology and architectural determinism', *Architect's Journal*, 4(August), pp. 253–262.

Lees, L. and Warwick, E., (2022) *Defensible Space on the Move*. London: Wiley.

Lennon, M. (2020) 'The art of inclusion: phenomenology, placemaking and the role of the arts', *Journal of Urban Design*, 25(4), pp. 449–466.

Leski, K. (2015) *The Storm of Creativity*. Cambridge MA: MIT.

Lipman, A. (1975) *Aspects of the Professional Ideology of Architects: Social Engineering and Design Theory*. Cardiff: Welsh School of Architecture.

Lu, S. and Sexton, M. (2009) *Innovation in Small Professional Practices in the Built Environment*. Oxford: Wiley Blackwell.

Lynch, M. and Woolgar, S. (1990) *Representation in Scientific Practice*. Cambridge, MA: MIT.

Maclennan, D. and Bannister, J. (1995) 'Housing research: making the connections', *Urban Studies*, 32(10), pp. 1581–1585.

Maclennan, D. and More, A. (1999) 'Evidence, what evidence? The foundations for housing policy', *Public Money and Management*, 19(1), pp. 17–23.

Macmillan, S. (2006) 'Added value of good design', *Building Research & Information*, 34(3), pp. 257–271. doi:10.1080/09613210600590074.

Madden, D. and Marcuse, P. (2016) *In Defense of Housing: The Politics of Crisis*. London: Verso.

Madgin, R. and Lesh, J. (eds.) (2021) *People-Centred Methodologies for Heritage Conservation: Exploring Emotional Attachments to Historic Urban Places*. London: Routledge.

Malpass, P. (1968) *People and Plans: Essays on Urban Problems and Solutions*. New York: Basic Books.

Matrix (1984) *Making Space: Women and the Man Made Environment*. London: Pluto.

Mazzucato, M. (2018) *The Value of Everything: Making and Taking in the Global Economy*. London: Allen Lane.

Morris, R.N. and Mogey, J. (1965) *The Sociology of Housing*. London: Routledge Kegan Paul.

Moulaert, F. et al. (eds.) (2010) *Can Neighbourhoods Save the City? Community Development and Social Innovation*. Abingdon: Routledge.

Nelsen, M.D. (2021) 'Cultivating youth engagment: race & the behavioral effects of critical pedagogy', *Political Behavior*, 43, pp. 751–784.

Nottinghamshire County Council. (2021) *Style Guide*. Available at: https://www.nottinghamshire.gov.uk/global-content/digital-design-manual/style-guide.

Nowotny, H., Scott, P. and Gibbons, M. (2001) *Rethinking Science: Knowledge and the Public in an Age of Uncertainty*. London: Wiley.

Parnell, R. (2010) 'The potential of children's architectural education', *arq: Architectural Research Quarterly*, 14(4), pp. 297–299.

Phillips, A. and Erdemici, F. (eds.) (2012) *Actors, Agents and Attendants: Social Housing-Housing the Social: Art, Property and Spatial Justice*. London: Sternberg Press.

Polizzi, G. (2020) 'Digital literacy and the national curriculum for England: Learning from how the experts engage with and evaluate online content', *Computers & Education*, 152. doi:10.1016/j.compedu.2020.103859.

Rawling, E. (2020) 'How and why national curriculum frameworks are failing geography', *Geography*, 105(2), pp. 69–77.

Ray, N. (2008) 'Studio teaching for a social purpose', *Open House International*, 33(2), pp. 18–25.

Reizenstein, J.E. (1975) 'Linking social research and design', *Journal of Architectural Research*, 4(3), pp. 26–38.

Renold, E. *et al.* (2020) 'The 4Ms project: young people, research and arts-activism in post-industrial place', in McDermot, M., Cole, T., Newman, J., Piccini, A. (eds.), *Imagining Regulation Differently: Co-Creating Regulation for Engagement*. Bristol: Policy Press.

Rex, J. and Moore, R. (1969) *Race, Community and Conflict: A Study of Sparkbrook*. Oxford: Oxford University Press.

Ruonavaara, H. (2017) 'Theory of housing, from housing, about housing', *Housing Theory and Society*, 35(2), pp. 178–192.

Russo, A. *et al.* (2017) 'Edible green infrastructure: an approach and review of provisioning ecosystem services and disservices in urban environments', *Agriculture, Ecosystems and Environment*, 242, pp. 53–66.

Ryan-Collins, J., Lloyd, T. and Macfarlane, L. (2017) *Rethinking the Economics of Land and Housing*. London: Zed Books.

Samuel, F. (2008) 'Suburban self-build', *Field*, 2(1), pp. 111–124.

Samuel, F. (2014) 'The way we were: the changing relationship of research and design', March. Available at: http://www.ribajournal.com/pages/march_2014__intelligence_research_230015.cfm.

Samuel, F. (2018) *Why Architects Matter: Evidencing and Communicating the Value of Architects*. London: Routledge.

Samuel, F. *et al.* (2013) *RIBA Home Improvements: Report on Research in Housing Practice*. RIBA. Available at: www.architecture.com/research.

Say, M. (2021) *DLUHC Gives Councils Over £1million for Digital Planning Pilots*. UK Authority. Available at: https://www.ukauthority.com/articles/dluhc-gives-councils-over-1-million-for-digital-planning-pilots/.

Sharr, A. and Thornton, S. (2013) *Demolishing Whitehall*. London: Routledge.

Sheldrake, M. (2020) *An Entangled Life*. London: Bodley Head.

Shrubsole, G. (2019) *Who Owns England?* London: William Collins.

Sprunt, R. (1975) 'Building knowledge and building law', *Journal of Architectural Research*, 4(3), pp. 10–16.

Statistics Authority. (2021) *The UK Statistical System*. Available at: https://www.statisticsauthority.gov.uk/.

Steel, C. (2020) *Sitopia*. London: Penguin.

Stephens, M. (2011) 'Comparative housing research: a "system-embedded" approach', *International Journal of Housing Policy*, 11(4), pp. 337–355.

Stevenson, F. (2019) *Housing Fit for Purpose: Performance, Feedback and Learning*. London: RIBA Publishing.

Super Slow Way. (2020) *Super Slow Way*. Available at: https://superslowway.org.uk/.

Temenos, C. and Lauermann, J. (2020) 'The urban politics of policy failure', *Urban Geography*, 41(9), pp. 1109–1118.

Uittenbroek, C.J. *et al.* (2019) 'The design of public participation: who participates, when and how? Insights in climate adaptation planning from the Netherlands', *Journal of Environmental Planning and Management*, 62(14), pp. 2529–2547.

UKRI. (2020) *The UK's Research and Innovation Infrastructure: Opportunities to Grow Our Capability*. UK Research and Innovation. Available at: https://www.ukri.org/wp-content/uploads/2020/10/UKRI-201020-UKinfrastructure-opportunities-to-grow-our-capacity-FINAL.pdf.

UNESCO. (2020) *How Much Does Your Country Invest in R & D?* Available at: http://uis.unesco.org/apps/visualisations/research-and-development-spending/.

Visual Capitalist. (2017) *A Global Look at R & D Spending*. Available at: https://www.visualcapitalist.com/global-leaders-r-d-spending/.

Wang, V. and Shepherd, D. (2020) 'Exploring the extent of open government data - A critique of open government datasets in the UK', *Government Information Quarterly*, 37(1), 101405.

Wilson, A. and Tewdwr-Jones, M. (2022). *Digital Participatory Planning: Citizen Engagement, Democracy and Design*. New York: Routledge.

Whitehead, C. (2014) 'The neo-liberal legacy to housing research', in Clapham, D., Clark, W., and Gibb, K. (eds.) *The Sage Handbook of Housing*. London: Sage, pp. 113–130.

Part II

The impact of housing and neighbourhoods on hope and wellbeing

Chapter 4

Measuring wellbeing and social value

We know at a visceral level what makes good housing, but in order to be accounted for in a neoliberal system we are forced to try to capture it in a numerical way. Wellbeing is a dimension of 'intrinsic value' (Bunting, 2008), an aspect of experience that is traditionally 'best evaluated qualitatively, or with a mixture of qualitative and quantitative methods' (Crossick and Kaszynska, 2016, p. 8). Until recently the qualitative dimension of wellbeing measurement has made it difficult to build into the spreadsheets that dominate the value management of our built environment but all this is set to change with the advent of new technologies. This chapter briefly reflects on the meaning of value, the value of design, the need for audit and the emergence of social value and its permutations. As Justin Welby notes, social value can be of 'immense benefit to society as a whole, not least as it is likely to show that investing in community is not a public sector cost but a significant public sector saving' (2018, p. 143).

Value and audit

Value, the worth of something, is a contradictory word. On the one hand it is 'the capitalist category par excellence' (Phillips, 2015) and a medium of control, on the other it can be a tool for accountability, and inclusion (Groak, 1992, p. 117). Value also relates to our ability to live out our values. The way in which we talk about 'value' has to change, not least because it designates as valueless all 'forms of economic activity that are informal, community based, and driven by collaboration and sharing' (Fioramonti, Coscieme and Mortensen, 2019). That there is an inherent problem in the way economies are measured and audited is widely recognised (Raworth, 2017; Mazzucato, 2018).

Gross domestic product, which tracks and celebrates spending, however toxic for society, has come to be used in ways it was never intended for, most notably as a 'performance assessment tool for society' (Fioramonti, Coscieme and Mortensen, 2019). The case against the use of gross domestic product as a measure of national success is growing (Nussbaum, 2011), with some arguing for instead for a measure of gross domestic value to take in a range of important less tangible impacts (Raworth, 2012). Small business guru Holly Tucker makes the case for 'gross domestic happiness' (Tucker, 2021). She has a point.

In an audit culture organisational performance is measured against predetermined targets. Audit always begins with classification and classifications are 'powerful technologies' that are both 'political and ethical' (Bowker and Leigh Star, 1999). The basis for government decision making in the UK is the Treasury *Green Book* (UK Gov, 2013) which weighs up costs against benefits, something that it is doing in an increasingly evidence-based way (Donovan, 2013, p. 4). Recent positive improvements to the *Green Book* point in the direction of a system based on environmental and social, as well as economic value, in other words the triple bottom line of sustainability. While there is a long tradition of economic valuation, however flawed, and some solid measures for environmental value – carbon (embodied and operational), biodiversity and so on – social value, the focus of this book, is very much a work in progress. I argue that housing must be valued against social, environmental and economic indicators over long periods of time, taking both short and long term impacts into account. Social value, according to the UK Green Building Council (Figure 0.1), 'encompasses environmental, economic and social wellbeing' (UKGBC, 2021, p. 7). Notice the slippage here between 'value' and 'wellbeing', one that is extremely useful to me in this argument as I want to get away from the use of the word value as it is so tied up with a monetary view of the world, preferring instead to use the term 'wellbeing' as the UKGBC team have done here.

The value of design

During the late 1990s the value of design had a powerful champion in the form of New Labour Deputy Prime Minister John Prescott (under Tony Blair) who believed that 'in the broadest sense [good design] is the key to respect for people whether they be users of the building or passers by' (Macmillan, 2004, p. 4). One result was the foundation of the Commission for Architecture and the Built Environment (CABE), the aim being to bring about a real improvement in design quality, while being a 'thinly disguised ploy to temper the damaging excesses of neoliberalism' (Punter, 2011, p. 2). While there wasn't much public rented housing being built under New Labour CABE did a significant amount towards developing an evidence base for placemaking and good housing (Carmona and Natajaran, 2016), but its emphasis was more on towns and cities than their relationship with their rural hinterland. CABE's funding was cut during the Conservative 'war on quangos' reducing its research capability considerably. The CABE *Value Handbook: Getting the Most from Your Buildings and Spaces* appears to mark a pinnacle in the organisation's optimism, with the authors advising local authority planners to 'use value rather than cost when making the business case' (2006, p. 10), a sentiment that seems to have been largely ignored for reasons that have emerged over the last few chapters, but remains sound to this day.

The recent history of construction in the UK has been one in which quantitative performance indicators, notably economic performance, dominate. 'Value management' (BSI, 2000), 'value engineering' (Kelly, Male and Graham, 2010) and 'value analysis' (Designing Buildings Wiki, 2017) – 'an approach by which supposed sub-systems in a design are further optimized against a constant performance requirement' (Groak, 1992, p. 93) – are processes in which costs can be squeezed until the pips come out. The first thing to go in such situations, tends to be any aspirations for good design.

In response to the Social Value Act 2012 in England, which requires that social value needs to be demonstrated when spending government money, local authorities began to look at the way that social value is generated through their procurement chains. It is not surprising therefore that social value was quickly taken up by big construction and infrastructure firms (and their clients) and aligned to their needs with emphasis being placed on 'tick box' type outcomes, things that could be readily measured, such as jobs and apprenticeships created during the construction project, with little or no consideration given to the intrinsic long-term social value (wellbeing impacts), of the buildings and projects that were being delivered.

It all comes back to building procurement. Rather than using vast, and complex building contracts (as set in Chapter 2), in which the only winners are lawyers, shrewd clients are starting to use a system that encourages all the members of the team to club together to deliver on predetermined outcomes while sharing project liabilities – value or outcomes based procurement. This way of proceeding can save both money and time while encouraging collaborative innovation (Samuel, 2018). However the whole thing relies on the ability of the team to demonstrate value with evidence. Anne Bentley, author of the important report *Procuring for Value* (Bentley, 2018), has been instrumental in the development of the Construction Innovation Hub Value Tool. This will enable clients to decide on the kinds of value they want to generate with their project and set the parameters accordingly. Refreshingly the Value platform takes into consideration the long-term return of projects as well as a range of wellbeing considerations and seems set to determine the future trajectory of construction procurement.

Local authorities have been turning to social value experts to help them with the evaluation of their offerings. Given the current supremacy of financial value there has been strong interest in the potential of Social Return on Investment (SROI), a form of accounting that enables the monetisation of social value outcomes, for example, the cost of a depressed person for a year to UK PLC. There are a variety of existing systems for capturing social value – the National TOMS Framework is sometimes used by local authorities for procurement and now includes a Real Estate Plug-in (TOMS, 2019). HACT's Social Value Bank is another with strong relevance for housing (HACT, 2015). Kelly Watson's work on healthcare buildings used SROI to prove fairly unequivocally that paying for good design is worth it in terms of long-term SROI (Watson and Whitley, 2016). Whether the social value of housing ought to be monetised is another matter. My prediction, discussed in later chapters, is that this way of working will be disrupted by technology which will soon enable social value to be accounted for spatially in real time using data mapping techniques.

Social value of housing and neighbourhood design

It was out of a sense of frustration with the problematic and erratic way in which project bids are evaluated and won that we, a group of leaders on research in architectural practice, began work on the *RIBA Social Value Toolkit for Architecture* which set out a range of ways in which the design of housing could impact on the wellbeing of people (Samuel, 2020). We started by reviewing the literature of 'wellbeing', defined in the *Oxford Dictionaries* as 'the state of being comfortable, healthy or happy. We also examined measures relating to the value of green spaces such as 'natural capital' (Natural England, 2011; GLA, 2017) and 'ecosystem services' which also address the positive impacts of nature on people. Some dimensions of social sustainability are included in a variety of well established post occupancy evaluation systems such as WELL and LEED (Hay et al., 2017). The New Economics Foundations *Five Ways to Wellbeing* (Aked *et al.*, 2011) was a particularly useful resource as was the Canal and River Trust review of wellbeing literature, *Waterways and Wellbeing* (2017). Our conclusion was that although there was much agreement on the constituent attributes of wellbeing across a range of grey (industry and charity) literature reports, a wide variety of different wordings were being used for the same thing. At the same time there are a multitude of overlapping definitions of social value, social assets and social capital out there (Alesina and La Ferrara, 2002; Rocco and Suhrcke, 2012, p. 2). This lack of clarity on what constitutes wellbeing is typical of a private sector driven field which lacks government leadership.

Drawing together the findings of the literature review we argued that the social value of housing is in: fostering positive emotions whether through connections with nature or offering opportunities for an active lifestyle, connecting people and the environment in appropriate ways and in providing freedom and flexibility to pursue different lifestyles (autonomy). Participation, supporting communities to help design and build their homes and neighbourhoods has social value too. These, we argued, could be used as headline outcomes for capturing the social value of housing. Affordability is obviously a key consideration. Whether this should probably sit within the more economic value of triple bottom line accounting or within social value has yet to be established. We offered a range of post occupancy evaluation (POE) questions which could then be used to tease out aspects of each theme, for example, 'my neighbourhood gives me opportunities to stop and communicate with other people'. The *Social Value Toolkit for Architecture* has since been published by the Royal Institute of British Architects, enshrined in their *Sustainable Outcomes Guide* (RIBA 2020) and 'social purpose' has been built into its (Post Brexit) educational requirements meaning that, at last, budding architects will learn how to take it into consideration (RIBA, 2021).

It is important to note that the *Social Value Toolkit for Architecture* focusses on contemporary housing and fails to address the issue of heritage sector which has its own distinct social evaluation categories such as Historic England's 'communal value' (2021), and Historic Scotland's 'social interest'. Elizabeth Robson has developed a Social Value Toolkit for heritage professionals, an important first step in aligning social value with heritage value (Robson, 2021) but considerably more work is needed in this area.

During the process of writing the *Social Value Toolkit for Architecture* we realised that social value was a fairly meaningless term without knowing where the social value actually happens. The spatialising of social value in maps was the focus of the *Mapping Eco-Social Assets* project which involved the making of layered

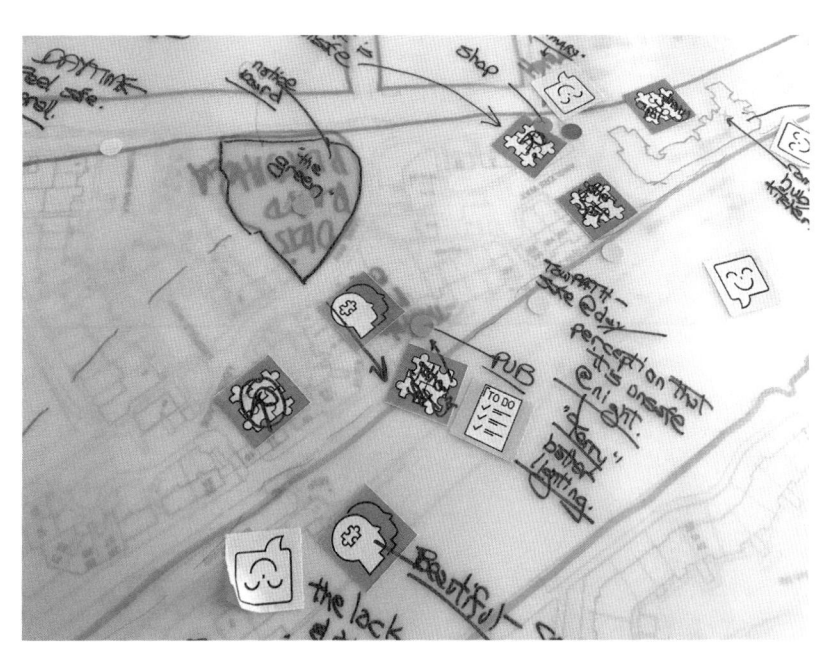

Figure 4.1
Making maps with community for *Mapping Eco Social Assets* Project. Source: © Flora Samuel.

maps using the measures set out in the *Social Value Toolkit for Architecture*. Focussing on council owned estate in Reading we led a series of workshops with residents of different ages and backgrounds, including school children asking them to help us co-create maps of their area (Figure 4.1). Armed with stickers indicating things like 'connection to people' and fat pens they adorned our base maps with a rich set of observations about where they lived. Cartography seemed to come naturally to the communities we worked with. The handmade maps were then redrawn as digital maps (this required discernment from Eli Hatleskog who drew the maps up giving weightings to different kinds of comments (Hatleskog and Samuel, 2021). They were then overlaid over one another revealing strong hot spots of social value (Figures 4.2 and 4.3). At the time that we were making the maps the local authority closed down a swimming pool in order to sell the site for keyworker housing. We realised that we could have used the maps to demonstrate the impact of this decision on local people, a powerful capability that I will return to in Chapter 9.

There is a lot of debate about whether it is best to collect data from people by asking them questions, *active* data, or to use the census and other sources to infer what is needed, *passive* data. Stated preference research shows how little correlation there can be between what people say and what they do (revealed preferences) (Engstrom and Forsell, 2018). In one interesting case the citizens of Yarmouth complained of misrepresentation through the statistics about levels of social infrastructure (Thomas, 2021). Their lived experience was at odds with the things that had been measured. There is a delicate balance to be achieved between active and passive data, the main thing being that communities must have the power to understand, and contest if necessary, the data that is being

The impact of housing and neighbourhoods on hope and wellbeing

Figure 4.2
Positive Emotions layer of community made map of an estate in Reading.
Source: © Eli Hatleskog and Flora Samuel.

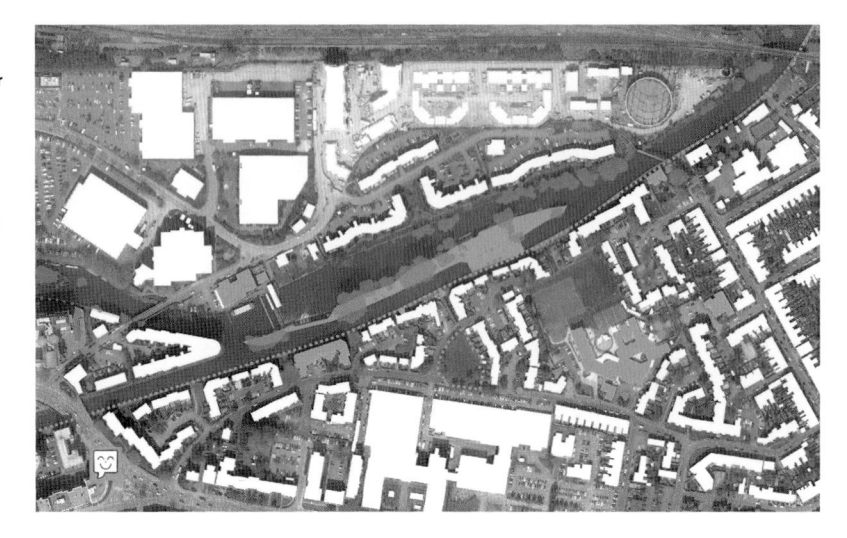

Figure 4.3
Detail of community made map, part of *Mapping Eco Social Assets* Project, Reading.
Source: © Eli Hatleskog and Flora Samuel.

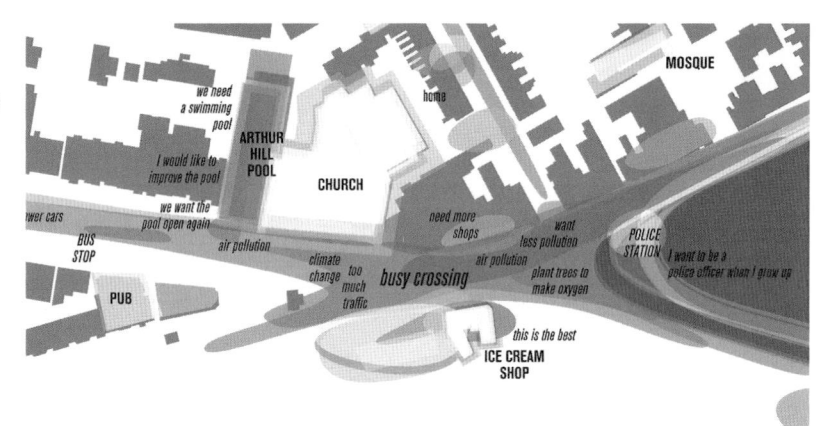

collected about them as well as the methodologies used to collect it. As Caroline Criado Perez has made clear in her book *Invisible Women* the way that data is collected is rarely objective (2019).

Social value is a metric that attempts to capture wellbeing in a way that enables the 'social' can be seen alongside other kinds of valuation in national, local authority and project accounting and procurement. The capabilities approach resists the idea that important elements of wellbeing 'can be reduced to a single metric without distortion' (Nussbaum, 2011, p. 18) but offers a means to 'package comparative information in such a way as to reorient the development and policy debate' (Nussbaum, 2011, p. 17). That there is potential to use a capabilities approach as a foundation for measurement of wellbeing is an underexplored area (Robeyns, 2016), particularly in the context of the built environment. There is work to be done in aligning social value with capabilities. My hope is that social value can be captured in a baggy enough way to honour choice in people's lives while offering a way of framing and visualising those choices.

Conclusion

Agendas of economic growth and sustainability are fundamentally at odds with one another (Webb, Hawkey and Tingey, 2016). Instead 'degrowth' offers 'a social imaginary guiding new political thinking for the Anthropocene', as well as 'a self-binding commitment to think creatively about achieving a liveable system of communities for all humankind' (Rechel and Perey, 2018, p. 247). This presents a challenge to cultural expectations of economic acceleration and the way in which value is conceived. A rebalancing of value to include social and environmental value, as well as economic value, is needed to make sure we get the communities and housing that work for wellbeing. This requires the creation of new categorisations and definitions of value. These categorisations must be regularly reviewed to ensure that they are fit for purpose. While there are reasonably robust existing indicators (largely quantitative) for economic and environmental value, there is considerable agreement on what constitutes social value, but little agreement on how it can be demonstrated. Getting agreement on terminology is fundamental to data gathering and predicting outcomes, a process that can be greatly enhanced through the making of maps as data needs to be spatialised. We need to know with some accuracy what is happening where.

Part 2 of *Housing for Hope and Wellbeing* focusses on some of the different ways in which housing can contribute to social value which I correlate with eudaimonic wellbeing, a sense of purpose beyond the self, in other words hope. The chapter headings – connecting people, physical health, self actualisation and community identity – represent my current distillation of some of the classic social value themes presented in the *Social Value Toolkit for Architecture* and its younger sister the *Quality of Life Framework*, recently developed by URBED for the Quality of Life Foundation (URBED, 2021). The development of these categories is an ongoing project. Categories should regularly be reviewed to make sure that they are fit for purpose (Bowker and Leigh Star, 2000) so these categories are currently in the process of being tested and revised through a succession of research projects with the Quality of Life Foundation at the helm.

Note

Justin Welby quotes, © Justin Welby, 2018, *Reimagining Britain*, Bloomsbury Continuum, an imprint of Bloomsbury Publishing Plc.

References

Aked, J. *et al.* (2011) *Five Ways to Wellbeing*. NEF (The New Economics Foundation). Available at: https://neweconomics.org/uploads/files/8984c5089d5c2285ee_t4m6bhqq5.pdf.

Alesina, A. and La Ferrara, E. (2002) 'Who trusts others?' *Journal of Public Economics*, 85(2), pp. 207–234.

Bentley, A. (2018) *Procuring for Value*. CIC. Available at: http://www.constructionleadershipcouncil.co.uk/wp-content/uploads/2018/07/RLB-Procuring-for-Value-18-July-.pdf.

Bowker, J. and Leigh Star, S. (2000) *Classification and Its Consequences*, Cambridge, MA: MIT.

BSI. (2000) *Value Management BS EN 12973:2000*. Available at: http://shop.bsi-group.com/ProductDetail/?pid=000000000030012919.

Bunting, C. (2008) 'What instrumentalism? A public perception of value', *Cultural Trends*, 17(4), pp. 323–328. doi:10.1080/09548960802615463.

CABE. (2006) *The Value Handbook: Getting the Most From Your Buildings and Spaces*. Available at: http://webarchive.nationalarchives.gov.uk/20110118095356/http://www.cabe.org.uk/files/the-value-handbook.pdf#page=1&zoom=auto,36,643.

Canal and River Trust. (2017) *Waterways and Wellbeing: Building the Evidence Base*. London: Canal and River Trust.

Carmona, M. and Natajaran, L. (2016) *Design Governance: The CABE Experiment*. London: Routledge.

Criado Perez, C. (2019) *Invisible Women*. London: Chatto and Windus.

Crossick, G. and Kaszynska, P. (2016) *Understanding the Value of Arts and Culture: The AHRC Cultural Value Project*. AHRC. Available at: http://www.ahrc.ac.uk/documents/publications/cultural-value-project-final-report/.

Department of Health. (2014) *What Works to Improve Wellbeing*. Available at: https://assets.publishing.service.gov.uk/government/uploads/system/uploads/attachment_data/file/277593/What_works_to_improve_wellbeing.pdf.

Designing Buildings Wiki. (2017) *Value in Building Design and Construction*. Available at: https://www.designingbuildings.co.uk/wiki/Value_in_building_design_and_construction (Accessed: 3 January 2017).

Donovan, C. (2013) *A Holistic Approach to Valuing Our Culture - Publications - GOV.UK*. Available at: https://www.gov.uk/government/publications/a-holistic-approach-to-valuing-our-culture (Accessed: 15 January 2014).

Engstrom, P. and Forsell, E. (2018) 'Demand effects of consumers' stated and revealed preferences', *Journal of Economic Behavior & Organisation*, 150(June), pp. 43–61.

Fioramonti, L., Coscieme, L. and Mortensen, L.F. (2019) 'From gross domestic product to wellbeing: how alternative indicators can help connect the new economy with the sustainable development goals', *The Anthropocene Review*, 6(3), pp. 2017–222.

GLA. (2017) *Natural Capital Accounts for Public Green Space in London*. Available at: https://www.insidehousing.co.uk/news/news/giant-equity-investor-to-compete-head-on-with-associations-for-section-106-53821.

Groak, S. (1992) *The Idea of Building: Thought and Action in the Design and Production of Buildings*. Oxford: Taylor and Francis.

HACT. (2015) *Procurement and Social Value*. Available at: https://www.hact.org.uk/sites/default/files/uploads/Archives/2015/9/Procurement%20and%20Social%20Value%20-%20A%20white%20paper%20for%20Wandle%20LOGOS.pdf.

Hatleskog, E. and Samuel, F. (2021) 'Mapping as a strategic tool for evidencing social values and supporting joined-up decision making in Reading, England', *Journal of Urban Design*, 26, 5, pp.591-612.

Hay, R., Bradbury, S., Dixon, D., Martindale, K., Samuel, F., and Tait, A, (2017) *Building Knowledge: Pathways to Post Occupancy Evaluation*, RIBA. Available at:

file:///Users/vw911381/Downloads/BuildingKnowledgePathwaystoPOEpdf%20(1).pdf.

Historic England. (2021) *Conservation, Principles, Policies and Guidance*. Available at: https://historicengland.org.uk/advice/constructive-conservation/conservation-principles.

Kelly, J., Male, S. and Graham, D. (2010) *Value Management of Construction Projects*. 1 edition. Oxford ; Malden, MA: Wiley.

Macmillan, S. (2004) *Designing Better Buildings: Quality and Value in the Built Environment*. New York: Spon.

Mazzucato, M. (2018) *The Value of Everything: Making and Taking in the Global Economy*. London: Allen Lane.

Monbiot, G. (2017) *Out of the Wreckage: A New Politics for an Age of Crisis*. London: Verso.

Natural England. (2011) *No charge? Valuing the Natural Environment*. Available at: http://publications.naturalengland.org.uk/publication/36019.

Nussbaum, M. (2011) *Creating Capabilities*. Cambridge MA: Harvard University Press.

Punter, J. (2011) 'Urban design and the English urban renaissance 1999–2009: a review and preliminary evaluation', *Journal of Urban Design*, 16(1), pp. 1–41.

Raworth, K. (2012) 'Want to know how to get beyond GDP? Start here.' Available at: https://www.kateraworth.com/2012/07/01/want-to-know-how-to-get-beyond-gdp-start-here/.

Raworth, K. (2017) *Doughnut Economics: Seven Ways to Think Like a 21st Century Economist*. London: Random House.

Rechel, A. and Perey, R. (2018) 'Moving beyond growth in the anthropocene', *The Anthropocene Review*, 5(3), pp. 242–249.

RIBA (2021) *The Way Ahead*. Available at: https://www.architecture.com/knowledge-and-resources/resources-landing-page/the-way-ahead

RIBA (2020) *Sustainable Outcomes Guide*. Available at: https://www.architecture.com/knowledge-and-resources/resources-landing-page/sustainable-outcomes-guide.

Robeyns, I. (2016) 'Capabilitiarianism', *Journal of Human Development and Capabilities*, 17(3), pp. 397–414.

Robson, E. (2021) *Social Value Toolkit for Heritage Professionals*. University of Stirling. Available at: https://socialvalue.stir.ac.uk/about/introduction/.

Rocco, L. and Suhrcke, M. (2012) *Is Social Capital Good for Health? A European Perspective?* World Health Organization. Available at: http://www.euro.who.int/__data/assets/pdf_file/0005/170078/Is-Social-Capital-good-for-your-health.pdf.

Samuel, F. (2018) *Why Architects Matter: Evidencing and Communicating the Value of Architects*. London: Routledge.

Samuel, F. (2020) *Social Value Toolkit for Architecture*. London: RIBA. Available at: https://www.architecture.com/knowledge-and-resources/resources-landing-page/social-value-toolkit-for-architecture.

Serin, B. *et al.* (2018) *Design Value at Neighbourhood Scale*. CACHE: Glasgow University. Available at: http://housingevidence.ac.uk/publications/design-value-at-the-neighbourhood-scale/.

Thomas, T. (2021) '"We have plenty": community spaces study is disputed in Yarmouth North', *The Guardian*. 28 June. Available at: https://www.theguardian.com/society/2021/jun/28/we-have-plenty-community-spaces-study-disputed-yarmouth-north.

TOMS. (2019) *National TOMS - Social Value Portal*, *Social Value Portal*. Available at:https://socialvalueportal.com/solutions/national-toms/

Tucker, H. (2021) *Do What You Love, Love What You Do*. London: Virgin Books.

UKGBC, (2021) *Framework for Defining Social Value*. Available at: https://www.ukgbc.org/ukgbc-work/framework-for-defining-social-value/

UK Gov. (2013) *The Green Book: Appraisal and Evaluation in Central Government - Publications - GOV.UK*. Available at: https://www.gov.uk/government/publications/the-green-book-appraisal-and-evaluation-in-central-governent (Accessed: 16 January 2014).

URBED. (2021) *Quality of Life Framework*. Available at: https://www.qolf.org/wp-content/uploads/2021/02/PD20-0742-QOLF-Framework_v09_LR.pdf.

Watson, K.J. and Whitley, T. (2016) 'Applying social return on investment (SROI) to the built environment', *Building Research & Information*, pp. 1–17. doi:10.1080/09613218.2016.1223486.

Webb, J., Hawkey, D. and Tingey, M. (2016) 'Governing cities for sustainable energy: The UK case', *Cities*, 54, pp. 28–35.

Welby, J. (2018) *Reimagining Britain*. London: Bloomsbury.

Chapter 5

Connection

The success of our species is down to working collectively, pooling resources. It is for this reason that evolutionary biologists categorise us as some of the most sociable of mammals (Krznaric, 2020). Connectivity in some form is recognised as being vital for eudaimonic wellbeing and is a feature of pretty much all well-being indicators (Samuel, 2020), and it isn't just connection to each other that matters – connectivity to other creatures in the natural world is equally important. Extending our networks in new and unexpected directions can come with a whole range of benefits, not least the alleviation of loneliness, ideas, connections and jobs (Cottam, 2018), but these connections need to be more than clicks on our computer. Digital communication as it stands fails to fulfil our need for 'social connectedness' (Nguyen, Gruber and Marler, 2021). This chapter starts with a discussion of mix and density, prerequisites for connection and sharing, before moving onto connective social infrastructure at the scale of the neighbourhood and on what can be done to connect people at the scale of housing.

Density and mix

Prior to the pandemic increased density was seen as the panacea for a wide range of sustainable and social ills but the need for social distancing has put paid to all that. Density is intimately connected with transport, shops and other facilities as a certain level of density is necessary to sustain infrastructure, a particular issue in rural areas. Just what makes the right level of density is not known despite considerable study. Density always has to be examined in context but it is generally agreed that there is a need for higher density towards the middle of settlement and around transport hubs (RTPI, 2018). Arguments for density include: reduced loneliness; more access to facilities and less time spent travelling. It can support features and activities that low density can't (for example, specialist services and shops). Negatives of density include noise, lack of light, an absence of nature and lack of privacy and a lack of human scale (Channon and Kriekler, 2020).

In her book *The Death and Life of Great American Cities* (1961) the pioneering urban activist Jane Jacobs argued for concentration, diversity and sociability in city planning, with its important corollaries of 'city surveillance and city safety' (Jacobs, 1961, p. 53). Her work heralded a drive towards mixed development (Joseph and Chaskin, 2010) which has stayed with us ever since. Just as teachers have to offer a range of different types of learning to suit different learning styles, neighbourhoods have to offer a range of opportunities for connection, for example, inclusive spaces like libraries for a broad constituency of people as well as more intimate spaces like hairdressers where trusting relationships can be forged (Mayor of London, 2021). Independent shops and farmers markets help employ local people, keeping money in the local economy while being crucial places of interaction (see, for example, Emerson *et al.*, 2021). The local fruit stall at the end of my street has been there for decades. It isn't just a source of cheap fruit and vegetables, it is a place to meet people, exchange greetings and news with the stallholders and complain about local politics. The owners offer useful surveillance to the street, regularly look after heavy shopping for people, and leave free old fruit out in the evening for people who can't afford to pay for it. In this way the fruit stall makes a considerable contribution to our quality of life but it can only exist because of an increase in generosity of the pavement in that area. Physical interventions at the scale of the mix and at the scale of the pavement, a particular concern for Jane Jacobs, can have dramatic impacts on interaction.

Connective social infrastructure

The Mayor of London's Office *Connective Social Infrastructure* report is a heartening and useful document. It sets out a 'social integration strategy' encompassing three key interconnected themes – relationships; participation and equality – all of which can be promoted through 'connective social infrastructure' (Mayor of London, 2021, pp. 22–23). The research in the report (undertaken by Social Life and Hawkins Brown) shows just how extremely important local places – formal and informal infrastructure – are for spending time with 'people from a different background' and therefore social cohesion, with community centres, green spaces, places of worship, cafes, pubs and restaurants being particularly important across the case study areas (Figure 5.1). 76% of people surveyed said that they took part in some sort of 'local network, group or club'. Of this group 90% reported that they had come to know new people through these groups, the majority being from different backgrounds (p. 58). A further London based study, this time by Blanc, Scanlon and White, makes the interesting point that a sense of security and community correlates to the number of long term residents in a development (2020), yet another argument against housing precarity.

Suzanne Wessendorf's forensic study of Hackney suggests that people are comfortable with people mixing with their own kind at home as long as they mix more freely in public. There is a 'fine balance between what residents in a super-diverse area experience as acceptable and unacceptable social divisions, and the ways in which people interpret their social surroundings in terms of the participation of their fellow residents in local life' (2013, p. 419). This is one reason why it is so important to build diverse opportunities into the lives of places. This includes volunteering opportunities which can be signposted through the design of the neighbourhood environment in small but important ways that signal

Connection

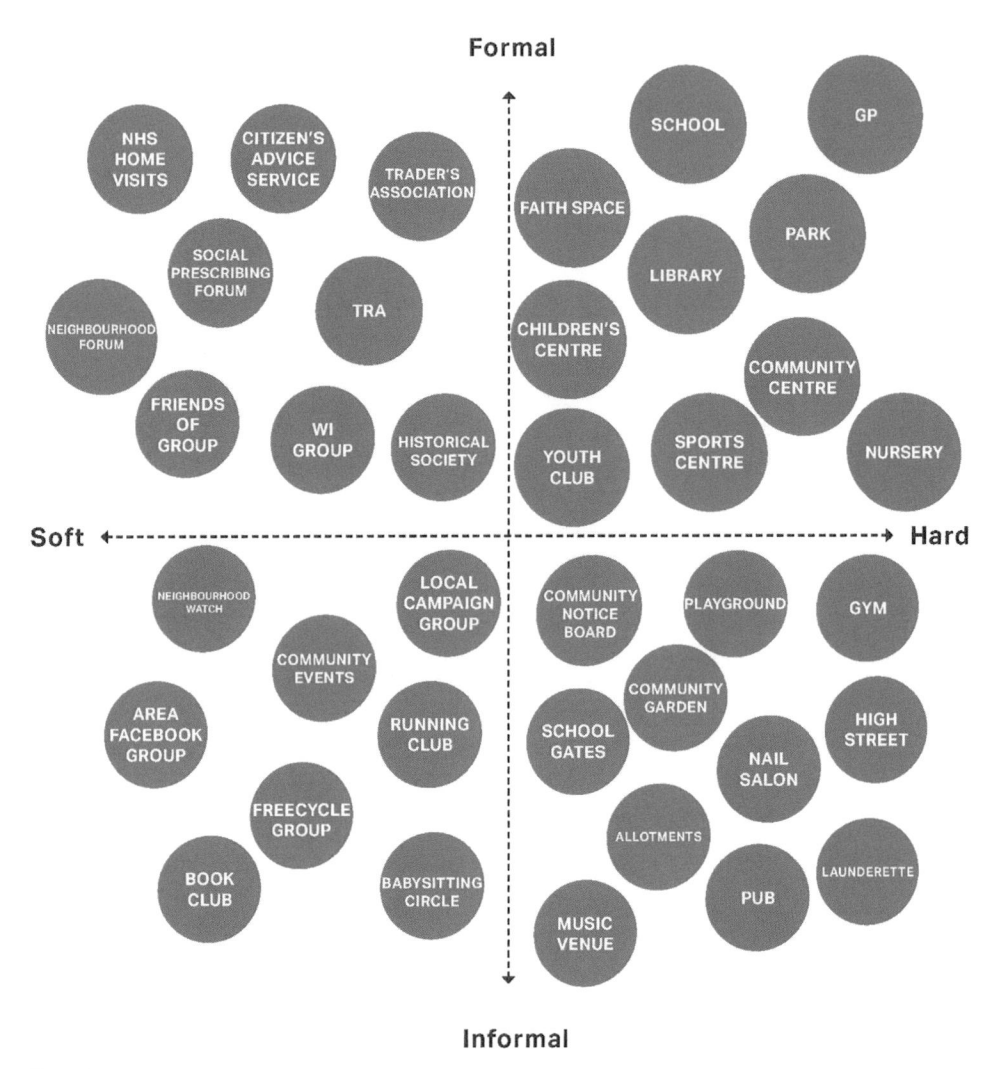

Figure 5.1
Understanding different types of social infrastructure. Source: © Connective Social Infrastructure, GLA, 2021.

abundance to those around – a box of free windfall apples outside a house, a community planter that needs weeding, or a bench designated for chatting for anyone who feels like it. Chatbench.org is a charity that assists with the provision of such facilities, but there are many more. Providing places for people to exercise their innate generosity is key to the development of a more caring society (Trogal, 2019). We have to make opportunities to volunteer, however small and informal easy.

Perceived levels of social support are important to relieve a sense of social isolation (Emerson *et al.*, 2021). 'Neighbourhoods that are welcoming attractive, feel safe and have amenities for all residents can help people from becoming lonely' (Age UK, 2018). Older people suffer from a 'creeping marginalisation' in which their needs and desires are poorly represented or stereotyped, with city discourse tending to focus on young urban populations (Handler, 2014, p. 29). There is a growing body of evidence that links the quality of the physical fabric of neighbourhoods with reduced loneliness, particularly for older people (Scharf and de Jong Gierveld, 2008; Age UK, 2018). Most of all a community has to feel safe. The presence of CCTV cameras does not offer the same tangible feeling of safety as physical surveillance, particularly for women (Criado Perez, 2019).

There is ample evidence that the act of volunteering, the sharing of time, actually makes us happier (Lawton, Gramatki and Fujiwara, 2020) and healthier (for example, Tabassum et al., 2016). Independent from government and from the private sector, the voluntary sector was worth about £23 billion in 2014 – '2% of the total value of unpaid work' (ONS, 2017). Without wishing to go down the wormhole of what constitutes 'unpaid work' it seems that 52% of the population volunteered informally at least once in 20018/2019. Faith groups have a particular role in this – for example, Christians contribute over 100 million volunteer hours and nearly £400 million to social action every year (Welby, 2018, p. 257). An example is the local mosque in North Kensington that opened itself up immediately as a place of refuge for everyone in the aftermath of the Grenfell fire, a more agile organisation than the local authority which took some time to respond to the situation (Doherty, 2018). That volunteering shot up during the pandemic is widely evident even if only from the email feed from my local neighbourhood facebook group which was full of people volunteering to fetch medicine, deliver groceries and so on.

The importance of food sharing in reducing inequalities, forging links and building new possibilities is receiving wide acknowledgement in research (Marovelli, 2019). 'Commensality', eating together is fundamental for forging family bonds, good eating habits and developing communication skills but it requires reviving the cultures associated with growing, cooking (Hennchen and Pregernig, 2020) and eating food while developing the skills of sociability. Food can be used, not only to provide sustenance for those in need, but also to bring together groups that rarely interact – intergenerational lunches are one example. Food is also great bringing together people of different cultures. Food solidarity is a growing arena, see, for example, the Felix project in Homerton, East London that redistributes food that would be wasted otherwise (The Felix Project, 2021). People in my area are using the Olio App for redistributing waste food but this only works for those who are online. The City of Milan won the 2021 Earthshot prize for its work in this area showing just what is possible when a whole city gets behind an initiative to help redistribute food whether people are online or not.

None of this can happen without the availability of free or affordable space in which the community can congregate. It isn't just about quantity of space, quality matters too with particular groups needing particular kinds of spaces, for example, those on the autistic spectrum who can find some kinds of space too overwhelming. In such situations the availability of quiet intimate space with relaxing lighting is important. The Men's Sheds movement has developed across the UK to provide places for men to 'connect, converse and create' in a supportive atmosphere where it is also possible to broach health and other issues that they might otherwise be reluctant to discuss (Men's Sheds Association, 2021). The very name 'men's shed' speaks of the particular kind of space they need.

Existing space needs to be programmed for more intensive use, an example being nightclubs which can be used by day by older communities for dancing (Handler, 2014). They can also be used to bring targeted networks together – an example is MISERY which is a sober club night for queer, trans and intersex black people and people of colour in London, that was started to 'fill a huge gap of much needed mental health and community support in a crowded, busy, yet isolating city', one of a series of such initiatives across the UK (Erdem and Mirza, 2020).

The need to choreograph new types of mix of people is a subject that repeats itself across this book. The Intergen project 'a tried and tested model for sharing place and space to promote wellbeing in neighbourhoods for old and young citizens' brought older people into schools to share their experiences and knowledge with young people to share experiences in schools in London and Greater Manchester. Results included an improvement in pupil performance and wellbeing while the older people felt valued and useful. Generally there was a reduction in age related stereotyping across the group which was considered good value by participating schools (Raynes, 2020).

R-URBAN in Paris is a beautiful exemplar of what is possible when a neighbourhood gets a bit of programming (Figure 5.2). 'R-URBAN provides tools and resources to facilitate citizen involvement in this project, including accompanying

Figure 5.2
R-URBAN's L'Agrocité de Gennevilliers 2019. Source: © Atelier d'Architecture Autogérée.

emerging projects at local and regional levels that are working to meet the same ends' (R-Urban, 2016). Their first pilot unit at Colombes in France, comprising urban agriculture, residential space, recycling and community gardens, explores the development of community resilience through co-production of community assets. It provides a good example of the way in which 'architects and researchers could play an important role in designing and creating new conditions for resilient living through communing' (Stevenson, Baborska-Narozny and Chatterton, 2016). R-URBAN have brought their toolkit to London where they are working on a project in Hackney Wick.

Sharing at the scale of housing

Housing has to be seen as part of a web of local facilities that enables sociability at multiple levels. Balancing the needs of the individual and the community is a complex task (King, 2017). Matter Architecture usefully describe a range of scales that need to be considered when planning intergenerational – or indeed any kind of connected – living situations: location; configuration; management; shared space and homes (Figure 5.3). Particular attention has to be paid to in-between spaces where people meet. 'Collective inventiveness flourishes in the production and use of threshold spaces' (Stavrides, 2016). In the 1960s and 1970s architects like Herman Hertzberger alerted the architectural community to the importance of designing such moments of encounter into their housing schemes. This can be as simple as making sure that the kitchen sink looks out onto a communal garden or play space or providing a sunny seat outside the home where you might encounter neighbours going by.

Housing that allows for doorstep play under the watchful eye of parents can help even the smallest of children develop in confidence and autonomy. The charity Playing Out offers a range of tactics for promoting street play, with one beautiful and simple example being the use of drawing to delineate play space. Sitting on your front step with your children and saying hello to people who pass, chalking some pictures together on the pavement, getting bikes and scooters out for young children, or even just starting to think differently about your street are all simple starting points (Playing Out, 2021). Playing Out make the significant point that seeing their parents take control of space can encourage children to feel that they too can have a voice as they grow up.

The need for flexible space, both at the scale of the home and at the neighbourhood, has become very apparent during the pandemic. Empowering people to utilise shared space in positive ways is a delicate balance. We have to feel a sense of responsibility for shared space to take care of it, but this requires a particular kind of culture. Placemaking lore suggests that responsibility for space needs to be clearly defined for it to be useful but this fails to take into account the activities of children who use space in renegade and unexpected ways if they are allowed. A tract of grass outside a housing block peppered with signs saying 'No Ball Games Allowed' and dog excrement, bereft of wildlife because of a thoughtless and expensive mowing regime, is unlikely to be cared for by anyone. The advent of 'guerilla gardening' in which people plant flowers and trees in unloved

Connection

Location

A new scheme should be located where there is an opportunity to connect with and enhance local networks

Schemes should be located in areas with local facilities, public transport and amenities, to connect with them and act as a catalyst for community networks. Where these are lacking, schemes should consider how they could provide for the local neighbourhood through such provision. Opportunities should be identified for schemes to fill 'gaps' in local services and networks.

Building Configuration

Building configuration should cater to providing permeable environments that enhance health and wellbeing

Buildings should be configured to optimise the amenity for health and wellbeing whilst fostering relationships between residents and with the wider community. Relationships between public, communal, semi-communal spaces and individual homes must be a key guiding consideration in the configuration of the scheme.

Homes

Homes within the new scheme should be adaptable and facilitate independant living for longer

Homes must be designed for adaptability to suit changing lifestyles. The core provision is likely to be 'super-sized' one bedroom homes that can be converted to generous 2 person homes, Part M4(3) wheelchair accessible and home offices. A minor proportion of smaller and larger (including some family homes) may be appropriate. Sustainability, health and wellbeing must be optimised through the design of all the homes.

Shared Spaces

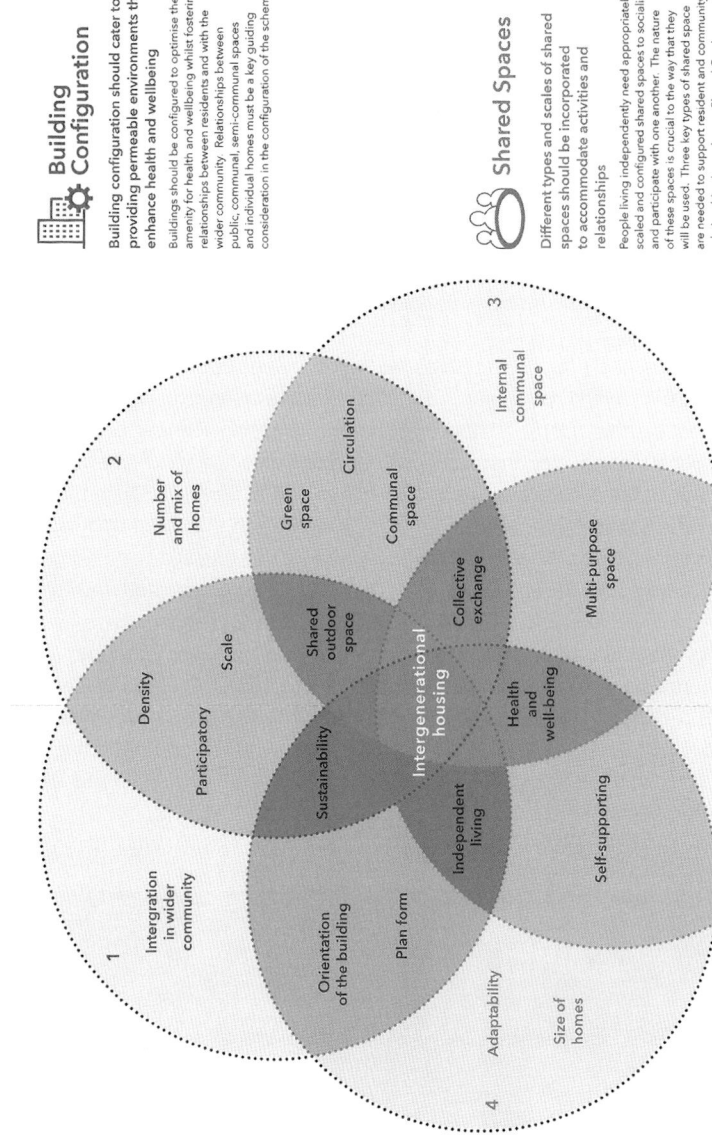

Different types and scales of shared spaces should be incorporated to accommodate activities and relationships

People living independently need appropriately scaled and configured shared spaces to socialise and participate with one another. The nature of these spaces is crucial to the way that they will be used. Three key types of shared space are needed to support resident and community relationships in a scheme: Shared Gardens, public rooms and break-out spaces. Each of these has particular characteristics.

The public room and shared garden spaces will work best when linked with, or accommodating services and facilities, depending on the scale, whilst the break-out spaces must be informal, small and requiring minimal maintenance.

Design for Management

A new scheme should be designed to facilitate management and be adaptable for future changes

Underpinning all the design principles is a requirement that they are designed to facilitate management. This must remain adaptable to allow for changing methods, whilst ensuring maintenance costs are kept low and considering how management can be integrated with the participation of the residents.

Figure 5.3 **Rethinking Intergenerational Architecture. Source: © Matter Architecture.**

89

spaces such as roundabouts and verges has given licence to people to start looking after public space but these efforts need the backing of local authorities.

Oscar Newman's 1972 book *Defensible Space* has been very influential in the UK in terms of 'designing out crime', ensuring neighbourhood surveillance through the layout of homes, providing good street lighting and reducing dark doorways and places for villains to hide (Armitage, 2013), but it remains a poorly defined and contested concept (Lees and Warwick, 2022). Whether having communal space really contributes to neglect and crime is not really known. The devil of course is in the detail. Reynald and Elffers argue for a merging of defensible space and 'routine activities perspectives' to find out how space and usage come together to make defensible places (Reynald and Elffers, 2009). This would seem to be the way to go.

Multigenerational households increased 38% between 2009 and 2014 (NHBC Foundation, 2017), while more and more young people are opting to remain living with their parents (ONS, 2022).There are an increasing number of positive examples globally of housing that has been designed specifically to bring generations together and to promote active ageing (Farrelly, 2014; Dove, 2020). In the UK one example is Castlemaine Court in Byfleet Surrey designed to offer affordable, fully accessible, high-quality, multigenerational, sustainable one and two bedroom homes for people of all ages (Figure 5.4). The scheme was designed with residential walkways which (post occupancy evaluation shows) residents use as an extension of their homes, a place to sit in the summer and view the communal gardens. The design by Archadia was based on 'Housing our Ageing Population' HAPPI (2012) principles showing their applicability for people whatever the age (Housing LIN, 2015). When families are on good terms with one another intergenerational living can bring great benefits, not least access to childcare. 40% of UK's grandparents assist substantially with looking after children (Age UK, 2017).

Figure 5.4
**Castlemaine Court multigenerational housing by Archadia.
Source:
© Charlotte Wood.**

Research shows that people who live in community led housing are measurably less lonely (Hudson et al., 2021). 'Residents who share a collective sense of purpose, who jointly participate in the design and management of their home environment, behave differently as a collective entity to those who inhabit aesthetically similar developer-led projects where residents are not bound together in shared endeavour' (Jarvis, 2019, p. 63). Helen Jarvis identifies three kinds of sharing that are happening in intentional communities: physical sharing (space and time); collective governance, working together to agree goals and lastly 'instrumental sharing' which is about 'reciprocal actions of care and assistance' (Jarvis, 2019, p. 69).

Cohousing is a model of collective living built around the principle of sharing space (Scanlon and Fernandez Arrigoitia, 2015) that has much potential for the development of affordable living environments (RICS, 2020). LILAC near Leeds (Figure 5.5) provides a well-documented and pioneering example (Chatterton, 2013). Another often-cited example is Marmalade Lane in Cambridge (Figure 5.6). Here connection happens in shared spaces and through shared facilities such as the use of electric vehicles. The list of facilities grows with new initiatives from within the community, for example, the recent installation of a pizza oven. Interaction between residents is further promoted through the presence of a local produce shop, gym and workshop. The only street in the development has been closed off, allowing children to play safely under the sheltering eye of nearby adults. Important lessons can be drawn from cohousing as an integrated practice to meet today's societal and environmental challenges but we have to find ways to diversify its appeal (Graham, 2022).

Figure 5.5
LILAC – Low Impact Living Affordable Community in Leeds.
Source: Magda © Baborska-Narozny.

The impact of housing and neighbourhoods on hope and wellbeing

Figure 5.6
Marmalade Lane, Cambridge. Source: © Saul Golden.

Our lives are intimately intertwined with plants and wildlife with whom we must share our homes. 'British gardens, as a collective, have the potential to form a network of nature reserves unparalleled in Europe' (McDonald, 2020, p. 215). Apparently approximately 48% of households put out food for birds (Davies *et al.*, 2009), suggesting that the British public has an enjoyment of wildlife and is willing to support it. Organisations like the National Trust (over 3 million members) regularly provide advice on making wildlife friendly gardens through things like making a pond, constructing bee hotels, providing holes in walls for hedgehogs, making space for composting and so on. The design of homes and the planning of places must make this easy. 'Planning strategies which neglect the role of gardens within estimates of greenspace, particularly those in urban areas, undervalue the extent of the resource' (Davies *et al.*, 2009, p. 768).

Technological avatars for nature are better than nothing. Even recorded birdsong can bring up a range of positive associations in our minds, the sound of running water slowing our breath and calming the heart. 'Classic burning fireplace' videos on You Tube have been viewed millions of times presumably because a screen showing a flaming logs in a fireplace feels more cosy and relaxing than no fire at all. It is difficult for people to care about nature when they have never really experienced it.

Digital connection

Digital connection is already permeating our lives, nowhere more so than the home. Sharing, both physical and digital, is fundamental to 'truly smart and sustainable cities' (McLaren and Agyeman, 2017). 'Smart' tends to be used as a zip file for innovative technology that includes some sort of artificial intelligence (Marikyan, Papagiannidis and Alamanos, 2019). Smart home technologies fall largely into four major categories, the first providing services to the residents, the second being about storing and retrieving multi-media captured in the smart home (with implications for privacy), the third being surveillance and the last being about reducing energy consumption (De Silva, Morikawa and Petra, 2012). Adam Juniper sets out the extraordinary range of ways in which digital technologies are infiltrating our homes: 'ecosystems' such as Alexa or Siri; 'smart home systems'; entertainment, games and TV; temperature; lighting; kitchen appliances and ordering of food; securing and monitoring (for example, baby); wellbeing appliances that measure exercise, body fat, blood pressure and so on; robotic gadgets that enact tasks on a sequenced basis such as pet care and lawnmowers as well as the modems and cables that facilitate all this (2018) and this doesn't include our communication devices like smart phones and computers. At present smart home technologies focus less on changing behaviour than on making existing behaviours more easy (Furszyfer *et al.*, 2020, p. 7).

The amount of technology in our homes is having a profound change on the way we experience our housing and neighbourhoods. While these devices offer new kinds of technology enabled sharing the real benefit is perhaps to the multinationals who are selling our data. This may be why they are so intent on offering us 'frictionless' connections between the digital and analogue worlds when actually that 'friction' is so important for human learning and empowerment (Drake, 2019). The infiltration of other digital realities into our lives makes the real physical experience of space feel delicate and poignant and in some way enchanting if we can only see it. It is no surprise that greater contact with nature has even been seen to temper excessive mobile phone use (Wang, Geng and Rodriguez-Casallas, 2021), which, in turn, must enable us to be more present for one another.

Conclusion

Homes and neighbourhoods have a strong influence on friendship and group formation (Halpern, 1995, p. 119) by offering opportunities for connection both informal – saying hello to your neighbour across the garden wall, semi-formal – a street party or community event – or formal – local authority organised drop in sessions. Digital connectivity will be increasingly important for data gathering on how to make homes and neighbourhoods fit for purpose but we have to find a way to prevent technology from deflecting our attention away from our environment and one and other. The need for face-to-face connection is well known as a fundamental precept of wellbeing whether we think we want to connect or not.

References

Age UK. (2017) *5 Million Grandparents Take on Childcare Responsibilities*. https://www.ageuk.org.uk/latest-news/articles/2017/september/five-million-grandparents-take-on-childcare-responsibilities/

Age UK. (2018) *All the Lonely People: Loneliness in Later Life*. Available at: https://www.ageuk.org.uk/globalassets/age-uk/documents/reports-and-publications/reports-and-briefings/loneliness/loneliness-report_final_2409.pdf.

Armitage, R. (2013) *Crime Prevention Through housing Design: Policy and Practice*. Basingstoke: Palgrave Macmillan.

Blanc, F., Scanlon, K. and White, T. (2020) *Living in a denser London: How residents see their homes*. London: LSE. Available at: https://www.lse.ac.uk/cities/Assets/Documents/Research-Reports/2020-LSE-Density-Report-digital.pdf.

Channon, B. and Kriekler, F. (2020) *The Myth: Density Equals Worse Health and Wellbeing Outcomes*. Available at: http://assael.co.uk/news/2020/myth-busting-density-and-wellbeing/.

Chatterton, P. (2013) 'Towards an agenda for post carbon cities: lessons from Lilac, the UK's first ecological, affordable, cohousing community', *International Journal of Urban and Regional Research*, 37(5), pp. 1654–1674.

Cottam, H. (2018) *Radical Help*. London: Virago.

Criado Perez, C. (2019) *Invisible Women*. London: Chatto and Windus.

Davies, Z.G. *et al.* (2009) 'A national scale inventory of resource provision for biodiversity within domestic gardens', *Biological Conservation*, 142(4), pp. 761–771.

De Silva, L.C., Morikawa, C. and Petra, I.M. (2012) 'State of the art of smart homes', *Engineering Applications of Artificial Intelligence*, 25, pp. 1313–1321.

Doherty, G. (2018) *Grenfell Hope*. London: SPCK.

Dove, C. (2020) *Radical Housing: Designing Multigenerational and Co-Living for All*. London: RIBA Publishing.

Drake, L. (2019) *Frictionless Technologies: The Innovation of Human Obsolescence*, *Posthumanity.ai*. Available at: https://posthumanity.ai/wp-content/uploads/2019/06/Laura-Drake-Frictionless-Technologies-Human-Obsolescence-2019.pdf.

Emerson, E. *et al.* (2021) 'Loneliness, social support, social isolation and wellbeing among working age adults with and without disability: Cross-sectional study', *Disability and Health Journal*, 14(1), 100965.

Erdem, N. and Mirza, A. (2020) 'Let's dance: how club culture can create community mental health support'. Available at: https://neweconomics.org/2020/12/lets-dance-how-club-culture-can-create-community-mental-health-support.

Farrelly, L. (2014) *Designing for the Third Age: Architecture Redefined for a Generation of 'Active Agers'*. Architectural Design, London: Wiley.

Felix Project. (2021) *The Felix Project*. Available at: https://thefelixproject.org/about/our-story.

Furszyfer, D.R. *et al.* (2020) 'Critically reviewing smart home technology applications and business models in Europe', *Energy Policy*, 144, 111631.

Graham, P. (2022) *Adjustable Housing*. University of Reading. Unpublished Thesis.

Halpern, D. (1995) *Mental Health and the Built Environment: More than Bricks and Mortar?* London; Bristol: Taylor & Francis.

Handler, S. (2014) *An Alternative Age Friendly Handbook for the Socially Engaged Urban Practitioner*. Manchester: University of Manchester Library. Available at: www.micra.manchester.ac.uk/research/population-ageing/research-activity.

HAPPI. (2012) 'HAPPI 2- housing our ageing population: plan for implementation'. All Party Parliamentary Group on Housing and Care for Older People. Available at: www.homesandcommunities.co.uk.

Hennchen, B. and Pregernig, M. (2020) 'Organizing joint practices in urban food initiatives - a comparative analysis if gardening cooking and eating together', *Sustainability*, 12, p. 4457. doi:doi:10.3390/su12114457.

Housing LIN. (2015) *Multi-Generational Homes: Building a Community for all Ages*. Available at: https://www.housinglin.org.uk/_assets/Resources/Housing/Practice_examples/Housing_LIN_case_studies/HLIN_CaseStudy_116_CastlemaineCourt.pdf.

Hudson, J. *et al.* (2021) '"A slow build-up of a history of kindness": exploring the potential of community-led housing in alleviating loneliness', *Sustainability*, 13(11323). Available at: https://wwww.mdpi.com/2071-1050/13/20/11323.

Jacobs, J. (1961) *The Death and Life of Great American Cities*. New York: Random House.

Jarvis, H. (2019) 'Age-friendly community resilience', in Trogal, K., Bauman, I., Lawrence, R. and Petrsecu, D. (eds.) *Architecture and Resilience*. London: Routledge, pp. 61–73.

Joseph, M. and Chaskin, R. (2010) 'Living in a mixed-income development: resident perceptions of the benefits and disadvantages of two developments in Chicago', *Urban Studies*, 47(11), pp. 2347–2366. doi:10.1177/0042098009357959.

Juniper, A. (2018) *The Smart Smart Home Handbook*. Paris: Hachette.

King, P. (2017) *Living Alone, Living Together*. Bingley: Emerald Publishing.

Krznaric, R. (2020) *The Good Ancestor: How to Think Long Term in a Short Term World*. London: WH Allen.

Lawton, R.N., Gramatki, J. and Fujiwara, D. (2020) 'does volunteering make us happier, or are happie people more likely to volunteer? Addressing the problem of reverse causality when estimating the wellbeing impacts of volunteering', *Journal of Happiness Studies*, 22, pp. 599–624.

Lees, L., and Warwick, E. (2022) *Defensible Space on the Move*. London: Wiley.

Marikyan, D., Papagiannidis, S. and Alamanos, E. (2019) 'A systematic review of the smart home literature: a user perspective', *Technological Forecasting and Social Change*, 138, pp. 139–154.

Marovelli, B. (2019) 'Cooking and eating together in London: food sharing initiatives as collective spaces of encounter', *Geoforum*, 99, pp. 190–201.

Mayor of London. (2021) *Connective Social Infrastructure*. Available at: https://www.london.gov.uk/sites/default/files/connective_social_infrastructure.pdf.

McDonald, B. (2020) *Rebirding*. London: Pelagic.

McLaren, D. and Agyeman, J. (2017) *Sharing Cities: A Case for Truly Smart and Sustainable Cities*. Cambridge, MA: MIT.

Men's Sheds Association. (2021) *Men's Sheds Association*. Available at: https://menssheds.org.uk/.

Nguyen, M.H., Gruber, J. and Marler, W. (2021) 'Staying connected while physically apart: digital communication when face-to-face interactions are limited', *New Media and Society* [Preprint]. doi: 10.1177/1461444820985442.

NHBC Foundation. (2017) *Multigenerational Living: An Opportunity for UK Housebuilders?* Available at: https://www.nhbcfoundation.org/publication/multigenerational-living-an-opportunity-for-uk-house-builders/.

ONS (2022) *Families and Households in the UK 2021*. Office for National Statistics. Available at: https://www.ons.gov.uk/peoplepopulationandcommunity/birthsdeathsandmarriages/families/bulletins/familiesandhouseholds/2021

ONS. (2017) *Changes in the Value and Division of Unpaid Volunteering in the UK: 2000–2015*. Office for National Statistics. Available at: https://www.ons.gov.uk/economy/nationalaccounts/satelliteaccounts/articles/changesinthevalueanddivisionofunpaidcareworkintheuk/2015.

Playing Out. (2021) *Playing Out*. Available at: https://playingout.net/about/our-vision-to-play-out/.

Raynes, N. (2020) 'Sharing place and space to promote wellbeing for old and young people in a neighbourhood', *European Journal of Public Health*, 30 (Supplement_5). doi: 10.1093/eurpub/ckaa166.1170.

Reynald, D.M. and Elffers, H. (2009) 'The future of newman's defensible space theory: linking defensible space and the routine activities of place', *European Journal of Criminology*, 6(1), pp. 25–46.

RICS. (2020) *Car-Free, Co-Housing Community is the UK's Project of the Year*, *Royal Institute of Chartered Surveyors*. Available at: https://www.rics.org/uk/news-insight/latest-news/press/car-free-co-housing-community-is-the-uks-project-of-the-year/.

R-Urban. (2016) *R-Urban: About*, *R-Urban*. Available at: http://r-urban.net/en/sample-page/.

Samuel, F. (2020) *Social Value Toolkit for Architecture*. London: RIBA. Available at: https://www.architecture.com/knowledge-and-resources/resources-landing-page/social-value-toolkit-for-architecture.

Scanlon, K. and Fernandez Arrigoitia, M. (2015) 'Development of new cohousing: lessons from a London scheme for the over-50s', *Urban Research and Practice*, 8(1), pp. 106–121.

Scharf, T. and de Jong Gierveld, J. (2008) 'Loneliness in urban neighbourhoods: an Anglo-Dutch comparison', *European Journal of Ageing*, 5(2), 103.

Stavrides, S. (2016) *Common Space*. London: Zed Books.

Stevenson, F., Baborska-Narozny, M. and Chatterton, P. (2016) 'Resilience, redundancy and low-carbon living: co-producing individual and community learning', *Building Research & Information*, 44(7), pp. 789–803.

Tabassum, F., Mohan, J. and Smith, P. (2016) 'Association of volunteering with mental well-being: a lifecourse analysis of a national population-based longitudinal study in the UK', *British Medical Journal Open*, 6(8). Available at: https://bmjopen.bmj.com/content/6/8/e011327.short.

Trogal, K. (2019) 'Resilience as interdependence', in Trogal, K., Bauman, I., Lawrence, R. and Petrsecu, D. (eds.) *Architecture and Resilience*. London, pp. 190–203.

Wang, C., Geng, L. and Rodriguez-Casallas, J. (2021) 'The role of nature-deficit disorder in the associations between Mobile phone overuse and well-being and mindfulness', *Current Psychology* [Preprint]. doi: 10.1007/s12144-021-01453-9.

Welby, J. (2018) *Reimagining Britain*. London: Bloomsbury.

Wessendorf, S. (2013) 'Commonplace diversity and the "ethos of mixing": perceptions of difference in a London neighbourhood', *Global Studies in Culture and Power*, 20(4), pp. 407–422.

Chapter 6

Physical health

Housing and neighbourhoods have a strong impact on our physical wellbeing (Wood *et al.*, 2017). Over the last few decades there has been an expansion of interest in the health benefits of a good environment and the impact of design on wellbeing (UK Gov, 1998; The King's Fund, 2017; Design Council, 2018), an interest that has taken a new turn in the wake of the pandemic. Researchers have for a long time been aware of the health benefits of giving access to nature and greenery into hospital environments, resulting in speedier recovery and the need for less painkillers as well as positive impacts on staff and carers (Ulrich, 1984; Ulrich and Delani, 1999). The very fact of being in a homely space, as opposed to an impersonal institutional space, makes us feel better, helping with recovery and the alleviation, for example, of pain in childbirth (Duque *et al.*, 2020). A recent 'relational turn' across many fields is acknowledging the complex interconnections that we have with our environment (Karvonen and Yocom, 2011). Not only do homes impact on our bodies but the home environment also impacts on other things like educational attainment (Clapham, 2019) and mental health (Clark and Kearns, 2012), the two obviously being intimately connected. This chapter gives an overview of a second dimension of social value, the complex impact of housing and places on the physical body as it emerges in the literature of placemaking and health. I start by examining the role of the built environment in promoting activity, play and rest, and therefore in helping us to stay healthy, and finish with a discussion of community gardening, not only as a source of food but also as an important way to stay fit while alleviating loneliness, now recognised as the killer that it is.

Active travel
The National Travel Survey shows that some 83% of journeys in England are under 10 miles which makes them well suited for active travel. Active travel – walking and cycling – have been correlated with a range of positive outcomes, including fitness, stress reduction, positivity, general psychological wellbeing and reduced absenteeism from work (Urban Transport Group, 2016). Interestingly it isn't just the actual walkability of neighbourhoods that is important for encouraging activity, the perception of walkability is important too (Jack and McCormack, 2014). A feeling of safety and trust in neighbourhoods can

Figure 6.1
Reconfigured access road at the Wintles.
Source: © Bob Tomlinson and Village Makers.

have a significant impact on rates of walking (Mason, Kearns and Livingston, 2013). Perceptions of danger real or imagined can have a serious impact on whether people go out and take exercise, particularly after dark. The look of a road can also make a considerable difference to how people use it. Bob Tomlinson of Village Makers recounts how his community was required to provide a five metre road to give access to their homes in the Wintles. Being the only wide straight stretch of road in the area it became a locus of antisocial behaviour, a problem that was only rectified when a Highways Officer worked with the organisation to recast the road as something much more attractive and user friendly (Figure 6.1).

Transport strategy has major implications for the quality of community making as the way we move around influences the way that space is allocated for certain functions. The Urban Transport Group note that increased rates of walking and cycling bring about a series of 'identifiable benefits to the urban realm, many of which are not included in conventional transport benefits or transport scheme appraisal' (Urban Transport Group, 2016, 7.6). Low traffic neighbourhoods which filter motor vehicles off residential streets have been shown to be particularly beneficial for quality of life, particularly in more deprived areas (Voce and Walker, 2021). Ironically it is the people who are less likely to own cars who suffer most from the pollution that it generates. Traffic noise even reduces schoolchildrens' ability to learn (Foraster, Esnaola and Lopez-Vincente, 2022). The slowing of traffic to 20 mph in our neighbourhoods not only reduces the risk of fatal injury but can also impact upon the sociability of neighbours. A Bristol-based study showed that the slowing of traffic also led to a marked increase in children walking to school (Pilkington et al., 2018).

Statistics suggest that walking and cycling are more dangerous than other types of transportation however they are not dangerous activities per se, the

Figure 6.2
The pleasure of swimming in the harbour of Copenhagen for free.
Source: © Flora Samuel.

health benefits of cycling far outweigh its dangers. Further the risk of a cyclist getting injured goes down as levels of cycling go up (Jacobsen et al., 2012). Addressing cycling safety leads to more cyclists on the road which, in turn, improves safety. Germany and the Netherlands are notable for putting in place a variety of policies to increase usage including the expansion of their cycle networks, segregation of cycle lanes, traffic calming and the restriction of vehicle use in urban areas with traffic regulations in favour of pedestrians and cyclists. Bicycle sharing schemes too are also considered good for health (Woodcock et al., 2014). The Mini-Hollands programme in three outer London boroughs is an investment of around £100 million into safe cycling, Dutch style, a part of the Mayor of London's *Healthy Streets* approach (2020). This shows what is possible in the context of England.

Reducing traffic speed has a range of positive outcomes, including improving connections between neighbours and placemaking. Shared space, an idea proselytised by the late Ben Hamilton Baillie, is the idea that traffic can be calmed by clear prompts in the environment, changes in road surface, obvious presence of children playing, lack of motorway type signage (Laker, 2019). The proliferation of road signage, crash barriers and crossings are not only ugly, expensive and bad for placemaking, they also send motorists the potent message that cars take priority over everyone else (let's not forget the need for wildlife crossings too). Shared space has been criticised by the visually impaired and others for making it difficult to get about, but surely we can take forward some of his lessons while also assisting the less differently able. Highways teams have a vital role to play in making great communities.

Suffice to say, homes and neighbourhoods must be designed with active travel in mind. One of the reasons that mixed developments are so successful is that they offer a variety of interesting destinations (FIT, 2018, p. 17). Living Streets is a charity dedicated to getting people walking. Its vision until 2025 is around three outcomes; making walking the top of the travel hierarchy for shorter journeys; making better streets for walking and striving for equality and inclusion (Living Streets, 2020), accessibility for wheelchairs is a particular issue (Hutabarat Lo, 2009).

For people to get walking they obviously need to have safe enjoyable places to walk leading them to a choice of useful and interesting destinations in both urban and rural locations. Lively environments that offer positive distractions at ground level and feel safe are obviously going to encourage walking yet so many of our buildings are designed with dull impenetrable ground floor walls interspersed with eddying currents of litter. Such places are particularly nasty for small children, sending them messages about what they can expect from the world – 'babies and toddlers are the fastest learners on the planet' (Jang *et al.*, 2022).

Walkability as a free resource has major implications for equality and autonomy. Ironically walkability can be really bad in rural areas where pavement less roads are a hazard to walkers and cyclists alike and so much land is private and out of bounds. The Countryside and Rights of Way Act (CROW) has already been enacted in Scotland, enabling people to walk and campm responsibly pretty much anywhere within reason, and is needed across the UK (Right to Roam, 2021). The impact on quality of life at multiple levels would be profound.

Fostering exercise and play at the scale of the neighbourhood

The overall attractiveness or 'livability' of a place is an obvious incitement to get up and get out there. Copenhagen has topped the livability leagues for many years and with good reason. One simple joy is being able to swim freely in the harbour waters at the centre of the capital (Figure 6.2). Building on its successful Urban Life Strategy for 2009–2015 the City of Copenhagen's new strategy is Co-Creation Copenhagen (2015–2025) a primary goal of which is that people stay outside 20% longer in 'urban nature' with all the benefits that this brings in terms of sociability, commerce, exercise and climate change awareness (Saaby and Bauman, 2019). There are eight indicators of success for the programme include the stipulation that urban nature must be included in all the phases in the city planning system, another is that 90% of residents in a new area should have easy access to a park or green area. With regard to urban nature in private areas, one indicator is that '10% of Copenhageners should experience active engagement in the work to create more and better urban nature', with the second indicator being that 'Copenhagen city should facilitate 50 partnership projects with urban nature' (Saaby and Bauman, 2019, p. 258). This all links to the climate change plan for the city.

The manifold health benefits of access to green space (van den Bosch and Bird, 2018) have been explored by the National Health Service (NHS) 2012–2017 Greenspace Demonstration project (Centre for Sustainable Healthcare, 2020; NatureScot, 2020) building on the idea of a 'Natural Health Service'. That there are considerable wellbeing benefits in exposing people to urban nature (not just about exercise) is by now well documented and tools are being developed to measure it happening on a constant basis (McEwan *et al.*, 2020).

Even the temporary use of green space is better than nothing. Ideally green space needs to be easily to get to which is one reason why the provision of pocket parks and other smaller interventions is so important. 'Both the number of parks near to participants homes, and the total spatial area of accessible parks matters' as well as a range of different leisure provisions within them (Wood et al., 2017, p. 70). Size isn't the only thing that matters, the design, layout of space, biodiversity, colour, texture and mix impact on usage and the benefits derived from these places (see, for example, Clark et al., 2014).

Space is experienced in uneven and unequal ways (Boys, 2014). Good design is inclusive, universal and intergenerational offering opportunities for all to extend and surprise themselves through new challenges. It tactfully extends an invitation to play across the spectrum, something that requires diplomacy in a designer. Exercise prompts in my local area target the most able (think pull-ups), leaving the less vigorous well and truly out if it. Women in particular need to take more exercise but lack outdoor places that meet their needs (Kilgour and Parker, 2012). In my local park women in hijabs use the early morning cover of darkness as their opportunity to run in peace. Some imagination is needed here to encourage greater inclusion.

Clever landscapes offer multiple opportunities for play and exercise to different sectors of the population (and their pets) at different times of the day and night. Girls and boys use space very differently so both their needs need to be accommodated (Criado Perez, 2019). Make Space for Girls is a charity that campaigns for public space with girls in mind. HerCity, a division of UN Habitat, offers a 'toolbox' for making sure girls across the world get what they need from their places. Think, for example, of a child challenging herself to jump down over increasing numbers of steps or the incredibly creative challenges thought up by the parkour group Storror through very close analysis of the relationship between the body and space. Yes such places may also be potentially dangerous, but children have to learn how to manage risk in their lives. Skipping ropes and French skipping elastics, the mainstay of my childhood, were banned from my daughter's school playgrounds leaving the girls, in particular, with nothing to do but mind games. In recent years discussion has moved to the question of whether play is over-regulated, driving children indoors to participate in, also potentially dangerous, digital games. 'Failing to allow children to take any risk will reduce their experiences and learning, and is, in turn, likely to create vulnerability in their adult life' (Hewitt-Taylor and Heaslip, 2012).

Making flexible space for different kinds of play takes imagination. Nothing does this better than water – whether in pools, runnels or exciting squirts – it is sure to get everyone joining in. In Wales legislation about the inclusion of swales, grassy ditches to carry off and absorb excess rainwater, in housing developments can be reframed as play places. This is a real opportunity to make space for beauty, fun and biodiversity in the public realm.

There is a growing body of evidence that shows that children in denser areas are less likely to succumb to obesity because children in these areas have better connectivity to parks and other destinations. A recent Sheffield study found that having good quality green space within 300m of a child's home made them less likely to become obese (Mears *et al.*, 2020). Further pop-up parks and temporary street closures can allow children to reclaim territory that benefits creativity and empowerment and engagement in the wider public realm (Pitsikali, Parnell and McIntyre, 2020). Parks and playgrounds, including school playgrounds, allow children and parents to meet other families and also provide important contact with nature (Puhakka et al., 2019), a benefit for every generation. All in all well-conceived housing and neighbourhoods can have a major impact on children's early life experiences (Alderton *et al.*, 2019).

Of course the same goes for experiences of later life. In *An Alternative Age-Friendly Handbook* Sophie Handler offers a range of 'age-inclusive initiatives' that go 'beyond a baseline of bodily needs' (Handler, 2014, p. 53). These can be large scale (and expensive) or extremely small. A nice simple example is a tile in the pavement that reminds walkers to stop and do a shoulder rotation. In order to get people up and moving, there is need for enough basic things like wide flat footways, easy transitions between levels, simple clear signage, the regular and frequent availability of warm and supportive seating as well as well maintained, safe and sufficient toilets (Handler, 2014). Women's advancement into the public realm can be charted against the advent of the public lavatory. Things that can be an inconvenience in youth can be magnified in old age.

Small initiatives have a big role to play in the making of inclusive communities. They just require a bit of thought. A simple example is water fountains. Public water fountains have been at the centre of community life for time immemorial but over the last few years they have been knocked down and covered up as water, arguably a human right, has become an increasingly commercialised, resulting instead in a flood of rarely to be recycled plastic bottles (Perkins, 2019). In response to this need the Mayor of London's office is currently working with Thames Water to install 100 new fountains in busy and accessible parts of London. That David Chipperfield Architects recently managed to include a new water fountain in their refurbishment of Selfridges in London is a bigger achievement than it might sound.

Comfort and sleep

Whether cold or hot, excesses of temperature can kill, particularly the old and the vulnerable. Sometimes these deaths are caused by poor housing and sometimes they are caused by poverty and an inability to pay the bills. Well-designed sustainable housing reduces running costs and alleviates the chances of overheating (Zhang and Liu, 2018). It is worth noting that not only do people living in Passivhaus sustainable homes have low running costs, they also enjoy better air quality than those in conventional housing (Moreno Rangel *et al.*, 2020). Temperature and air quality are also important conditions for sleep.

A recent IKEA publicity campaign features duvets and pillows tumbling out of a brown pill bottle. The message is clear – sleep stops you getting ill. The importance of sleep and dreams for cognitive function and overall health is undeniable. Further loss of sleep can have disastrous consequences in terms of accidents. More people are working night shifts than ever before, with major implications for health, transportation and city planning. Sleep deteriorates with age so, as our society ages, it is likely to become a topic of increasing importance. The design of housing can have major implications for this most sensitive and important of processes.

While mixed neighbourhoods may be a good thing for vitality and safety they can be really noisy, particularly in the hot months when you have to keep your windows open and the hum of industrial fans cuts across the evening air. I myself am woken most nights in the wee small hours by the arrival of a succession privatised rubbish trucks removing rubbish from the shops behind my home with each business using a different company. Design for sleep requires careful planning at the neighbourhood scale and careful planning within the home to ensure bedrooms are kept as much as possible away from noise. Extensive sound proofing between properties is needed, with implications for the layout and overlap of units. There are other ways to reduce the impact of noise such as moving water and vegetation which mask out sounds with something more pleasant (Lugten *et al.*, 2018).

There is also the issue of light pollution which not only leads to shallow sleep, waking frequently but has a 'persistent negative' effect on the brain (Cho *et al.*, 2013) and can mess with our circadian rhythms. Completely blocking out light while providing good ventilation and the cool environment that is also important for sleeping is a design challenge indeed. Not only this but you need to feel secure to sleep well too (Walker, 2017).

Although it is well known that natural light impacts on our circadian timing system, the arousal system and affective system (van Creveld and Mansfield, 2020) the impact of light, particularly natural daylight on wellbeing is largely unexplored field (Osibona, Solomon and Fecht, 2021). The importance of exposure to sunny south light, particularly for older people, is however relatively well understood which is why adequate daylight is central to the Housing our Ageing Population Panel (HAPPI) principles of good home design. Artificial lighting has a range of psychological impacts well known in retail and office design that I've yet to see properly discussed in the context of housing.

All homes should have balconies and access to outdoor space – for daylight, for stretching, for reconnecting with the earth and the elements – good design can make these experiences more accessible, special and seductive through the framing of enticing views, harnessing all the senses to make ritual moments of connection. If we've been working on a computer, we can be crackling with static, something that needs to be drained away through earthing (grounding) standing with your bare feet on the earth (Menigoz, Latz and Ely, 2020), but people need access to earth to stand on. Innumerable books on mindfulness recommend that people get out into the fresh air in the morning, with or without bare feet, to greet the world and send out positive feelings for a new day. Such ritual moments can be built into architecture of homes and neighbourhoods. Green space varying from our own gardens and balconies to national parks, pocket parks to the weedy patches of earth at the base of patient sentinel urban trees all play a role in re-connecting us to what matters.

Community gardening

As a species we have built ourselves on community gardening. A literature review of community gardens by Guitart et al reveals the wide extent of the benefits delivered by community gardens in terms of cohesion, improved health, access to fresh food, saving and making money, as well as education. Further benefits can include reduced crime, environmental sustainability, the enhancement of cultural heritage, life satisfaction and levelling up as well as increased biodiversity (Guitart, Pickering and Byrne, 2012). As well as more obvious health benefits such as weight loss and improved nutrition. Gardening can also contribute to pain relief, help people deal with difficult times and improve mental health (Schmutz and Lennartsson Turner, 2014). The lovely thing about it is that gardening has something for everyone no matter their ability or stamina.

Research shows that community gardens can provide young people with an opportunity to do something constructive, to contribute to the community, to develop interpersonal skills including 'social control as well as opportunities for improved nutrition' (Ober Allen *et al.*, 2008). Gardening can also have important benefits in providing opportunities and food for refugees who have a very hard time being moved around while awaiting the outcomes of their cases. The Cardiff Salad Garden offers refugees something to do while they aren't allowed to work, giving them a sense of community and free salad while funding itself through the provision of salad to local restaurants. Much has been written, particularly by geographers, about connections between memory and identity for migrant, exploring the ways in which 'cultural identity is at once deterritorialized and reterritorialised' (Fortier, 2020). Reconnecting with the land may help with this.

Architects Bohn & Viljoen envisage 'productive urban landsapes' (CPULs) in which leftover spaces in cities are enlisted for urban food production (Viljoen, 2005) (Figures 6.3 and 6.4). In the UK allotments afford the lucky few a chance to grow your own at a very low cost. Local authorities have a duty to provide space for allotments (Shrubsole, 2019). I pay roughly £120 a year for the use of my one in Cardiff. Unsurprisingly people with allotments worried less about food security at the start of the pandemic (Mead *et al.*, 2021). Allotments tend to be adult environments dominated by a health and safety culture that emanates from the Highways departments with which they are associated. They need to be more child (and nature) friendly. Allotments, subject to regular inspection by the local authority, can feel like quite a responsibility and can be quite far from people's homes so other opportunities to get involved in gardening are needed near at hand to allow people to dip in and out as and when they can.

Incredible Edible in Todmorden on the Yorkshire Lancashire border, not an affluent area, is an extremely inspiring example of local food production (Figures 6.5 and 6.6). Begun as an experiment in guerrilla planting of fruit and vegetables it quickly took off as a joined up local movement aiming for self sufficiency in terms of food production, benefitting from Lottery funding on the way. The original idea was planting food by the sides of roads, in public gardens and in planters with people being encouraged to help themselves to food. Others have tried to replicate the experiment in other places revealing the need for strong

Figure 6.3
Spiel/Feld Marzahn is a CPUL urban agriculture project in the Berlin borough of Marzahn-Hellersdorf.
Source: © Bohn & Viljoen Architects 2012.

Figure 6.4
A CPUL project in Kokubunji, Japan, a city within the Tokyo metropolis.
Source: © Bohn & Viljoen Architects, Laboratories for urban agriculture study 2019.

community champions to facilitate the process. Studies of Incredible Edible show an overwhelmingly positive response to the project (Hardman et al., 2019). It is not so much the food production that has been the central achievement of Incredible Edible, but more the community cohesiveness that has been generated by the whole approach (Thompson, 2012).

Figure 6.5
Pollination Street, Incredible Edible, Todmorden.
Source: © Incredible Edible Todmorden.

Figure 6.6
Policeman with children, Incredible Edible, Todmorden.
Source: © Incredible Edible Todmorden.

Isobel Tomlinson notes an emergent 'political discourse' within the UN and other key organisations around 'agroecology' which brings together the science of developing sustainable food systems with an approach to food provision that gives equal attention to sustainability goals of resilience and equity (2013, p. 87). With some ingenuity, and a more plant based diet, Britain could be self sufficient in terms of food (Fairlie, 2010). And what a difference that would make to health (and carbon production) – the benefits of a plant-based diet for reducing risk of cancer, heart disease and a range of chronic diseases are well known (see for example Feher *et al.*, 2020).

Conclusion

'Blue Zones' are communities where people enjoy longer lives than anywhere else. Here stress reducing activities like walking and resting are part of their daily routines which also include meals that are very largely plant based. What is particularly distinctive about these societies is that people have a strong sense of purpose, a sense of their place in the world (Blue Zones, 2021). This chapter set out some of the ways in which homes and places can impact on the physical health of our bodies, fostering active lifestyles, encouraging play, sleep and the growing of local food. Not only this but 'the promotion of self-esteem, resilience and the coping skills of individuals and communities' can have a positive impact on both quality of life and longevity (Rocco and Suhrcke, 2012, p. iv). These are the focus of the next two chapters on the social value of housing.

References

Alderton, A. *et al.* (2019) 'Reducing inequities in early childhood mental health: how might the neighbourhood built environment help close the gap? A systematic search and critical review', *International Journal of Environmental Research and Public Health*, 16(9). Available at: https://emergingminds.com.au/resources/the-role-of-neighbourhoods-in-young-childrens-mental-health-what-does-the-evidence-tell-us/.

Blue Zones. (2021) *Blue Zones*. Available at: https://www.bluezones.com/.

van den Bosch, M. and Bird, W. (2018) *Oxford Textbook of Nature and Public Health*. Oxford: Oxford University Press.

Boys, J. (2014) *Doing Disability Differently: An Alternative Handbook on Architecture, Dis/ability and Designing for Everyday Life*. London: Routledge.

Centre for Sustainable Healthcare. (2020) *NHS Forest*. Available at: https://nhsforest.org/

Cho, J.R. *et al.* (2013) 'Let there be no light: the effect of bedside light on sleep quality and background electroencephalographic rhythms', *Sleep Medicine*, 14(12), pp. 1422–1425.

Clapham, D. (2019) *Remaking Housing Policy: An International Study*. London: Routledge.

Clark, J. and Kearns, A. (2012) 'Housing improvements, perceived housing quality and psychosocial benefits from the home', *Housing Studies*, 27(7), pp. 915–939. doi:10.1080/02673037.2012.725829.

Clark, N. *et al.* (2014) 'Biodiversity, cultural pathways, and human health: a framework', *Trends in Ecology and Evolution*, 29(4), pp. 198–204.

van Creveld, K. and Mansfield, K. (2020) 'Lit environments that promote health and wellbeing', *Building Services Engineering Research and Technology*, 41(2), pp. 193–209.

Criado Perez, C. (2019) *Invisible Women*. London: Chatto and Windus.

Design Council. (2018) *Healthy Placemaking*. London: Design Council/Social Change UK. Available at: https://www.designcouncil.org.uk/sites/default/files/asset/document/Healthy_Placemaking_Report.pdf.

Duque, M. *et al.* (2020) 'Homeliness in health care: the role of everyday designing', *Home Cultures*, 16(3), pp. 213–232.

Fairlie, S. (2010) *Meat: A Benign Extravagance*. Vermont: Chelsea Green.

Feher, A. *et al.* (2020) 'A comprehensive review of the benefits of and barriers to the switch to a plant-based diet', *Sustainability*, 12(10), p. 4136.

FIT. (2018) *Transport for New Homes: Summary and Recommendations*. Foundation for Integrated Transport. Available at: https://www.transportfornewhomes.org.uk/wp-content/uploads/2018/07/transport-for-new-homes-summary-web.pdf.

Foraster, M., Esnaola, M. and Lopez-Vincente, M. (2022) ds/2018/07/t road traffic noise and cognitive development in schoolchildren in Barcelona, Spain: A population-based cohort study', *Plos Medicine*, 19(6). Available at: https://journals.plos.org/plosmedicine/article?id=10.1371/journal.pmed.1004001.

Fortier, A.-M. (2020) *Migrant Belongings: Memory, Space, Identity*. London: Routledge.

Guitart, D., Pickering, C. and Byrne, J. (2012) 'Past results and future directions in urban community gardens research', *Urban Forestry and Urban Greening*, 11, pp. 364–373.

Handler, S. (2014) *An alternative age friendly handbook for the socially engaged urban practitioner*. Manchester: University of Manchester Library. Available at: www.micra.manchester.ac.uk/research/population-ageing/research-activity.

Hardman, M. *et al.* (2019) 'Critically evaluating the role of the incredible edible movement in the UK', in Certoma, C., Noori, S. and Sondermann, M. (eds) *Urban Gardening and the struggle for social and spatial justice*. Manchester Scholarship Online. Available at https://manchester.universitypressscholarship.com/view/10.7228/manchester/9781526126092.001.0001/upso-9781526126092

Hewitt-Taylor, J. and Heaslip, V. (2012) 'Protecting children or creating vulnerability?', *Community Practitioner*, 85(12), pp. 31–33.

Hutabarat Lo, R. (2009) 'Walkability: what is it?', *Journal of Urbanism: International Research on Placemaking and Urban Sustainability*, 2(2), pp. 145–166.

Jack, E. and McCormack, G.R. (2014) 'The association between objectively-determined and self-reported urban form characteristics and neighborhood based walking in adults', *International Journal of Behavioural Nutritional and Physical Activity*, 11(71). https://doi.org/10.1186/1479-5868-11-71.

Jacobsen, P.L. *et al.* (2012) 'Cycling Safety', in Pucher, J. and Buehler, R. (eds.) *City Cycling*. Cambridge, MA: MIT Press, pp. 141–156.

Jang, C. *et al.* (2022) *Access and Babies, Toddlers and Their Caregivers*. Bernard Van Leer Foundation. Available at: https://www.itdp.org/wp-content/uploads/2022/01/Access-for-All-Babies-and-Toddlers_December-2021-pages_final-3.pdf.

Jensen, H., Rasmussen, B. and Ekholm, O. (2019) 'Neighbourhood noise annoyance is associated with various mental and physical health symptoms', *BMC Public Health*, 19(1508).

Karvonen, A. and Yocom, K. (2011) 'The civics of urban nature; enacting hybrid landscapes', *Environment and Planning A*, 43(6), pp. 1305–1322. Available at: http://journals.sagepub.com.idpproxy.reading.ac.uk/doi/abs/10.1068/a43382.

Kilgour, L. and Parker, A. (2012) 'Gender, physical activity and fear: women, exercise and the great outdoors', *Qualitative Research in Sport, Exercise and Health*, 5(1), pp. 43–57.

Living Streets. (2020) *Walk with Us: Living Streets Strategy 2020–2025*. Available at: https://www.livingstreets.org.uk/media/5777/lsstrategy_20-25.pdf.

Lugten, M. *et al.* (2018) 'Improving the soundscape quality of urban areas exposed to aircraft noise by adding moving water and vegetation', *The Journal of the Acoustical Society of America*, 144(5), p. 2906. doi:10.1121/1.5079310.

Mason, P., Kearns, A. and Livingston, M. (2013) '"Safe Going": The influence of crime rates and perceived crime and safety on walking in deprived neighbourhoods', *Social Science and Medicine*, 91, pp. 15–24.

Mayor of London. (2020) *Transforming Cycling in Outer Boroughs: Mini-Hollands Programmes*, Mayor of London. Available at: https://www.london.gov.uk/what-we-do/transport/cycling-and-walking/transforming-cycling-outer-boroughs-mini-hollands-programme.

McEwan, K. *et al.* (2020) 'Schmapped: development of an app to record and promote the well-being benefits of noticing urban nature', *Translational Behavioral Medicine*, 10(3), pp. 723–733.

Mead, B. *et al.* (2021) 'Urban agriculture in times of crisis: the role of food growing in perceived food insecurity and well-being during the early COVID-19 lockdown', *Emerald Open Research*, 3(7). Available at: https://emeraldopenresearch.com/articles/3-7/v1.

Mears, M. *et al.* (2020) 'Neighbourhood greenspace influences on childhood obesity', *Pediatric Obesity* [Preprint]. doi:10.1111/ijpo.12629.

Menigoz, W., Latz, T.T. and Ely, R.A. (2020) 'Integrative and lifestyle medicine strategies should include earthing (grounding): review of research evidence and clinical observations', *Explore*, 16(3), pp. 152–160.

Moreno Rangel, A. *et al.* (2020) 'Indoor air quality in Passivhaus dwellings: a literature review', *International Journal of Environmental Research and Public Health*, 17(13), p. 4749.

NatureScot. (2020) *NHS Greenspace Demonstration Project*. Available at: https://www.nature.scot/nhs-greenspace-demonstration-project-bringing-outdoors-activity-resource-pack-mental-health.

Ober Allen, J. *et al.* (2008) 'Growing vegetables and values: benefits of neighborhood-based community gardens for youth development and nutrition', *Journal of Hunger and Environmental Nutrition*, 3(4), pp. 418–439.

Osibona, O., Solomon, B.D. and Fecht, D. (2021) 'Lighting in the home and health: a systematic review', *Environmental Research and Public Health*, 18(2). Available at: https://doi.org/10.3390/ijerph18020609.

Perkins, T. (2019) 'The fight to stop Nestle from taking America's water to sell in plastic bottles', *The Guardian*. 29 October. Available at: https://www.theguardian.com/environment/2019/oct/29/the-fight-over-water-how-nestle-dries-up-us-creeks-to-sell-water-in-plastic-bottles.

Pilkington, P. *et al.* (2018) *The Bristol Twenty Miles Per Hours Limit Evaluation (BRITE) Study*. University of West of England. Available at: https://uwe-repository.worktribe.com/output/875541.

Pitsikali, A., Parnell, R. and McIntyre, L. (2020) 'The public value of child-friendly space: Reconceptualising the playground', *Archnet_IJAR*, 14(2), p. 149.

Puhakka, R. et al. (2019) 'Greening of Daycare Yards with Biodiverse Materials Affords Well-Being, Play and Environmental Relationships', *International Journal of Environmental Research and Public Health*, 16(16).

Right to Roam. (2021) *Right to Roam*. Last accessed on November 2021: https://www.righttoroam.org.uk/.

Rocco, L. and Suhrcke, M. (2012) *Is social capital good for health? A European perspective?* World Health Organization. Available at: http://www.euro.who.int/__data/assets/pdf_file/0005/170078/Is-Social-Capital-good-for-your-health.pdf.

Ross, A. and Chang, M. (2013) 'Planning healthier places. Report from the reuniting health with planning project.' TCPA & Public Health England.

Saaby, T. and Bauman, I. (2019) 'From city policy to the neighbourhood: an interview with Tina Saaby', in Trogal, K., Bauman, I., Lawrence, R. and Petsrecu, D. (eds.) *Architecture and Resilience: Interdisciplinary Dialogues*. London: Routledge, pp. 251–258.

Schmutz, U. and Lennartsson Turner, M. (2014) *The Benefits of Gardening and Food Growing for Health and Wellbeing*. Ryton and London: Garden Organic and Sustain.

Shrubsole, G. (2019) *Who Owns England?* London: William Collins.

Thompson, J. (2012) 'Incredible edible - social and environmental entrepeneurship in the era of the "Big Society"', *Social Enterprise Journal*, 8(3), pp. 237–250.

Tomlinson, I. (2013) 'Doubling food production to feed the 9 billion: A critical perspective on a key discourse of food security in the UK', *Journal of Rural Studies*, 29, pp. 81–90.

Ulrich, R. and Delani, A. (ed.) (1999) 'Effects of Gardens on Health Outcomes', in *Design and Health: Proceedings of the Second International Conference on Health and Design*. Stockholm: Svensk Byggtjanst. Available at: http://www.majorfoundation.org/pdfs/Effects%20of%20Gardens%20on%20Health%20Outcomes.pdf.

Ulrich, R.S. (1984) 'View through a window may influence recovery from surgery', *Science*, 224(4647), pp. 420–421. doi:10.1126/science.6143402.

Urban Transport Group. (2016) *The Case for Active Travel: How Walking an Cycling Can Support More Vibrant Urban Economies*. Available at: https://www.urbantransportgroup.org/system/files/general-docs/The%20Case%20for%20Active%20Travel_0.pdf.

Viljoen, A. (ed.) (2005) *CPULs Continuous Productive Urban Landscapes: The Urban Agriculture Design Book for Sustainable Cities*. London: Architectural Press.

Voce, A. and Walker, P. (2021) 'Low-traffic schemes benefit most-deprived Londoners, study finds'. Available at: https://www.theguardian.com/world/ng-interactive/2021/mar/02/low-traffic-schemes-benefit-most-deprived-londoners-study-finds.

Walker, M. (2017) *Why We Sleep: The New Science of Sleep and Dreams*. London: Allen Lane.

Wood, L. *et al.* (2017) 'Public green spaces and positive mental health - investigating the relationship between access, quantity and types of parks and mental wellbeing', *Health & Place*, 48, pp. 63–71.

Woodcock, J. *et al.* (2014) 'Health effects of the London bicycle sharing system: health impact modelling study', *British Medical Journal*, 348, p. 425.

Zhang, L. and Liu, H. (2018) 'Turning green into gold: a review on the economics of green buildings', *Journal of Cleaner Production*, 172, pp. 2234–2245.

Chapter 7

Self actualisation

> *The basic, the sufficient – or in current jargon, the sustainable – is that which is our ordinary and commonplace environment. This ordinary dwelling provides the limits, the secure boundary that allows us to exclude, that helps us achieve sufficiency. It offers this secure boundary as a means to ensure that we are free.*
>
> (King, 2008, pp. 133–135)

Changes in work and leisure, coupled with increased life expectancy should lead to a 'rise in reflexivity' about the lives people want to construct and where they want to construct them (Gratton, 2011). The self actualistion of a couple, household or a family unit, and its relationship to their physical home environment is an under-explored and complex negotiation (Reimer and Leslie, 2004). In many ways it is implicit in the 'capabilities' approach that underpins my argument, which is about allowing people's lives to unfold in the way that they want them to, in this way respecting 'people's powers of self-definition' (Nussbaum, 2011, p. 18). In this chapter I will unpack some of the ways in which housing and neighbourhood design can impact on the process of individual self-building. I begin with a discussion of the way in which building and home making can be used to inform the process of self actualisation including the important acts of home making, collecting, decluttering and cleaning. I will then move on to ways in which the housing delivery system can foster choice and empower people to get involved with the design of their homes. The next chapter will widen the scale of the conversation to that of the community.

World building

Self actualisation has a fundamental link with eudaimonia, the connection with a sense of purpose beyond the self that is at the core of this book. Across the globe and over time there have been many different cultural ways of describing and naming the journey of fulfilling the purpose that we were born with. This journey has been enshrined in myths, fairytales, philosophy, literature and blockbuster movies. It is the journey from being lost to being found and happens in correspondence with some mysterious other that holds the blueprint. The Welsh word 'hiraeth' captures this sense of homesickness and longing to achieve the 'homeland in the mind' (Griffiths, 2013, p. 354).

Figure 7.1
Jung's Tower at Bollingen.
Source:
© Andrew Taylor.

The house is a widely recognised symbol of the self in dreams and art. To change your home is to change yourself, an idea that underpins art and occupational therapy in which creativity and play are tools for teasing out what lies within (Reed and Sanderson, 1999). This is an idea that emerged out of the work of analytical psychologist Carl Jung who built his tower at Bollingen, a form of therapy (Samuel and Menin, 2006) and a way of manifesting the figures that populated his inner cosmos (Figure 7.1). Other similar examples are the Black Forest farmhouse built by philosopher Martin Heidegger and his colleague Ludwig Wittgenstein's cabin in the woods (Sharr, 2017). These are particularly self conscious examples of what we all tend to do in our homes, if allowed.

The theories of psychoanalyst Donald Winnicott are useful to unpack some of the ways in which home design can be for the exploration of inner and outer worlds. Winnicott believed that to grow physically and psychologically a person needs to use their natural creativity to try to integrate fragmentary experiences into a cohesive narrative (Menin and Samuel, 2002, p. 4). For Winnicott, breaks or absences within a child's primary holding environment (the relationship with the primary carer) could be alleviated through a child's use of 'transitional phenomena' things that can be holding objects of affection (for example, a teddy), a 'potential space', a place that facilitates the explorations of the interplay between inner and outer worlds. Sarah Menin and I illustrated the way this idea played out in the architecture of two modernist architects, and friends, Alvar Aalto and Le Corbusier, both known for their consummate skill in designing 'inside outside spaces' that connect us with the natural world. We also drew on the ideas of Edith Cobb, author of *Ecology of the Imagination in Childhood,* who has shown how, as an alternative to retreating into psychosis, traumatised children can engage in 'world building', an attempt to structure their lives in analogy with an external system such as the natural world. This can give structure to an otherwise chaotic childhood, a hope of being otherwise. On this note a fascinating Sheffield-based study found that young people felt a real sense of 'mental health support' from urban nature.

> [This natural place would] just like give me a hug basically, like 'here's a hug', this is a gift from me to you and like these are all of the resources that you'll ever need: you've got the ground to ground you, you've got the sky to inspire you, [laughs] you've got the trees and how well rooted they are and, that offer you security and like you can recognise the cycles of death and life and you can let them come and go as you please.
>
> (Mina quoted in Birch *et al.*, 2020)

It is no surprise that Wilderness Therapy is proving itself to be very effective in helping young people suffering from mental health issues to develop greater self knowledge, self awareness and self regulation (Ribe Fernee and Einar Gabrielsen, 2021). This is yet another reason why we have to make sure children get access to natural environments.

If self-actualising is supported by nature then this can be helped by bringing more of it into the home. Common methods used by architects to allude to nature in homes include obvious ones such as: the inclusion of trees and plants in the design, views of nature, borrowed landscapes, including ritual moments (often windows) for contemplation of specific things (the bark of a tree, fire, water), natural lighting that tracks the path of the days and seasons across the interior of the home as well as other elements that embrace ageing and the passage of time such as the inclusion of colour, texture, natural materials and forms (Samuel, 2007). Designing places to connect with nature can be as simple as a window to the sky.

In the case of bespoke home design the task of the professional becomes one of supporting self actualisation, an attendant on the journey into new kinds of lifestyles. Architects such as Jane Burnside spend long hours developing mood boards and other methodologies to get under the skin of what clients might really want or need (2015). Commissioning a garden, home or a house extension is an opportunity to get to know yourself and to reflect on your life's journey. In this situation the house becomes less of an object and more of a process of development with the architect assisting in the task of reconfiguring or even reducing space in line with personal priorities. Mary Reynolds, a garden 'designer' in Ireland (a better word is needed for this kind of environment based therapy) understands this well. She has conceived a radical new way of implementing garden design, one that specifically includes the client in the conception and care of an evolving landscape that is true to its place, its geology, weather, biodiversity and culture (Reynolds, 2016). Her principles owe a lot to Rudolph Steiner's concept of biodynamic farming, a conversation with the land that fully acknowledges the mysterious connection between people and their places.

Collections and the development of taste

A house can also be an engine of display and acculturation (Maddrell and Sidaway, 2010). The accumulation, or not, of Winnicott's 'transitional phenomena', stuff, on the way to self-realisation is important. Sigmund Freud himself had a tableful of little statues on his desk in his consulting room in Hampstead, these objects 'reflecting his state of mind' (Davies, 2020). One of the ways in which Le Corbusier built connections to nature into his interiors was through the inclusion of what he called 'objects that inspire a poetic reaction' (Samuel, 2007). These included stones, bones, 'primitive art' and things that he collected on his travels. These were displayed as a sacred object on an altar, much as the ancient Romans worshipped their *lares* and *penates*, household gods. Here he was following in the tradition of the 17th-century grand tour whereby young men of affluent households travelled around Europe and beyond in pursuit of culture, collecting along the way, an inverted form of colonialism. The fruits of these journeys were collected in cabinets of curiosities (a Renaissance conception) several of which form the basis on important museum collections today. The Sir John Soane museum in London provides a beautiful example of the interface between collecting and his ruminations on the meaning of life and indeed death. It was through these collective accumulations that such 'connoisseurs' of culture became arbiters of what was of value, in essence taste.

The development and acknowledgement of individual taste is an important station on the spiral journey to self-hood. Taste, a word loaded with class distinction (Bourdieu, 1984), is very much in the eye of the beholder as Grayson Perry observed in this TV series on the subject *All in the Best Possible Taste* (2012). Paradoxically it is used both to differentiate ourselves and to fit in. Perry's art balances cleverly on this nexus between taste, ritual, gender, individuation, objects, contemporary culture and class. The House for Essex, Perry's collaboration with FAT Architecture (completed in 2014), plays upon all these themes

The aesthetics of home and places can have real impact on how people feel about themselves. A survey of homebuyers by CABE suggests that what home buyers actually want is 'character', a sense of richness in the detail of their homes whether modern or traditional looking (CABE, 2005, p. 18). They want to know that somebody cares. The advent of the industrial revolution, the mass production of objects and throw away culture was greatly disturbing to Victorian commentators such as William Morris who believed that makers should take pleasure in making things and that somehow that pleasure would be passed on to those who used them. This is an idea taken up by the priest and palaeontologist Pierre Teilhard de Chardin who argued that every last atom contains energy, an energy that we share in the very particles of our body bringing us into a humming resonance with our surroundings (Samuel, 1999). Taken to its logical extreme the things that you touch, the objects you own, the things that surround you speak to you all the time.

Historically the home is one of the few places where women have been able to express their creativity (Solnit, 2020, p. 152). In recent years there has been much commentary on the gender dimension of home décor, one of the few ways in which women traditionally have been able to express themselves while having limited opportunities in the outside world. In Victorian décor frills, curves and fripperies were associated with women with simple rectilinearity being associated with men. You need look no further than a large chunky whisky carafe and a curved decanter for sherry. Le Corbusier played upon the gender dimension of furnishings and objects in his collaborations with Charlotte Perriand as a prompt for women's liberation (Samuel, 2004). Bill Osgerby writes of the way it only became socially acceptable for men to think about home décor in the context of the 'playboy pad' for seduction, celebrated within the pages of *Playboy* magazine in the 1960s (Osgerby, 2001). Here articles on interior design and cooking were intermingled with sport and porn to make it somehow OK. I am thinking now of the popular US TV programme *Queer Eye* in which people are nominated for a life make over by the 'Fab Five'. This programme playfully faces cultural perceptions in this area head on while evidently having a transformative impact on its subjects. Fortunately the gender associations with interior décor have largely been dispelled, but echoes certainly remain.

Housework

A recent phenomenon that brings the excesses of our consumerist culture into relief, as well as its impact on mental health, is the world of decluttering as popularised by the Japanese decluttering expert and writer Mari Kondo and a range of other writers, not all Japanese (Kondo, 2017). While Kondo's method is built out of a very real need to use less space in constrained and expensive Tokyo flats it is also, quite evidently, built on a spiritual connection with material things. In line with the etiquette of visiting a Shinto shrine the first thing Kondo will do on arrival in a home is to kneel down to greet it, inviting the home owners that she will be working with to join her in the process. In doing so she acknowledges the home as a sacred space. According to the 'KonMari' method we need to go through layers of household objects, from least to most personal, discarding all those things that fail to 'spark joy'. It is best to try it before you cast judgement. I personally found that the process of interrogating my possessions and their memories enabled intensely helpful leading to a major restructuring of pretty much everything I held dear. I am not alone. The internet is full of testaments to Kondo's 'Lifechanging magic'. Other parallel movements in this direction include the rather more hipster 'Minimalism'. These stories of getting rid of things are inevitably accompanied by radical life changes, movement out of dull corporate jobs that allowed for the constant accumulation of consumer goods, 'downsizing' and the simple life moving out into the country to live a more connected lifestyle sometimes glorified in women's magazines, rather schizophrenically next to inducements to buy.

In his book *Goodbye Things* Fumio Sasaki writes of moving to a smaller home in order to enjoy his life more and have more time to do so – 'the next time I move I'd like to find an even smaller place to live' (Sasaki, 2017). There is some evidence that Generation Y is embracing its frugal and uncertain future in active rejection of 'boomer' excess. Who wants to be tied down to one place when job opportunities are fast moving and fluid? Other manifestations of minimalism and mobility include the tiny home movement and van life, one example being the You Tuber Jenelle Eliana whose timely search terms and tiny van home parked in and around Los Angeles earned her almost instant influencer status. Life in a van, the subject of the film *Nomadland* (2021) isn't always that glamorous.

As a woman born in the 1960s I feel that the cleanliness of my house has very direct links to my feeling of self worth and I will furiously set to cleaning if anyone is coming round. Women in the UK, despite holding down jobs, still carry the greatest burden in terms of domestic work. This brings me to the positive mental health impacts of cleaning celebrated in the work of contemporary blogger come writer such as Mrs Hinch author of Sunday Times No.1 bestselling non-fiction hardback of the 2019, *Hinch Yourself Happy* in which she recounts the way in which she cleaned herself out of depression, the delights of a well-ordered cupboard of chemical cleaning fluids of every fragrance and simple and cheap ways to make your home look its best. While it has obviously worked for Mrs Hinch I can't help wondering whether obsessive cleaning can have something to do with workaholism, an addictive behaviour adopted by many to avoid actually sitting still and being present. This is the essence of the Bible story in which Jesus gently reprimands Martha for complaining that her sister Mary was not helping with the housework, instead sitting to hear the words of their remarkable guest. Yet cleaning can be a form of therapy – the book *Hinch Yourself Happy*, is a tale of sadness and trauma contained through the delight delivered by cleaning products and a sparkling home, the popularity of Mrs Hinch's blogs evidence that the need to clean just doesn't go away (Hinch, 2019).

'The IKEA effect' refers to the fact that people value things that they have put effort in more than things that are ready-made (Norton and Mochon, 2011). I believe that the years of care and attention that have gone into the heavily polished patina of a stair banister are reflected back at the people whose hands sweep across it as they come down to breakfast each morning and that the love that goes into cleaning a house pays back down the line. For this to happen a house has to be a joy to clean, designed with cleaning in mind with beautiful textures to delight the hand. Le Corbusier, who was obsessed with lightening the load of housewives, carefully designed the steel kitchen of the Unité housing block in Marseilles with no edges so the whole thing could be cleaned with the swipe of a cloth (this was demonstrated to me by one resident such was her pride in her 50 year old kitchen). Domestic cleaners are typically overworked and underpaid, physical manifestations of the lack of fairness in our society. The architect Sarah Wigglesworth designed her home at Stock Orchard Street in London to be easily cleaned in part as a commentary on such inequalities (Figure 7.2). We are unlikely to have robot cleaners for some time yet so we ought to have homes that we can clean ourselves. There are many forms of home care that are also in a way self care. The decoration of the house for festivities springs to mind, a beautiful way to celebrate the home and to celebrate the passage of time, something that is always accompanied with the underlying tang of death.

Local authority blitz teams are regularly called in to do the unpleasant task of cleaning the homes of hoarders, a process that Sarah Krasnostein sensitively discusses in her book *The Trauma Cleaner* (2017). It is a strange thought that in a house not far away from me my neighbour has been collecting his faeces in jam jars. Edgar Allan Poe's classic *The Fall of the House of Usher* (1839) epitomises the uncanny home gone so very wrong. Tales of haunted houses are part of our cultural foundation. Exorcisms of people and of places are on the rise (Kingsbury

Figure 7.2
**Designed with cleaning in mind. Stock Orchard Street by Sarah Wigglesworh Architects.
Source: © Paul Smoothy.**

and Chesnut, 2019). Why pay for a dodgy damp proofing company when the mould in your basement could be caused by lingering spirits? Spiritual house cleansing is not unheard of even in 21st-century Britain. Why would we talk about a place having a good 'vibe' if we weren't somehow influenced by its energy. Such ideas are of course central to Chinese feng shui. While it might be considered socially acceptable to ask a feng shui consultant to come round and tidy up the energies flowing around a house in an effort to improve the lives of those within. The subject of spirit or spiritual cleansing of the home is rarely mentioned. yet people in the UK are making a living doing this very thing using ancient techniques such as dowsing for this purpose, reportedly with some success. The idea that homes can be inhabited by malevolent energies is as old as the hills, indeed ghost stories are a fundamental part of our mythology. I mention this aspect of self actualisation through the home partly to make the point that we are not so far removed from our 'primitive' ancestors as we might purport to be. Narratives, rituals and ceremonies all have a place in the making of our homes and ourselves.

Ageing and growing

We are never too old to change – the need for self actualisation extends into old age which has to be seen as part of a continuing adventure. On this note Andrea Jones' remarkable thesis on housing choices in later life recasts the decisions made by the people examined in her study as 'unclaimed forms of housing activism' (2016). That older people, and indeed any people, thrive on having just a little autonomy, was made clear in one classic study by Langer and Rodin in which they gave pot plants to two groups of elderly people in a nursing home. The group that fared much better in terms of wellbeing was the group that was asked to care for the plant themselves (1976). This is one reason why the ability to age in place with the support of the local community is so important. People need as much autonomy as they can get, even into deepest old age. The Village movement, started in Beacon Hill, Boston, USA, in 1999 provides one important model of the way neighbours can be mobilised to help one another (Cavendish, 2019, pp. 152–155). Options need to be available for downsizing while leading a meaningful and active life. The Humanitas Deventer retirement home, east of Amsterdam in the Netherlands combines 160 people between 79 and 100 with six university students who provide a breath of outside air. Key to the success of such a scheme is a group of people who 'gel' (Cavendish, 2019, p. 159). The development, which is now oversubscribed, places focus on happiness with new arrivals being asked to reflect on who they are and who they want to be in the future. It is the curation of the community that is key here. As an increasing proportion of the population enters into old age the resources to look after us will be thinly spread so surely we have to look to positive examples such as this as a way forward. The process of self actualisation doesn't stop with age.

Our homes and neighbourhoods – memorials, cemeteries and shrines – are places of life but also in some way also 'deathscapes' (Maddrell and Sidaway, 2010), momento mori, a reminder to live our lives well for the next generation which will soon take on our mantle. Death is arguably the ultimate moment of self actualisation – an examined life likely leading to a more philosophical attitude to death. It is not surprising that the vast majority of people want to die in their own homes, a process that is facilitated at the intentional community of Findhorn where real efforts are made to enable people to remain at home even during the process of dying and death (Jarvis, 2019).

Conclusion

This chapter has offered a brief overview of some of the ways in which homes can facilitate self actualisation through world building, collecting, housework and ageing. These are some of the most intangible and least explored aspects of social value to be discussed in this book but it is vitally important nonetheless. Homemaking and self making are interconnected acts through which we explore who we are. This is one reason why it is so important to ensure that people have real choices when it comes to choosing where to live. It is also why it is so important to let people adapt and decorate their own homes, something that is very difficult in precarious rental accommodation. The journey towards finding yourself is a journey towards belonging, one in which you actually feel at home in your own skin. It is a process that, in reality, happens through our relationship with others, the subject of the next chapter.

References

Birch, J., Rishbeth, C. and Payne, S. (2020) 'Nature doesn't judge you - how urban nature supports young people's mental health and wellbeing in a diverse UK city', *Health & Place*, 62, 102296. doi:10.1016/j.healthplace.2020.102296.

Bourdieu, P. (1984) *Distinction: A Social Critique of the Judgement of Taste*. Cambridge, MA: Harvard University Press.

Burnside, J. (2015) 'Co-design for new lifestyles', in Dye, A. and Samuel, F. (eds.) *Demystifying Architectural Research*. Newcastle: RIBA Enterprises, pp. 55–61.

CABE. (2005) *What Homebuyers Want*. Available at: http://webarchive.nationalarchives.gov.uk/20110118095356/http:/www.cabe.org.uk/publications/what-home-buyers-want.

Cavendish, C. (2019) *Extra Time: 10 Lessons for an Ageing World*. London: Harper Collins.

Davies, B. (2020) 'Freud at Home: At His Desk'. Available at: https://www.freud.org.uk/2020/04/27/freud-at-home-at-his-desk/.

Gratton, L. (2011) *The Shift: The Future of Work Is Already Here*. London: Collins.

Griffiths, J. (2013) *Kith: The Riddle of the Childscape*. London: Penguin.

Hinch, M. (2019) *Hinch Yourself Happy*. London: Michael Joseph.

Jarvis, H. (2019) 'Age-friendly community resilience', in Trogal, K., Bauman, I., Lawrence, R. and Petrsecu, D. (eds.) *Architecture and Resilience*. London: Routledge, pp. 61–73.

Jones, A. (2016) *Alternative Capital, Friendship and Emotional Work: What Makes It Possible to Live in Intentional Communities into Older Age*. University of Sussex. Available at: http://sro.sussex.ac.uk/id/eprint/66690/1/Jones,%20Andrea.pdf.

Kingsbury, K. and Chesnut, A. (2019) 'Driving out the Devil: What's Behind the Exorcism Boom?', *Catholic Herald*. Available at: https://catholicherald.co.uk/driving-out-the-devil-whats-behind-the-exorcism-boom/.

Kondo, M. (2017) *Spark Joy*. London: Vermillion.

Langer, E.J. and Rodin, J. (1976) 'The effects of choice and enhanced personal responsibility for the aged: a field experiment in an institutional setting', *Journal of Personality and Social Psychology*, 34(2), pp. 191–198.

Maddrell, A. and Sidaway, J.A. (eds.) (2010) *Deathscapes: Spaces for Death, Dying, Mourning and Remembrance*. London: Routledge.

Menin, S. and Samuel, F. (2002) *Nature and Space: Aalto and Le Corbusier*. London: Routledge.

Norton, M.I. and Mochon, D. (2011) 'The "IKEA Effect": When Labor Leads to Love'. Harvard Business School. Available at: https://www.hbs.edu/ris/Publication%20Files/11-091.pdf.

Nussbaum, M. (2011) *Creating Capabilities*. Cambridge MA: Harvard University Press.

Osgerby, B. (2001) *Playboys in Paradise: Maculinity, Youth and Leisure-style in Modern America*. London: Bloomsbury.

Phillips, A. and Erdemici, F. (eds.) (2012) *Actors, Agents and Attendants: Social Housing- Housing the Social: Art, Property and Spatial Justice*. London: Sternberg Press.

Reed, K.L. and Sanderson, S. (1999) *Concepts of Occupational Therapy*. Hagerstown, MD: Lippincott Williams and Wlikins.

Reimer, S. and Leslie, D. (2004) 'Identity, Consumption, and the Home', *Home Cultures*, 1(2), pp. 172–210.

Reynolds, M. (2016) *The Garden Awakening: Designs to Nurture our Land and Ourselves*. Cambridge: Green Books.

Ribe Fernee, C. and Einar Gabrielsen, L. (2021) 'Wilderness Therapy', in Harper, N.J. and Dobud, W.W. (eds.) *Outdoor Therapies*. New York: Routledge, pp. 69–80.

Samuel, F. (1999) 'Le Corbusier, Teilhard de Chardin and the Planetisation of Mankind', *Journal of Architecture*, 4(149–165).

Samuel, F. (2004) *Le Corbusier: Architect and Feminist*. London: Wiley Academy.

Samuel, F. (2007) *Le Corbusier in Detail*. London: Wiley.

Samuel, F. and Menin, S. (2006) 'Self Building with Jung, Aalto and Le Corbusier', in Odgers, J., Samuel, F., and Sharr, A. (eds.) *Primitive*. London: Routledge, pp. 207–220.

Sasaki, F. (2017) *Goodybe, Things*. London: Penguin.

Sharr, A. (2017) *Heidegger's Hut*. Cambridge, MA: MIT.

Solnit, R. (2020) *Recollections of My Non-Existence*. London: Granta.

Chapter 8

Identity and belonging

So it seems that our homes play a significant role in the formation of our identities (Forrest and Kearns, 2001), reflecting back at us a sense of our place in the world. It is for this reason that the neighbourhood plays a critical role in the dynamics of social exclusion (Hulse *et al.*, 2011), in other words belonging. Sixty-two per cent of the UK population report that they 'feel they belong to the immediate neighbourhood' (UKGov, 2019). This varies little across the demography and geography of the UK apart from London where a sense of belonging is significantly diminished, possibly because of levels of multiculturalism. Belonging is that much harder for recent immigrants (Hirsch, 2018). I begin this swift review with a discussion of the land and its role in the shaping of identity before discussing a range of things that can contribute positively to a sense of belonging including the use of local services, produce and materials, the development of identity through framing narratives of the past, present and future through arts, culture and heritage. Ultimately, as was seen in the last chapter, having a sense of control is all important for the collective co-creation of identity (JRF, 2011).

The land

Our cardinal reference point in developing identity has to be the land which itself is working towards a kind of self actualisation in conversation with our own, sometimes referred to as its genius loci. An impoverishment of the land results in an impoverishment of our own beings, an idea that is emerging in so much contemporary writing. My reading of the land is ecological not nationalistic. The land, like the British people, is the product of migration. It has been heavily altered by an influx of humans who have killed all the large carnivores that were such an important part of our early rainforest ecosystems as well as waves of immigration by flora and fauna with things we consider as deeply British, for example, sheep (Egypt) and rabbits (France), being introduced over the centuries. We in Britain have low expectations of levels of biodiversity, with our ecosystems being a bare shadow of what they once were. This includes our seas which, despite their contribution to climate change and food production, are being trawled almost to oblivion. An environment that is impoverished offers few opportunities for caring, wonder and taking notice, key determinants of wellbeing (see, for example, Aked *et al.*, 2011).

Figure 8.1
Behind the Byker Wall. Newcastle.
Source: ©
Andrew Curtis (cc-by-sa/2.0).

Housing, whether new or refurbished, has to enhance the environmental and social value that is already there. New housing must unfold out of the conditions of the land and its people. This takes expertise from historically sensitive designers. There is a long tradition within architecture of building on and reconstituting what is already there as a precursor to the new. Ralph Erskine's Byker Wall project in Newcastle (Figure 8.1) is a particularly interesting example. Erskine set up an office in a disused funeral parlour on the site, his open door policy meaning that residents could pop in to share their thoughts with him at any time (Spatial Agency, 2016). By inputting their ideas into his proposal Erskine assisted in creating a sense of community among the contributors. The relocation and preservation of historic fragments in the landscaping of the new scheme helped in preserving a sense of collective history and identity that has lasted over time (Pendlebury, Townshend and Gilroy, 2009).

Local materials and services

To accrue identity materials and services need to reflect the local landscape and culture. When I tried to find a local brick to build a shed in my back garden I drew a complete blank – nobody in my local brick supplier knew the origin of the bricks they were selling. Yet in the 19th century every area had its own brick – this is one of the things that make our local terrace houses distinctive (different areas can have their own typical house plans too; Muthesius, 1984). Local stones, local timber and local clay resonate beautifully with the local environment and tend to suit more local ways of building with inevitable benefits in terms of reducing carbon footprint, but also in connecting with cultural memory.

Figure 8.2
Use of local materials at Nansledan, Cornwall.
Source: © Adam Architecture/ Duchy of Cornwall.

Memories are highly sensory - 'If we can hear and smell something we can often see it' (Tuan, 2007, p. 11). Unfortunately the use of local materials and services is made difficult by local authority processes and building regulations. Adam Architecture had to negotiate extensively with the local highways team in order to use local stone in the streetscape of Nansledan in Cornwall (Figure 8.2), a recent housing development for the Duchy of Cornwall, something that was worth the effort.

Eating local and using local food supply chains is one of the first things we can do to reinforce local economies, in doing so reinforcing a distinct sense of community. Neighbourhoods are places for the sharing of food which, as we know well, plays a strong role in cultural identity and in the creation of shared social history (Autio et al., 2013). Rural populations are growing (ONS, 2020) as are new kinds of food business. Craft beers, are, for example, described as 'tools of local identity' (Schell and Reese, 2003) and are strongly linked to their place of provenance. Linking people back to the terroir of place through 'taste-scapes' is an unexplored area with much potential (Everett, 2019). Local food also plays an important role in sustainable tourism enhancing the 'visitor experience by connecting consumers to the region and its perceived culture and heritage' (Sims, 2009). It is something to be proud of.

Distinctiveness of place has multiple benefits including significant impact on inward investment and R&D spend (CaSE, 2020), which is why an industry has developed around 'place branding', the artificial curation of identity to compensate for barren privatised, globalised built environment. Policy makers and businesses, cynically using 'brandscape' to maximise economic benefits, while tugging our hearts, starved of meaningful narratives. The development of community identity has to be an authentic bottom-up thing built out of the intangible heritage of the past and the social value of the present. I am not talking about

Figure 8.3
East Quay, Watchet.
Source: © Flora Samuel.

a return to a pre-industrial era. A beautiful example of a thoroughly 21st-century community initiative built very strategically on a survey of existing activity in the area is the work of the Onion Collective in Watchet, a seaside town in Dorset. As well as building a major community arts building (Figure 8.3), they have set up an R&D facility for bio building materials in a redundant factory in order to promote a new kind of vernacular (Onion Collective, 2018). The decision to do this builds on a careful inventory of existing social value of the town and its hinterland. The Onion Collective's work in Watchet has done much to revive the embers of its distinctive industrial identity while creating new kinds of narrative of place and community.

There is a very broad consensus of agreement about the importance of involving people in the 'visioning' of their places. Community involvement in urban design, the sharing of ideas about the future of places, can enrich social networks with direct benefits for social capital, wellbeing (Semenza and Tanya, 2009) and health (Lewis, Bambra and Barnes, Amy, 2019). 'Visioning has become an integral part of corporate governance in the UK, a key feature of civic entrepreneurialism and place-marketing'. Further it has a particularly important role to play in conveying desirable urban futures and building public consensus to deliver them (Punter, 2011). A study based in Hull revealed that residents derived 'comfort' even from the predictability of 'kitsch' developer led place branding exercises

(Atkinson, 2007) so imagine how much more powerful a community generated, participatory vision might be (Kavaratzis and Kalandides, 2015). All manner of techniques – for example, storytelling and performance – can be used to solicit and capture shared community aspirations (Roe and Scott-Bottoms, 2020) and to make them happen, the very act of working together, once again contributing to a sense of community identity.

The role of stories, in the construction of identity and relationships is widely recognised across a range of fields (Mildorf, 2019). 'Constructive pride in local, history and identity' are key (Civic Revival, 2021). A New Economics Foundation study based in Peckham in London found that 'the use of local designers and artists in the development of the streetscape in the Bellenden neighbourhood roused curiosity in residents and bestowed the place with a uniqueness and distinctiveness, features which are thought to be important for a shared sense of belonging' (NEF, 2012). It is all about creating new narratives out of the old.

Arts and culture

You need look no further than Amanda Gorman's recitation of 'The Hill We Climb' at US President Biden's 2021 Inauguration to see the tingling impact of poetry on a nation's selfhood. A good deal of research has gone into showing, what we should already know, that arts and culture have a major role in developing a collective sense of identity, community and belonging (Parkinson, 2019, p. 18) yet the arts remain continually underfunded as though a 'nice to haves'.

Art is not a monolithic entity. The kind of art that assists community identity is generally rather different to the kind of art that attracts large amounts of cultural funding (Holmes, 2010) or is attractive to investors as 'a fungible hedge' (Joselit, 2013, p. 1). This kind of high cultural capital art is led by 'intelligentsia managed institutions' (Olds, 2002, p. 155), skewed by politics (Bertelli *et al.*, 2014) and bought by highly mobile transnational elites with little loyalty to place. What value does art have, for example, the Little Mermaid Statue in Copenhagen harbour, if it is taken away from its home? The Chinese artist Ai Wei Wei has been particularly successful in riffing on this topic. Art becomes part of a 'world culture' which is then overlaid on local culture (King, 1991), leading ultimately to its dilution. Some artists position themselves in active resistance to the commoditised situation described above, yet both kinds of art have become a tool of global finance and 'bureaucratized, patronized, professionalized, and commercialized, culture' (Nowotny, Scott and Gibbons, 2001b, p. 27), a situation that has ironically left a generation of young artists dispossessed, their funding cut, unable to rent studios, unable to find jobs.

Not for profit artists such as those that work in communities (Alexiou, Zamenopoulos and Alevizou, 2012) tend to rely for their existence on public funding, their ability to attract funding being related to their cultural capital, accrued through shows in high art venues and so on. This is always going to help those who can afford to live and work in high cultural capital cities such as London, with the arts increasingly becoming the terrain of the independently wealthy (Dabiri, 2021).

The terrifyingly vague term 'artistic quality' is a major determinant of public support for the arts (Loots, 2019, p. 274). This can make it difficult for communities to access support for socially oriented projects. Despite these difficulties there are many communities that are very active in dreaming up events that create sense of place and civic pride (Govers, 2018). That the Belfast based activist group Array Collective won the prestigious Turner Prize in 2021, for their making of a highly performative Irish pub, has to be a step in the right direction, not least because they come from Northern Ireland.

In my own area Made in Roath is an entirely bottom-up annual arts festival that combines open studios, people opening up their homes and businesses as exhibition spaces with community events creating a web of community glue that keeps us together during the months between events. A Welsh Government investigation found that participation in cultural events has significant links to reports of life satisfaction and that there is a clear connection between deprivation, poor health and lack of access to culture. Culture was here is defined in the broadest sense – 'not just the arts, but also heritage and the historic environment, including the contribution of museums, libraries and the media' (Welsh Government, 2016, p. 10). Enjoyment of cultural happenings has also been shown to be effective as a form of social prescribing to address issues like anxiety and increase sense of purpose (Tierney and Mahtani, 2021).

Museums and libraries play a vital role in remembering who we are. They are also a very important resource for small children and their parents, not only as somewhere free to go out of the rain, but offering 'the start of a lifelong relationship with museums, their collections and their stories' (Wallis, 2018, p. 365). A recent study of the Museum of Scotland in Edinburgh revealed that the 'museum was a place where people actively made and remade their identities'. Here an exhibition on the history of an Edinburgh neighbourhood provided an opportunity to 'resurrect a sense of community based upon a shared identity, constructed using the social history of the area' reframing it as a source of pride'(Newman and McLean, 2006, p. 62). These are just a few of the reasons why museums need to be kept open and to be kept free. In our market driven world the value of museums tends to be measured in footfall, a very crude measure, this is forcing museums to develop a hybrid role as places of leisure and entertainment (McPherson, 2007). This can lead to the marginalisation of less powerful or visible narratives (Fredheim, 2018).

Libraries too are transforming into more hybrid community hubs, places to access the internet and do homework, but their fundamental role as a repository of community knowledge and a symbol of the communities learning remains the same. 'In the library, users are exposed to the plurality of the community and learn about otherness' (Aabo and Audunson, 2012). Libraries also play an important role in quality of life (Fujiwara, Lawton and Mourato, 2019). Consolidation into large city libraries doesn't really do it for the local communities when people so rarely make it into the centre of town. Sometimes community libraries emerge almost by themselves, a book repository at the base of a tower block in Redcliffe in Bristol or a 'lockdown library' in an old telephone box during the pandemic (Figure 8.4), instigated by community members these form vital parts of community glue.

Figure 8.4
Lock Down Library, Cardiff.
Source: © Flora Samuel.

Heritage

While it may be obvious that heritage plays a vital role in the creation of identity (Neill, 2004), organisations such as Historic England have had to go to great lengths to produce reports like *Wellbeing and the Historic Environment* (Reilly, Nolan and Monckton, 2018) to make this clear. The process of assigning significance to buildings is increasingly being recognised as a socio-cultural activity, not just a technical one (De La Torre and Mason, 2002). Cultural heritage, sometimes blurred with 'cultural heritage values' received one of its first definitions from the Convention on the Protection of the World Cultural and Natural Heritage (UNESCO, 1972). The case for intangible heritage was advanced through the Burra Charter (instigated by Australian ICOMOS in 1979 and regularly updated), a groundbreaking moment in conservation debate (ICOMOS, 1999). It sets out the meaning of 'cultural significance' to include 'aesthetic, historic, scientific, social or spiritual value for past, present or future generations'. Intangible cultural heritage is defined as 'the practices, representations, expressions, knowledge, skills – as well as the instruments, objects, artefacts and cultural spaces associated therewith – that communities, groups and, in some cases, individuals recognize as part of their cultural heritage' (UNESCO, 2003, p. article 2). This momentum gained traction in England with the publication of a series of *Heritage Counts* reports (English Heritage, 2006) which discussed the role of heritage on places, communities and 'big society', the political buzzword at that time. It isn't just about places, buildings, objects and things. Identity comes through shared practices however ephemeral, coffee mornings, street parties, talent contests, quizzes, bingo, flash mobs, jumble sales, quilting, cooking, knitting, dancing, dog shows and the simple act of hanging out. Eating, drinking and sport too are all critical to developing a sense of neighbourhood identity.

Conservation needs to be acknowledged as a highly political business (ICOMOS, 1994) – as with history it tends to be those in power who get to shape and choose what is retained from the past, often producing an idealised and tidy version of events (with a little murderous activity for added frisson) suitable for visitor attractions. Recent furore over acknowledging the role of slavery in the history of certain National Trust properties provides a case in point. Pretending that slavery never happened is not going to help those people who are still struggling from its ancestral traumas trying to find belonging in 21st-century Britain. Identity has a strong relationship with narratives of the past, and indeed the present (Urry, 1995).

If decisions have to be made about what layer of history is to be preserved I argue it is better to try to be honest about this rather than pretend. Back in the 19th century William Morris set up the Society of Protection of Ancient Buildings (SPAB), a school of thought that requires restoration work to be done in a way that shows that it is new. The resultant effect of palimpsest, although maybe not as it might have looked in the past, can be very beautiful, a reminder of where we come from and helping to situate ourselves in the now.

Bozen's Cottage in Tasmania by Taylor and Hinds Architects is an example of a particularly sensitive refurbishment of a tiny landmark home reusing materials from the site, local materials and is full of references to its historic past (Figure 8.5). I was fortunate enough to interview the couple who live in the house to find out how they felt about the work. They attribute their own acceptance as

Figure 8.5
Bozen's cottage.
Source: © Adam Gibson

newcomers into the local community very much to the cultural sensitivity of the architecture of their new/old home and to the respect it offers to its former inhabitants. The details of the interior give constant cause to remember those who lived there before and to reflect on Tasmania's colonial past and future. In this way skilful architecture can help people to establish their sense of place in the world.

Conclusion

In this chapter I began with a discussion of the land and its pull on our identity. I made the argument for, where possible, using local materials and services for the building of local homes, not just for the local economy, but also for local identity. I moved onto the globalising tendencies of high art and culture and made the case for supporting home grown arts and culture, drawing on global links, in the name of fostering shared identity, shared narratives about our collective past present and future. Discussions of how we frame history, both in words and buildings, are key to framing our visions for the future and in setting a plan for what we valorise going forward. These narratives have to be inclusive if they are to foster the belonging so badly needed in an increasingly alienating world.

References

Aabo, S. and Audunson, R. (2012) 'Use of library space and the library as place', *Library & Information Science Research*, 34(2), pp. 138–149.

Aked, J. *et al.* (2011) *Five Ways to Wellbeing*. nef (the new economics foundation). Available at: https://neweconomics.org/uploads/files/8984c5089d5c2285ee_t4m6bhqq5.pdf.

Alexiou, K., Zamenopoulos, T. and Alevizou, G. (2012) *Valuing Community-Led Design*. Summary report for AHRC Connected Communities, pp. 1–13.

Atkinson, D. (2007) 'Kitsch geographies and the everyday spaces of social memory', *Environment and Planning A*, 39(3), pp. 521–540.

Autio, M. *et al.* (2013) 'Consuming nostalgia? The appreciation of authenticity in local food production', *International Journal of Consumer Studies*, 37(5), pp. 564–568.

Bertelli, A.M. *et al.* (2014) 'Politics, management, and the allocation of arts funding: evidence from public support for the arts in the UK', *International Journal of Cultural Policy*, 20(3), pp. 341–359.

CaSE. (2020) *The Power of Place: Maximising Local Economic Impacts of R & D Investment in the UK*. Campaign for Science and Engineering. Available at: https://www.sciencecampaign.org.uk/resource/placereport.html.

Civic Revival. (2021) *Civic Revival Mission*. Available at: https://www.civic-revival.org.uk/mission/.

Dabiri, E. (2021) *What White People Can Do Next: From Allyship to Coalition*. London: Penguin.

English Heritage. (2006) *Heritage Counts: Communities and Heritage*. Available at: c.english-heritage.org.uk/content/pub/HC_2006_NATIONAL_20061114094800.pdf.

Everett, S. (2019) 'Theoretical turns through tourism taste-scapes: the evolution of food tourism research', *Research in Hospitality Management*, 9(1), pp. 3–12.

Forrest, R. and Kearns, A. (2001) 'Social cohesion, social capital and the neighbourhood', *Urban Studies*, 38, pp. 2125–2143.

Fredheim, L.H. (2018) 'Endangerment-driven heritage volunteering: democratisation or "changeless change"', *International Journal of Heritage Studies*, 24(6), pp. 619–633.

Fujiwara, D., Lawton, R.N. and Mourato, S. (2019) 'More than a good book: contingent valuation of public library services in England', *Journal of Cultural Economics*, 43, pp. 639–666.

Govers, R. (2018) *Imaginative Communities: Admired Cities, Regions and Countries*. Antwerp: Reputo Press.

Hirsch, A. (2018) *Brit(ish): On Race, Identity and Belonging*. London: Vintage.

Holmes, J. (2010) 'Why we must fund the arts', *The Guardian*. 27 February. Available at: https://www.theguardian.com/commentisfree/2010/feb/27/arts-funding-reasons-subsidise-creativity.

Hulse, K. *et al.* (2011) *At Home and in Place? The Role of Housing Social Inclusion*. Australian Housing and Urban Research Institute. Available at: https://www.ahuri.edu.au/research/final-reports/177.

ICOMOS. (1994) 'The Nara document on authenticity'. Available at: http://www.icomos.org/charters/nara-e.pdf.

ICOMOS. (1999) *Burra Charter*. Available at: http://australia.icomos.org/publications/charters/ (Accessed: 9 November 2015).

Joselit, D. (2013) *After Art*. Princeton: Princeton University Press.

JRF. (2011) *Community Organisations Controlling Assets: A Better Understanding*. Available at: https://www.jrf.org.uk/report/community-organisations-controlling-assets-better-understanding.

Kavaratzis, M. and Kalandides, A. (2015) 'Rethinking the place brand: the interactive formation of place brands and EHT role of participatory place branding', *Environment and Planning A*, 47(6), pp. 1386–1362.

King, A. (1991) *Culture, Globalisation and the World System: Contemporary Conditions for the Representation of Identity*. Palgrave.

Lewis, S., Bambra, C. and Barnes, A. (2019) 'Reframing "participation" and "inclusion" in public health policy and practice to address health inequalities: evidence from a major resident-led neighbourhood improvement initiative', *Health and Social Care in the Community*, 27(1), pp. 199–206.

Loots, E. (2019) 'Strings attached to arts funding: panel assessments of theater organizations through the lens of agency theory', *The Journal of Arts Management, Law and Society*, 49(4), pp. 274–290.

McPherson, G. (2007) 'Public memories and private tastes: the shifting definitions of museums and their visitors in the UK', *Museum Management and Curatorship*, 21(1), pp. 44–57.

Mildorf, J. (2019) 'Narratives of vicarious experience in oral history interviews with craft artists', *Journal of Pragmatics*, 152, pp. 103–112.

Muthesius, S. (1984) *The English Terraced House*. New Haven, CT: Yale University Press.

NEF. (2012) 'Good foundations: towards a low carbon, high well-being built environment'. New Economics Foundation.

Neill, W.J.V. (2004) *Urban Planning and Cultural Identity*. Hove: Psychology Press.

Newman, A. and McLean, F. (2006) 'The Impact of Museums upon Identity', *The Impact of Museums upon Identity*, 12(1), pp. 49–98.

Nowotny, H., Scott, P. and Gibbons, M. (2001) *Rethinking Science: Knowledge and the Public in an Age of Uncertainty*. London: Wiley.

Olds, K. (2002) *Globalization and Urban Change: Capital, Culture, and Pacific Rim Mega-Projects*. Oxford: Oxford University Press.

Onion Collective. (2018) *Industry for Watchet: Putting Community at the Heart of Industrial Innovation*. Watchet. Available at: https://www.onioncollective.co.uk/contact.

ONS. (2020) *Rural Population*. Available at: https://assets.publishing.service.gov.uk/government/uploads/system/uploads/attachment_data/file/912408/Rural_population__August_2020.pdf.

Parkinson, A. (2019) *Value of Arts and Culture in Placeshaping*. Arts Council. Available at: https://www.artscouncil.org.uk/sites/default/files/download-file/Value%20of%20Arts%20and%20Culture%20in%20Place-Shaping.pdf.

Pendlebury, J., Townshend, T. and Gilroy, R. (2009) 'social housing as heritage: The Case of Byker, Newcastle upon Tyne', in Gibson, L. and Pendlebury, J. (eds.) *Valuing Historic Environments*. London: Ashgate, pp. 179–201.

Punter, J. (2011) 'Urban design and the English urban renaissance 1999–2009: a review and preliminary evaluation', *Journal of urban Design*, 16(1), pp. 1–41.

Reilly, S., Nolan, C. and Monckton, L. (2018) *Wellbeing and the Historic Environment*. Swindon: Historic England. Available at: https://historicengland.org.uk/images-books/publications/wellbeing-and-the-historic-environment/wellbeing-and-historic-environment/.

Roe, M. and Scott-Bottoms, S. (2020) 'Improvisation as method: engaging "hearts and minds" in the landscape through creative practice', *Urban Forestry and Urban Greening*, 47, 126547.

Schell, S.M. and Reese, J.F. (2003) 'Microbreweries as tools of local identity', *Journal of Cultural Geography*, 21(1), pp. 45–69.

Semenza, J.C. and Tanya, L. (2009) 'an urban community-based intervention to advance social interactions', *Environment and Behaviour*, 41(1), pp. 22–42.

Sims, R. (2009) 'Food, place and authenticity: local food and the sustainable tourism experience', *Journal of Sustainable Tourism*, 17(3), pp. 321–336.

Spatial Agency. (2016) *Participation*. Available at: https://spatialagency.net/database/participation.1970s.

Tierney, S. and Mahtani, K.R. (2021) *The Role of the Cultural Sector in Social Prescribing for Older People Through the Covid-19 Pandemic*, *What Works Wellbeing*. Available at: https://whatworkswellbeing.org/blog/the-role-of-the-cultural-sector-in-social-prescribing-for-older-people-through-the-covid-19-pandemic/.

Tuan, Y.F. (2007) *Space and Place: The Perspective of Experience*. Minneapolis: University of Minnesota Press.

UKGov. (2019) *Community Life Survey 2018–2019 Data Tables.* Available at: https://www.gov.uk/government/statistics/community-life-survey-201920.

UNESCO. (1972) 'Convention on the Protection of the World Cultural and Natural Heritage'. Available at: http://whc.unesco.org/en/conventiontext/.

UNESCO. (2003) 'The convention for the safeguarding of intangible cultural heritage'. Available at: https://ich.unesco.org/en/convention

Urry, J. (1995) 'How societies remember the past', *The Sociological Review*, 43(1), pp. 45–65.

Wallis, N. (2018) 'Titian, tapestreis and toilets; what do preschoolers and their families value in a museum visit?', *Museum and Society*, 16(3), pp. 352–365.

Part III

How to build a housing system for hope and wellbeing

Chapter 9

A planning system for hope and wellbeing

> *We advocate an integrated approach, in which all matters relevant to place-making are considered from the outset and subjected to a democratic or co-design process. And we advocate raising the profile and role of planning both in political discussions and in the wider debate concerning how we wish to live and what kind of a country we want to pass on.*
>
> *(BBBBC, 2020, p. v)*

In Part 2 of *Housing for Hope and Wellbeing* I set out some of the intangible ways in which housing and places impact on social value, in other words wellbeing. This concluding part of the book is a speculation on the series of ingredients needed to make a housing system that sees its purpose as delivering on eudaimonic wellbeing above all else.

The first ingredient of a housing system for hope and wellbeing is a reimagined planning system. Given that the Royal Town Planning Institute (RTPI) itself is saying the reimagining of planning is urgently needed (2020) this shouldn't be such a far-fetched idea. Indeed quite a few of the points I make here inadvertently echo the RTPI's excellent *Digital Planning Manifesto* (RTPI, 2019) and their *Planning for a Better Future* proposals (RTPI, 2021). The planning system that I describe here will be based around digitally driven mapping that constantly, fairly and transparently allows people to input into what happens in their local environment, not least the building of their own homes. Not only will this allow people to understand and take responsibility for the things going on around them, it will also oil the wheels of democracy and trust. The chapter begins with a discussion of map making at regional, local and hyper local levels, this leads into the use of codes for digitally based decision making (always with an option for meaningful appeal from local people). Delivering the routine and repetitive acts of planning through digital plans will give time to planners to focus on what really matters, working in collaboration with the community to ensure that the planning system is fuelling the particular social, environmental and economic impacts that are needed in the right places.

A holistic digital planning system

In the not so distant future the UK will be covered by a patchwork of maps that gather real-time data on the generation of social, environmental and economic value. Increasingly sophisticated algorithms will build the impact of topography into indicators of accessibility to all manner of opportunities, transport, jobs, health, education and leisure. A new field of 'adaptive planning', described as 'fluid spatial planning as strategic intelligence' by Mark Twedwr Jones (2012) is emerging for planning on the move. 'To survive, planners and planning must adapt to a world comprising the unplanned – and decidedly messy – configuration of multiple overlapping, competing and contradictory spatial imaginaries' (Harrison, 2021, p. 6). They also need to become 'digital guardians' of data in an era of false intelligence and news (Wilson and Tewdwr-Jones, 2022, p. 16).

Geographic Information System (GIS) technology has transformed the kind of information that can be held in maps as well as the way that they are made, offering opportunities for community map making and democracy that are being explored across many fields (Hung, Hang Tse and Saggau, 2020). Excitingly these maps could be used to forecast future scenarios or to 'backcast' from a desired future. Not only would this help us to understand where we are now, they could also be used to project our impact on future generations.

A fundamental prerequisite of making good places is the reduction of inequality. More equal places perform better in almost every way (Wilkinson and Pickett, 2019). There is much talk of 'levelling up' – indeed the Ministry for Homes Communities and Local Government (MHCLG) was recently renamed Department of Levelling UP, Housing and Communities (DLUHC) – but this can't happen without an understanding of what is already there, and where. We now have the digital tools to capture this with some accuracy if only there was the political will.

The Scottish Government is prescient in its understanding of the potential of digital tools for planning enshrined in the 'five missions' of its digital strategy *Transforming Places Together:*

1. Data – Unlock the value of planning data
2. Digital Technologies – Deliver and end to end digital planning experience
3. Ways of Working – Create the conditions for digital to flourish
4. People – Use digital tools to drive collaboration and engagement
5. Innovation – Embed a Culture of Digital Innovation (Scottish Government, 2021, p. 10).

We need a fully integrated and holistic system of plans for the UK overall, a 'UK Spatial Framework' (RSA, 2020), one that shows all the data we have on places (Batty and Yang, 2022). As discussed in Chapter 4 data has to be collected in a robust standardised format for geotagged integration into the map. Location data includes personal data that can be used to identify people, and non-personal data that can describe the location of things, features or population data aggregated together. Ethics and security need to be respected while allowing the overall integrity of the maps to be maintained. Interestingly a recent report by the UK Geospatial Commission found that people were more happy for their geolocation to be collected if they thought it was going to be used for good purposes (Cabinet Office, 2021).

There are some very useful datasets out there which begin to unpack the stories of social value of places. An obvious example is the data from the census.

The ONS is responsible for collecting and publishing statistics related to the economy, population and society at national, regional and local levels which it gathers using its own stated 'Census Geography' (ONS, 2021), its methodology for dealing with things like boundaries. There are a range of robust, standardised datasets that need to be brought together including the Department for Environment, Food and Rural Affairs' Multi-Agency Geographic Information for the Countryside (MAGIC) (DEFRA, 2021) online platform detailing the natural environment of Great Britain, Natural England's Green Infrastructure database (Natural England, 2021) and MHCLG's open data platform (MHCLG, 2021a). These robust, standard datasets set a precedent for strong analytical practice in planning for the built environment, with increasingly mature data science telling a rich story about what is needed for levelling up but they need to be aligned.

This is easier at the national level. Things becomes more challenging at a local level when data can be structured in a variety of ways depending on who owns or manages it, requiring additional work on ground surveys, collation and analysis. The Greater Manchester Infrastructure Framework 2040 is an innovative array of map based data which can be overlaid in different combinations (GMA, 2019) and is already being used to improve evidence based decision making in the city (Mulholland *et al.*, 2022). Questions remain about how to develop a single schema that allows map layers to be clustered in a uniform way both to offer simple overarching statistics – for example, on social, economic and environmental value – and also to facilitate comparison with other local authorities. As technology evolves we should be able to do this with greater ease, but investment needs to be put into datasets and data gathering to make sure that they talk with one another. The COVID-19 Community Fund Mapping Tool which tracked the use and impact of emergency funds in Scotland is a powerful example of how mapping can assist policy making (Scottish Government, 2021).

Wouldn't it be exciting farming and housing together as a map? Going forward planning has to have jurisdiction over forestry and farming activities as well as the built environment (Shoard, 1997). They have to be conceived as a seamless whole. Urban Metabolism, the modelling of throughputs of cities as though they were a living organism, provides a useful framework for this kind of systemic thinking (Perrotti and Stremke, 2018). The connections between social, environmental and economic value in the context of rural development are amply illustrated by Isabella Tree's value driven case for the rewilding of the Knepp Estate near Gatwick Airport (2018, pp. 304–307) and Benedict McDonald's carefully crafted economic case for the rewilding (ironically) of our national parks (2020). This involves planning for our entire land (also water and air) mass in a holistic way.

The potential of distributed working offers up so many possibilities for new forms of employment in more rural areas that will enhance, rather than destroy farmland environments while taking pressure off cities. This would require a reconfiguration of planning to allow farms to build homes on the footprints of their sheds and outhouses to make 21st-century hamlets. In rural areas farmers need to be able to repurpose their buildings easily for new kinds of communities working in a distributed way while bringing more affluence, as well

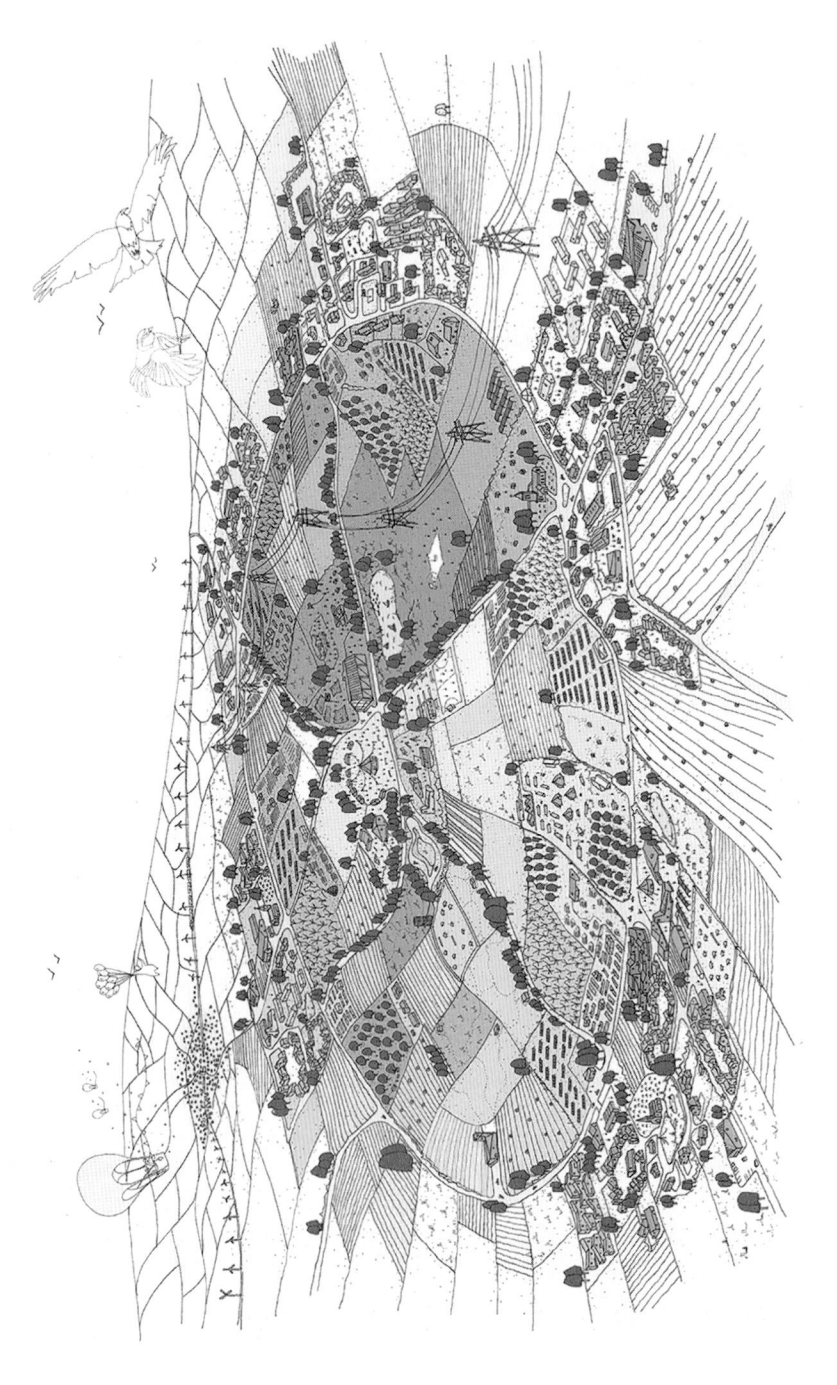

How to build a housing system for hope and wellbeing

Figure 9.1
VeloCity Big Back Garden.
Source:
© VeloCity.

as a diversity of people and wildlife to the countryside. In their report *Growing Villages Differently* VeloCity offer an important vision for the countryside (Figure 9.1), unlocking land for new places to live and work, connecting villages through active travel routes and sharing resources, all this while preventing sprawl (VeloCity, 2019).

The National Park City is a growing movement that recognises 'how our urbanised lives aren't served as well as they might be by the current static system of protected landscapes' (2020). I love the designation of London as a 'national park city' in recognition of its amazing flora and fauna as it turns the way we think about cities upside down. To this end 'we need to talk about the green belt' (Simons, 2020).The green belt (Gov.uk, 2019), which was enshrined in planning after World War II, has been an important force for protecting green space for both for the enjoyment of nature and for people but is currently failing on both these counts (CPRE, 2022). Bizarrely conservation charities such as Buglife are now calling for the preservation of brownfield sites because of their rich biodiversity while the 'greenfield sites' that are being so vociferously protected can have very little wildlife due to the zeal of agribusinesses. 'Brown is the new green' (Tree, 2018, p. 125). Either green belts are made to become more human and nature friendly or planning has to protect places that are already known to contribute to the quality of life of people, plants and wildlife whether in the green belt or not. In an ideal world both would happen simultaneously.

Mapping has a key role to play in providing a holistic understanding of the social, environmental and economic value that is happening in any area. An outcome of the *Mapping Eco Social Assets* project described in Chapter 4 was the development of the *Better Places Toolkit* by Stantec with our team at the University of Reading, an enabling framework for integrating social value into land value decision making at the level of the local authority (Stantec, 2022). To do this is calls upon a range of 'passive data', existing datasets such as the census, that offer a base line of information. This is combined with 'active data' developed through consultation with communities on the ground to create a comprehensive understanding of what is happening in a community (Figure 9.2). All of this information is spatially tagged meaning that a social value map can be made that is overlaid onto other maps (green infrastructure, blue infrastructure, topography, sites of archaeological and scientific interest, roads, rail and so on) in this way facilitating the creation of holistic, nuanced and truly Smart maps which can be programmed to show things like the ways in which major roads and other blockages impact on accessibility. Each data layer can also be subjected to a multiplier based on the quality of the source to ensure that the best quality data has more credence within the overall model.

The active community made social value maps are also core to a recent research project, *Community Consultation for Quality of Life*, a collaboration between the Universities of Reading, Cardiff, Ulster and Edinburgh with the Quality of Life Foundation and the digital platform Commonplace funded by the Arts and Humanities Research Council. The aim was to improve the way community consultation on planning happens, both digital and face-to-face through

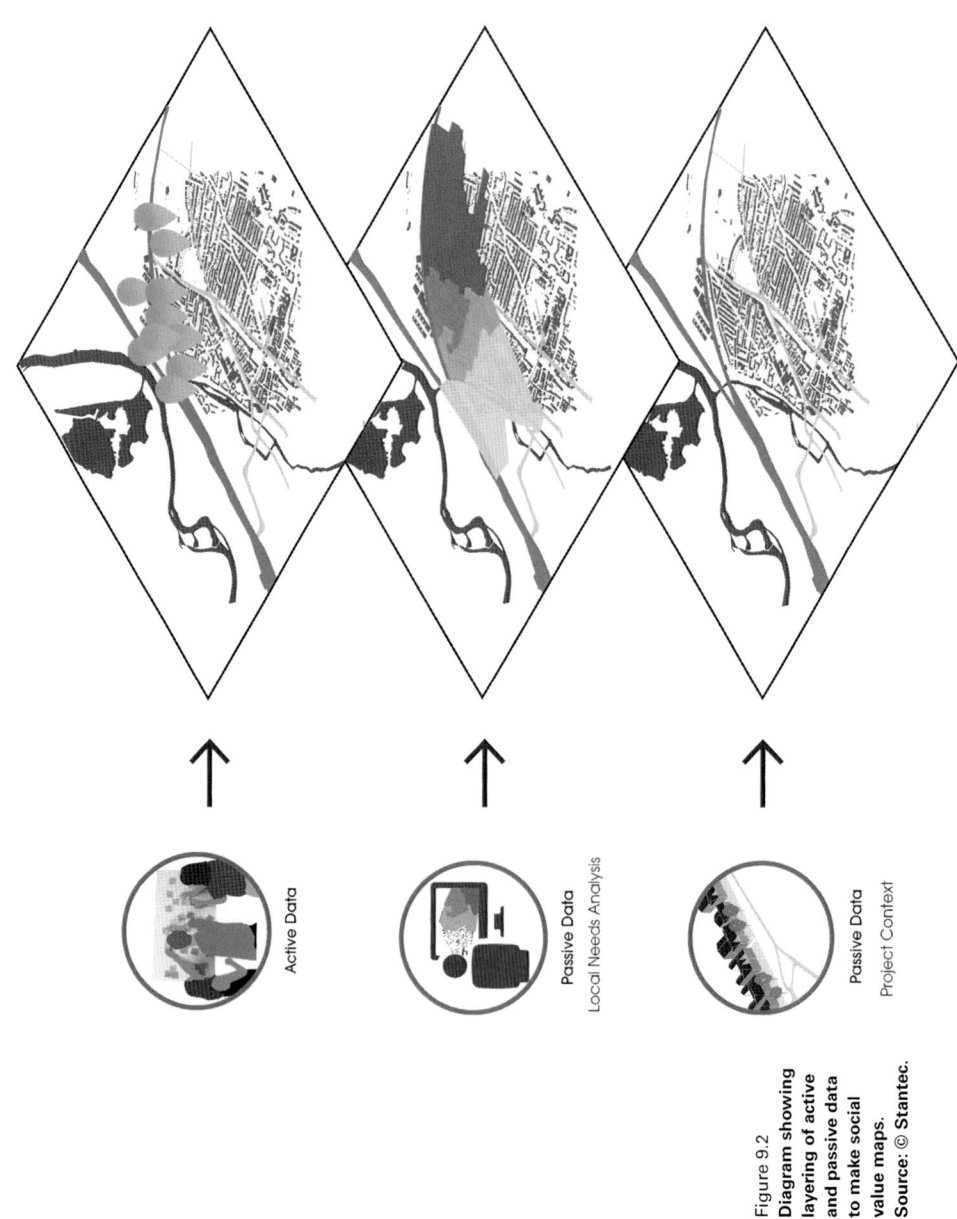

How to build a housing system for hope and wellbeing

Figure 9.2
**Diagram showing layering of active and passive data to make social value maps.
Source: © Stantec.**

142

the implementation of pilot projects across the UK. Consultations took place in an 'urban room', a community space, disused shop or pop up in the city with parallel, but interconnected, consultations on line in each of the four UK nations. The urban room, a concept with a rich history (Tewdwr-Jones, Sookhoo and Freestone, 2020), is a place to do collaborative resaerch on local issues. In the CCQOL urban room community members were asked to contribute to the making of quality of life/social value maps to show what they value in the area building on a digital format developed by Commonplace (Figures 9.3 and 9.4). A variety of experimental formats were used to make the consultations as engaging as possible, with the digital platform being refined based on feedback. Outputs include a code of conduct for planning consultation, a toolkit for undertaking face-to-face and digital planning consultations in each of the four nations, a digital format for delivering community consultation and lastly a social value map based on active community generated data for each of the four pilot cities. The potential, long term, is to develop a patchwork of social value maps of the UK constantly updated with real-time community generated data. These can be used alongside passive data sources to give an accurate and holistic picture of what is happening in a place at any one time. They won't be perfect, but they will be a start. We have some way to go to 'develop temporally dynamic models which are operational' (Batty, 2016, p. 253).

The options for deliberative democracy are growing. In a housing system for hope and wellbeing access to fast internet connection will be a utility and a right, giving people democratic control over the things that impact on our lives. One shining example of digital democracy at work (set out in the NESTA report *Digital Democracy* (Simon et al., 2017) is Better Reykjavik, a platform for generating ideas at city scale – over 18m euros has been allocated to 787 citizen-generated projects – (Better Reykjavik, 2021). Here Better Neighbourhoods facilitates annual participatory budgeting across the city, the culmination of a remarkable suite of participatory initiatives including Shadow City which sought innovation ideas

Figure 9.3 **Community Consultation for Quality of Life (CCQOL) Urban Room, Reading, 2022.** Source: © Flora Samuel.

Figure 9.4
Combining consultation with developing English language skills at CCQOL Urban Room, Reading.
Source: © Flora Samuel.

directly from citizens, and Shadow Parliament, which enabled citizens to comment on parliamentary activity, and Your Priorities, an open-source crowdsourcing tool developed by Iceland in 2008 in the wake of the banking crash, now being used across the globe, including a range of UK Local Authorities (Your Priorities, 2021). As digital voting becomes more and more easy participatory budgeting should become commonplace. Even the government in England is considering bringing in Street Vote to enable to locals to set their priorities (Phibbs, 2021). The advance of Citizen's Assemblies, supported by groups like the Involve Foundation and the Sortition Foundation, should be noted in this context. It is worth also mentioning Blockchain, the platform that facilitates the digital currency Bitcoin. Essentially it provides a decentralised database of transactions that can readily be seen by anyone on a network. Every new transaction must be validated by each computer on the network before being published on the exponentially developing database of transactions. As a method for counting votes it should, in theory, be tamperproof (Simon *et al.*, 2017).

Earlier in this book I mentioned the fact that we rarely account for wellbeing data because it has been so difficult to capture in a quantitative way. Forms of data gathering are needed that capture qualitative responses in quantitative ways, making it much easier to include wellbeing in the spreadsheets that govern the production of our built environment. Although still in its early stages text-mining (natural language processing) is of significant importance in this respect (Simon *et al.*, 2017). Within universities academics use programmes such as NVivo to scroll through reams of qualitative text using algorithms to pick out keywords and themes that can be presented by qualitatively or quantitatively. Researchers also text mine large bodies of open-source text, for example, tweets. It doesn't take much imagination to see that these kinds of techniques could be used together to inform action. Ultimately digital technology offers the potential for a planning system built on the democratic input of voters.

Local codes

A holistic value mapping system will enable planners to make sensitive decisions about earmarking land for housing and infrastructure. The recent publication of the MHCLG National Model Design Code provides detailed advice to local authorities on how to put together design codes, sets of rules to govern the form and nature of buildings and neighbourhoods building on what it calls the 'characteristics of well-designed places' clustered under the headings of climate, character and community (MHCLG, 2021b). The Department of Levelling Up Homes and Communities is encouraging communities to develop their own codes (DLUHC, 2022) which is a nice idea on the face of it, but is likely to exclude those people who are too busy surviving to get involved. If only the coding linked to the triple bottom line of sustainability – social, environmental and economic value – that is the basis of the National Planning Policy Framework and indeed the Treasury *Green Book*: then, finally, we just might get the joined up system that we need.

Rather than just coding the forms and materials of the built environment, coding should be used to designate places where social, environmental and economic value are needed – it will be easy to work this out from the value maps. The codes needn't be static, they can change in line with developments on the maps. This will enable the planning system to adjust sensitively to changes in places over time, planning on the move. A simple example might be low levels of social value caused by poor health outcomes. This could be alleviated by prioritising the creation of high quality green exercise space in that area. Some aspects of the code can be applied to an entire authority, some to particular areas (for example, villages), some to development sites and some to individual plots. Planning codes have to be baggy enough to allow for variation within the rules.

The 3D city modelling system Vu City offers food for thought as it has so much potential as a planning tool. The Vu City model can, for example, be programmed to include buildings that have been given planning permission but have not yet been built. This means that planners can easily consider the cumulative impact of all the planning permissions that have been awarded in an area whether built or not. Aerial surveys take place on a regular basis to update the Vu City model. The models will show up any discrepancies between buildings as proposed and buildings as built making it extremely easy for planners to spot planning violations. If planning codes are built into these kinds of 3D models it should be easy to check that they conform to local policy at the press of a button. Digital maps and models should make planning so much more easy and effective than it is at present.

A holistic mapping system could also play a crucial role in coding the ingredients for what has come to be known as a 20 minute neighbourhood, a place where people can walk to access all the facilities they need, a concept that is being promoted widely in the UK at this time (Sustrans, 2020). It should be noted that a walking distance of 20 minutes might be out of reach for people with mobility issues and small children (Jang *et al.*, 2022). Indeed it is debatable whether the things that are 20-minutes walk away are part of what we think of as a neighbourhood. I argue that we need another term to describe things that are accessible in 20 minutes by foot – I propose a change in terminology to '20-minute community' as it is all about a sharing buildings, services and things. Either way it is very slippery concept that can only really be operationalised through the use of digital mapping. The value maps could include an algorithm that alerts us to the facilities that are needed in an area, and planners can use a range of powers at their fingertips (see later chapters) to bring them into being. The value maps will also show where physical obstacles such as major roads and rivers distort the 20-minute community. Ultimately a 20-minute community needs a spatial algorithm to ensure that it is being achieved, backed up through legislation, or it will just be another nebulous planning concept to be violated at will.

Conclusion

The automation of the planning system will free up planners to develop sensitive strategy for the coding and balancing of social, environmental and economic values across our land mass. Perhaps more importantly it will give them the time and space to embed themselves in their communities to work with residents and others to design and build homes and places that foster hope and wellbeing, something that will be discussed further in Chapter 11. This will take major investment in the short term but will deliver on long-term value. Political will is needed to make sure that we have a truly joined up planning system. In the next chapter I will focus on the changes needed within government to enable it to happen.

References

Batty, M. and Yang, W. (2022) *A Digital Future for Planning Full Report*. Digital Task Force for Planning. Available at: https://digital4planning.com/wp-content/uploads/2022/02/A-Digital-Future-for-Planning-Full-Report-Web.pdf.

BBBBC. (2020) *Living with Beauty: Promoting Health, Well-Being and Sustainable Growth*. Available at: https://assets.publishing.service.gov.uk/government/uploads/system/uploads/attachment_data/file/861832/Living_with_beauty_BBBBC_report.pdf.

Better Reykjavik. (2021) *Better Reykjavik*. Available at: https://reykjavik.is/en/better-reykjavik-0.

Cabinet Office. (2021) *Public Dialogue on Location Data Ethics*. Available at: https://www.gov.uk/government/publications/public-dialogue-on-location-data-ethics.

CPRE (2022) *The Countryside Next Door*. Available at: https://www.cpre.org.uk/wp-content/uploads/2022/05/CPRE_Countryside_Next_Door.pdf

DEFRA. (2021) *MAGIC*. Available at: https://magic.defra.gov.uk/.

Dixon, T. and Farrelly, L. (2019) 'People can now see the past present and future of their cities with urban rooms', *The Independent*. 26 January. Available at: https://www.facebook.com/TheIndependentOnline/posts/10156770679991636.

DLUHC. (2022) *Communities Empowered to Shape*. Available at: https://www.gov.uk/government/news/communities-empowered-to-shape-design-of-neighbourhoods.

GMA. (2019) *Greater Manchester Infrastructure Framework 2040*. Greater Manchester Authority. Available at: https://www.greatermanchester-ca.gov.uk/media/1715/greater-manchester-infrastructure-framework-2040.pdf.

Gov.uk. (2019) *Green Belts*. MHCLG. Available at: https://www.gov.uk/guidance/green-belt.

Harrison, J., Galland, D. and Tewdwr Jones, M. (2021) 'Regional planning is dead: long live planning regional futures', *Regional Studies*, 55(1), pp. 6–18.

Hung, M.J., Hang Tse, L. and Saggau, D. (2020) 'Strengthening urban community governance through geographical information systems and participation: an evaluation of my Google map and service coordination', *Australian Journal of Social Issues*, 55, pp. 182–200.

Jang, C. et al. (2022) *Access and Babies, Toddlers and Their Caregivers*. Bernard Van Leer Foundation. Available at: https://www.itdp.org/wp-content/uploads/2022/01/Access-for-All-Babies-and-Toddlers_December-2021-pages_final-3.pdf.

McDonald, B. (2020) *Rebirding*. London: Pelagic.

MHCLG. (2021a) *Homes & Communities*. Available at: https://data-communities.opendata.arcgis.com/.

MHCLG. (2021b) *National Model Design Code*. Ministry of Housing Communities and Local Government. Available at: https://assets.publishing.service.gov.uk/government/uploads/system/uploads/attachment_data/file/957205/National_Model_Design_Code.pdf.

Mulholland, C. et al. (2022) *Delivering Better Place Outcomes through Use of Data: Building on the Emerging Digital Planning System*. Reading: Stantec. Available at: https://www.stantec.com/uk/projects/b/better-places-research-project.

National Park City. (2020) *London National Park City*. Available at: https://www.nationalparkcity.london/

NPPF (2021) *National Planning Policy Framework*, Available at: https://assets.publishing.service.gov.uk/government/uploads/system/uploads/attachment_data/file/1005759/NPPF_July_2021.pdf

Natural England. (2021) *Green Infrastructure*. Available at: https://designatedsites.naturalengland.org.uk/GreenInfrastructure/Home.aspx.

ONS. (2021) *Open Geography Portal*. Available at: https://geoportal.statistics.gov.uk/.

Perrotti, D. and Stremke, S. (2018) 'Can urban metabolism models advance green infrastructure planning? Insights from ecosystems services research', *Environment and Planning B: Urban Analytics and City Science*, 47(4), pp. 678–694.

Phibbs, H. (2021) 'Gove's backing for street votes is very welcome. Lets get a pilot scheme going', *Conservative Home*. Available at: https://www.conservativehome.com/localgovernment/2021/11/goves-backing-for-street-votes-is-very-welcome-lets-get-a-pilot-scheme-going.html.

RSA. (2020) *A One Powerhouse Framework for National Convergence and Prospeciry A Vision for Britain. Planned*. London: Royal Society of Arts.

Available at: https://onepowerhouseconsortium.co.uk/app/uploads/rsa_overarching_report_final.pdf.

RTPI. (2019) *A Digital Planning Manifesto*. Available at: https://www.rtpi.org.uk/policy/2019/september/a-digital-planning-manifesto/.

RTPI. (2021) *Planning for a Better Future*. Available at: https://www.rtpi.org.uk/policy-and-research/planning-for-a-better-future/#M-3.1.

Scottish Government. (2021) *Transforming Places Together: Scotland's Digital Strategy for Planning*. Digital Scotland. Last accessed on November 2021: file:///Users/vw911381/Downloads/transforming-places-together-scotlands-digital-strategy-planning%20(1).pdf.

Shoard, M. (1997) *This Land is Our Land*. London: Gaia Books.

Simon, J. et al. (2017) *Digital Democracy: The Tools Transforming Political Engagement*. NESTA. Available at: https://media.nesta.org.uk/documents/digital_democracy.pdf.

Simons, Z. (2020) 'We need to talk about England's green belt', *Financial Times*. Available at: https://www.ft.com/content/f240e825-eca0-4fba-8813-86dfaa0a6933.

Stantec. (2022) *Delivering Better Places Through Data*. Available at: https://www.stantec.com/uk/projects/b/better-places-research-project.

Statistics Authority. (2021) *The UK Statistical System*. Available at: https://www.statisticsauthority.gov.uk/

Sustrans (2020) *What Is a 20 Minute Neighbourhood?* Available at: https://www.sustrans.org.uk/our-blog/get-active/2020/in-your-community/what-is-a-20-minute-neighbourhood/

Tewdr Jones, M., Sookhoo, D. and Freestone, R. (2020) 'From Geddes' city museum to Farrell's urban room: past, present, and future at the Newcastle City Futures exhibition', *Planning Perspectives*, 35(2), pp. 277–297.

Tewdwr-Jones, M. (2012) *Spatial Planning and Governance*. London: Palgrave Macmillan.

Tree, I. (2018) *Wilding*. London: Picador.

VeloCity. (2019) *Growing Villages Differently*. Available at: https://velocity651476576.files.wordpress.com/2020/05/velocity_manifesto_may2020.pdf.

Wilkinson, R. and Pickett, K. (2019) *The Inner Level: How More Equal Societies Reduce Stress, Restore Sanity and Improve Everyone's Well-Being*. London: Penguin.

Wilson, A. and Tewdwr-Jones, M. (2022) *Digital Participatory Planning*. New York: Routledge.

Your Priorities. (2021) *Your Priorities*. Available at: https://yrpri.org/domain/3.

Chapter 10

Policy for hope and wellbeing in housing and neighbourhoods

> *Every government policy needs to reinforce the narrative of hope. Our housing, education, health, economy, foreign policy and approach to climate change must strengthen us as a hopeful society.*
>
> *(Welby, 2018, p. 32)*

What is meant by policy here is the government and its agencies. These set the tone for what David Clapham calls a 'housing regime', the 'set of discourses and social, economic and political practices that influence the provision, allocation, consumption and housing outcomes in a given country' (2019, p. 4). This chapter reviews some shifts in policy across the UK that would be necessary to create a housing regime for wellbeing in the long term. I do not pretend to be a political expert but am writing from the perspective of someone who is occasionally called to talk with civil servants in Westminster about this or that in relation to housing and who is continually baffled by the poor communication across departments and warring visions of what might be. This is not to say that exciting changes aren't already afoot, one being the cross party Healthy Homes Act which envisages a reformed planning system around health (Slade, 2021). The Homes (Fitness for Human Habitation) Act 2018 is already on the statute book and is ripe with potential, were it to be properly enforced. The Conservative backed Social Value Act (2012) is already making waves. Positive change can only really happen if policy makers and people work together so this account begins with a discussion of trust, before moving to units of governance, something that impacts strongly on people's sense of agency and wellbeing. I will argue that we need joined up policy on health, social care and housing delivery at every scale. This will impact on the character of communities and their ability to innovate and attract investment. The chapter finishes with discussion of land and tax, primary levers at the disposal of government to make this transformation possible.

Trust

Lack of trust in the government is impeding progress at every level. Politicians are the least trusted of all the professions covered by a recent Ipsos MORI survey, with only about 15% of people having any faith in them at all (Ipsos MORI, 2020).

There is a lot of work to be done if people are to regain trust in their elected representatives including, among other things 'structural reforms to the House of Lords, a move to more proportional forms of representation in the House of Commons, greater diversity amongst MPs in terms of their backgrounds, work experience, ethnicity and gender' as well as a range of other cultural changes (Simon *et al.*, 2017, p. 95).

Taylor Gooby and Leruth argue that, the reason for the well-known paradox that people want far higher spending on pensions, healthcare and education but are reluctant to pay higher taxes is because they simply don't trust government to spend their money well (2018). Some recent research on local libraries found that 'those using health services, attending lectures and using library space for socialising are willing to pay more on average to maintain all services at their local library' (Fujiwara, Lawton and Mourato, 2019, p. 639). It follows therefore that people might be prepared to pay higher taxes if they had some agency in how they were spent or at least understood why they were being spent in a certain way. The Department of Levelling Up Homes and Communities has a laudable aspiration to develop a 'more stringent regulatory regime to create and maintain a golden thread of information' (DLUHC, 2021). Placing the duty on the people responsible for a building or a place to maintain this information would definitely help.

Roman Krznaric has outlined what he calls the 'design principles of deep democracy'. These include political bodies that are charged with the task of ensuring representation for disenfranchised young people and future generations, Citizens' Assemblies which allow for decision making without reference to short-term party politics, legal mechanisms to safeguard the rights of future generations and lastly 'self governing city states' (Krznaric, 2020, p. 175). Oxford Citizens Assembly on Climate Change set up by Oxford City Council is one pioneering example (Oxford City Council, 2019). Power has to be devolved at every level so people have a stake in decisions made and money spent. As already mentioned the Scottish government has set up its National Outcomes Framework so that its residents can see how it is doing in relation to its promises with everything falling roughly into line behind such top-level indicators. This seems like a good start.

Units of governance

The idea that power should be devolved to the city state reducing the power of the elites in central government and making policy more locally relevant is strengthening, building on the activities of the devolved nations and the growing impetus of Combined Local Authority initiatives. The first ever meeting of a city-regional land commission in the UK was convened in September 2020 in Liverpool to influence decision making in the city region, to improve fairness and inclusivity and to change approaches to decision making (Thompson, 2020). Liverpool's Land Commission is 'participatory', its aim being to build 'community wealth', providing a beautiful example of the way in which positive things are already afoot. Another example is the One Powerhouse Consortium based in the north of England has recently made the case to government for a 'move to megaregions – not as top-down national agencies but as bottom-up collaborations between regional leaders' (RSA, 2020, p. 4). In its vision England should be divvyed up into 'the Northern Powerhouse, the Midlands Engine' and the 'super LEP' (Local Enterprise Partnership) areas in the South-East and South-West (an example would be Thames Valley) with devolution of fiscal control. Building on this proposal four regional ministers would be needed, one for each of the English megaregions, whose primary role is to represent the region to government and who will form a committee for regional rebalancing attended by Secretaries of State for Business, Energy and Industrial Strategy (BEIS), Housing, Communities and Local Government (HCLG), Department for Transport (DfT) and Department for Environment, Food and Rural Affairs (DEFRA) and chaired by the Chancellor of the Exchequer (RSA, 2020, p. 4). Advocates of city states tend to stress the economic benefits of the approach but city states could also deliver on a range of other kinds of values which are arguably more important (Axinte *et al.*, 2019).

There is wide recognition of the need to reform local government too, something that the Welsh are acting on at the moment. In an insightful report on reformation of local government in England for the Centre for Cities Simon Jeffrey notes that we have 'a vertical fragmentation, where powers are split between lower-tier district authorities and upper-tier counties with no rationale for why they are allocated as they are (2020, p. 3). I recently stood in front of a large map with of a town with the local mayor who explained to me the difficulties caused by these artificial boundaries for those who are trying to make good things happen in the council. Jeffrey argues for governance units encompassing populations of 3,00,000 to 8,00,000 aligned with economic units. 'Where local economies are larger than this, then Combined Authorities should be formed with personal services retained at the local level' (Jeffrey, 2020, p. 5). I argue that governance units should be aligned with social units delineated by the value maps described in the previous chapter. This builds on our discovery, during a social value mapping exercise in Reading (Hatleskog and Samuel, 2021), that the political boundaries of the study area had a very poor fit with what people identified with as their neighbourhood. Indeed there was a political fissure between two ward boundaries right at the heart of the community with major impacts on cohesion. The Boundary Commission does review political boundaries in consultation with the public on a regular basis but this it is not a well-publicised process.

Wherever realistic power and responsibility need to be given to the smallest, most local, political unit that is practical and efficient through the principle of subsidiarity (Wanzenbock and Frenken, 2020), potentially the 20-minute community and the neighbourhoods within it. A digital mapping system such could be used to ensure that things join up across scales and borders. The neighbourhood, an excellent hyperlocal unit of governance, has to be seen as part of a holistic system of cross neighbourhood exchange, cultivating linkages between deprived and affluent populations. According to Flint and Kearns this requires 'a new focus on the outcomes of relationships between different populations at neighbourhood, city, regional and national scales within multi-level governance processes' (p. 51). Governance has to be seen holistically with an emphasis on balancing the local, national and global.

Joining up healthcare, social care and home building

Ultimately health care, social care, housing delivery and planning need to be dealt with holistically at both policy and community levels if improvements in wellbeing are to be achieved. Health care provision needs to be delivered locally at a variety of scales allowing for cheap and easy access. The building of big hospitals is a very public way to demonstrate that something is appears to be being done about the National Health Service (NHS), while bringing together a lot of resources, but doesn't necessarily work well for patients if they and their loved ones have to travel long distances to get there, incurring cost and creating carbon as they go (Duane *et al.*, 2012). The decentralising of healthcare is already being explored in the Wales (Welsh Government, 2021a). New emphasis on the 20-minute community should presumably extend to healthcare provision, the return of the cottage hospital and local maternity units. Local General Practitioner (GP) practices have the potential for a hybrid offering including advice on exercise, nutrition and food as well as social events and opportunities for volunteering, consultation, learning and creativity. This is increasingly happening with the advent of social prescribing, connecting people to things in their community of benefit to their health, something that arguably should not require the intervention of a doctor.

A hopeful housing system has to develop alongside a properly resourced National Health Service (NHS) that puts less emphasis on expensive medicalised solutions and more emphasis on prevention. 'There is a huge moral difference between a policy that promotes health and one that promotes health capabilities – the latter, not the former, honors the person's lifestyle choices' (Nussbaum, 2011, p. 26). Multiple studies have demonstrated the long-term financial savings to the NHS which could be achieved through remedial work on housing (Nicol and Garrett, 2019, p. 2). They tend to examine the low hanging fruit of evidence – for example, the reduction of trip hazards and ensuring adequate levels of warmth – so imagine what a truly holistic calculation of the value of good housing might demonstrate (Breaking Barriers Innovations, 2020). Plans to expand 'green social prescribing' are a promising step in this direction (NHS, 2021). The need to recognise housing as a health intervention has to be reflected in the organisation of government departments and their budgets. Care homes too need to be conceived as part of our health infrastructure (Samuel, 2020), with a spectrum of choices being offered to people in later life. This will require a cultural shift in policy making and housing delivery towards more holistic solutions (Park and Ziegler, 2016, p. 13). Hilary Cottam's experiments on 'good health' and 'ageing well' illustrate just how much improvement can be made to people's quality of life by extending their local support networks, while saving money too (2018).

Experiments are currently under way in Wales on the introduction of Universal Basic Income, a set income regardless of means, focussing for the time being on people with caring responsibilities (Welsh Government, 2021b). The potential for rolling out such a system across the UK is exciting as it would free people up from worries about survival, enabling them instead to focus on creative and purposeful opportunities within their own communities, including building their own homes and support networks.

The importance of creating 'accessible opportunities for communities to help themselves' through self-build has been recognised by a recent independent report to government (Bacon, 2021). New kinds of communities need support so people have choice about where to live and where to end their days (Howard, 2021). The recent development of the 'Right to Regenerate' is a positive development that allows local communities to develop derelict buildings and disused land for community purpose (Gov.uk, 2021). Such endeavours need to be made easy. MHCLG has announced a fund for the promotion of self build, together with an action plan for its promotion (MHCLG, 2021), but without efforts to reach a wider constituency of people such initiatives may actually only serve to fuel division like the current Neighbourhood Planning system in England which tends to work in favour of people in the most affluent areas (Lawson et al., 2022).

The solutions to boost housing supply are very well known (Anacker, for example, 2019 sets out a useful list), but it requires the kind of investment that has so far not been forthcoming in the UK. The government needs to take charge of housing delivery and to build up the stock of public rented housing to the point that it becomes the desirable norm as in some parts of Europe. Although there are promising developments in the area of 'place based impact investment' (The Good Economy, 2021) and ethical investment funds which are increasingly being used to build housing, the magnitude and urgency of the problem is so great that it really needs government intervention. The private sector cannot be expected to pave the way for zero carbon, closed loop economies, cradle to cradle, modern methods of construction, post occupancy evaluation and the long-term view. Development is a risky business and governments with a large portfolio are in a much better position than developers to absorb or underwrite risk to facilitate the process (Clapham, 2019). The guarantee of large contracts is key to enabling suppliers further down the chain to upskill and invest in the development of new products and innovations. Nobody wants to buy a module if there is a danger that the factory will go into liquidation any time soon and the modules will not be forthcoming, or if the modules are likely to go out of production and it won't be possible to buy new parts and extra modules in the future. These are huge risks for housebuilders and developers that won't go away without government leadership. Major investment in state funded, public rented, housing is a necessary first step towards a wellbeing oriented housing system. This would not be the rushed, experimental, stigmatising and poorly executed housing of the post war years – it needs to be something built on lessons learnt.

Community-based innovation

Good places act as magnets for talent and creativity (Gratton and Scott, 2016). A growing body of evidence is showing the importance of physical location for transnational entrepreneurs who want to rub shoulders with like minded people (Brown et al., 2019). High-quality and affordable housing is key to all this, one reason why the University of Cambridge is so active in seeking to attract 'world class' academics and researchers by investing in the £1bn project for North Cambridge (Tolson and Rintoul, 2018, p. 4), a city where housing is too expensive for young, or even old, academics on dwindling salaries. Arguably the investment and care that is currently going to priming the already affluent 'Oxford to Cambridge arc' into a magnet, might better be better distributed across the rest of the nation, again in the name of 'levelling up'. International centres of excellence and bottom-up activity are both needed support to generate resilient, mixed, ecosystems that are in a virtuous cycle of learning and development across the land mass of the UK.

Bloom et al. offer a fascinating review of ways in which governments can most effectively incentivise innovation. To spread opportunity and value preferential treatment needs to be given to support small businesses to innovate, start up and scale up. Meanwhile the planning system needs to favour the development of innovation clusters (2019). Currently Research and Development (R & D) tax credits are available for innovative businesses but only really if they are working in technology. R & D tax credits need to be reframed to encompass social innovation, including community development. They also need to be readily available to the arts and humanities, as they play such a key role in these transformations (Flinders, 2015). At the same time a rebalancing is needed in favour of tiny businesses and 'informal' entrepreneurs (Williams and Nadin, 2012), all the while placing emphasis on the local. Procurement must be framed in favour of small suppliers. This has to be accompanied by a shift in government discourse from technology and efficiency to purpose (Jarvis, 2019), and in the right places.

Land and tax

Ultimately, to bring about a housing system for hope and wellbeing, we have to revert back to a situation in which the land is held by the public for community good and the generation of community wealth. This is not a new idea – indeed the Liberal Prime Minister Lloyd George tried to reform land ownership at the start of the last century as part of his famous People's Budget (Packer, 2001). Unsurprisingly his bill was blocked by the House of Lords (and their vested interests), but so key is this issue to the positive transformation of our society that it will not go away. This subject re-emerged in *Land for the Many* a report written by some of the key thinkers in this area for the Labour party in advance of the 2019 election (Monbiot et al., 2019), but land reform shouldn't just be seen as a Labour issue as it has ramifications for all parties as it is just as much about 'freedom' as 'theft' (Grayston, 2019).

Anthropologist Clifford Geertz has argued that 'man is an animal suspended in webs of significance that he himself has spun' (Geertz, 1973, p. 5). We have spun a world of property law and tax on top of historical injustices that have made it admissible for some to claim ownership of land which is at core a common good (Hayes, 2020). Surely there has to be a way out of this. I am going to make the case for land tax but there are other, more incremental ways to improve on the situation we have now, for example, by closing off inheritance tax loopholes exploited by some land owners and banning offshore ownership of land and property which, as Guy Shrubsole argues, would make sure taxes were paid, improve transparency and reduce risks of money laundering (2019).

The rules that govern tax and investment are key to the delivery of an inclusive and fair housing market (Clapham, 2019, p. 22). An easy win would be to make better use of existing stock, using the tax system and stamp duty to discourage the ownership of second and third homes (Gallent, Mace and Tewdwr-Jones, 2016), putting pressure on private landlords and putting more homes back onto the market. Research suggests that an empty homes tax of 1% would generate the equivalent to 11% of the current council tax (local government tax) (Bourne, 2019). There are many other ways in which tax can be used to stimulate housebuilding, support the environment and make a fairer system (Barker, 2014). Lunde et al have offered an excellent pan Europe examination of the pros and cons of different taxation systems from which governments can learn (2021).

There are obviously some significant practical hurdles to be overcome to make a land value tax, a recurring tax on landowners based on the value of 'unimproved land', viable including a comprehensive and up to date land registry (Hughes et al., 2020, p. 1), but it is worth holding out for as it would bring coherence to our current iniquitous system. One result would be a separation of the value of a building from the value of the land, potentially making homes more affordable. Martin Adams is not alone in proposing that landlords who have exclusive use of land should, in compensation for loss of amenity for the public, pay a 'community land contribution' (2015). This would, in turn, build community wealth for the buying back of land priced at current use value (Bentley, 2017, p. 2). An additional service charge, like council tax, would be paid for facility use (Denmark has a similar process). Another word for this is a 'lease'. Unfortunately the current government in the UK is moving away from leaseholds because of the confusions that it causes among buyers. One surveyor I spoke with suggested that the issue was more about the inability of surveyors to develop and communicate a clear and transparent leasehold system than any problem with leases per se.

The Scottish Land Commission has made a series of recommendations for improving supply of land that are less radical than a land tax. These would be implemented through a new kind of land agency built on a public interest-led approach to development (Scottish Land Commission, 2021b). These include ensuring that uplifts in land value are captured when public investment is involved as well as the provision of a steady stream of development ready sites in the right places and in the right timescale to ensure delivery of Scotland's targets. Most interestingly there is recommendation that there is a publicly available register of optional agreements on land accompanied by a regular statistical bulletin on land value. This would be vital to ensure that land is valued appropriately (Scottish Land Commission, 2021a), laying the ground for a transparent system of land value capture (potentially accounting for social value). This could bring very considerable money into community wealth. KPMG and Savills research suggests, for example, that 8 prospective Transport for London projects costing £36 billion could, for example, bring in £87 billion of value uplift (TfL, 2017).

Equivalent bodies to the Scottish Land Commission are needed in the other nations of the UK, tasked with the remit of land reform for social, environmental and economic value and the implementation of land value tax (Shrubsole, 2019). A key element of this would be the return of land to public, shared ownership. This would include leasing land to community groups interested in doing their own housing developments. A recent report on the promotion of custom and self build recommended the creation of a division within Homes England devoted to identifying land for this kind of community housing (Bacon, 2021). Whatever the land agency looks like it needs to be an organisation that puts communities, and wellbeing, first.

Conclusion

If only there was the political will the UK housing system could be reconfigured to deliver eudaimonic wellbeing, in the form of socially, environmentally and economically balanced communities. For this to happen the societal pact between government and people needs to be re-established, enabling both to work together to maximise capabilities. A rethinking of units of governance to facilitate local input into decision making around places would assist this process.

Health, social care, housing delivery and innovation need to be planned holistically to deliver housing and neighbourhoods that promote wellbeing. The bottom line is that people need places and spaces to grow their capabilities, which is one of the reasons why land reform is such a vital part of the journey. There are so many 'hard' levers that governments can use to effect change – some of which have been set out here – but the 'soft' systems, winning hearts and minds are equally important. Community-based policy has to be at the heart of every government agency, in particular local authorities, the subject of the next chapter. The urgent need for local government finance reform is not just a matter for accountants but will have serious repercussions for who we are as a community for England's future (Amin Smith and Phillips, 2019).

Note

Justin Welby quotes, © Justin Welby, 2018, *Reimagining Britain*, Bloomsbury Continuum, an imprint of Bloomsbury Publishing Plc.

References

Adams, M. (2015) *Land: A New Paradigm for a Thriving World*. Berkeley, CA: North Atlantic.

Amin Smith, N. and Phillips, D. (2019) *English Council Funding: What's Happened and What's Next?* Institute of Fiscal Studies. Available at: https://www.ifs.org.uk/publications/14133.

Anacker, K.B. (2019) 'Introduction: housing affordability and affordable housing', *International Journal of Housing Policy*, 19(1), pp. 1–16.

Axinte, L.F. *et al.* (2019) 'Regenerative city-regions: a new conceptual framework', *Regional Studies, Regional Science*, 6(1), pp. 117–129.

Bacon, R. (2021) *House: How Putting Customers in Charge Can Change Everything*. UK Gov Independent Review. Available at: https://assets.publishing.service.gov.uk/government/uploads/system/uploads/attachment_data/file/1013928/Bacon_Review.pdf.

Barker, K. (2014) *Housing: Where's the Plan?* London: London Publishing Partnership.

Bentley, D. (2017) *The Land Question: Fixing the Dysfunction at the Root of the Housing Crisis*. Civitas. Available at: http://www.civitas.org.uk/content/files/thelandquestion.pdf.

Bloom, N., Van Reenen, J. and Williams, H. (2019) 'A toolkit of policies to promote innovation', *Journal of Economic Perspectives*, 33(3), pp. 163–184.

Bourne, J. (2019) 'Empty homes: mapping the extent and value of low-use domestic property in England and Wales', *Palgrave Communications*, 5(9). Available at: https://www.nature.com/articles/s41599-019-0216-y.

Breaking Barriers Innovations. (2020) *Somerset Playbook Programme Final Report*. Available at: https://bbi.uk.com/reports/.

Brown, R. *et al.* (2019) 'Start up factories, transnational entrepreneurs and entrepreneurial ecosystems: unpacking the allure of a start-up accelerator programme', *European Planning Studies*, 27(5), pp. 885–904.

Clapham, D. (2019) *Remaking Housing Policy: An International Study*. London: Routledge.

Cottam, H. (2018) *Radical Help*. London: Virago.

DLUHC. (2021) *Golden Thread: Factsheet*. Available at: https://www.gov.uk/government/publications/building-safety-bill-factsheets/golden-thread-factsheet.

Duane, B. *et al.* (2012) 'Taking a bite out of Scotland's dental carbon emissions in the transition to a low carbon future', *Public Health*, 126(9), pp. 770–777.

Flinders, M. (2015) 'Participatory arts and active citizenship'. Available at: https://culturalvalueproject.wordpress.com/tag/social-value-of-arts/.

Fujiwara, D., Lawton, R.N. and Mourato, S. (2019) 'More than a good book: contingent valuation of public library services in England', *Journal of Cultural Economics*, 43, pp. 639–666.

Gallent, N., Mace, A. and Tewdr Jones, M. (2016) *Second Homes: European Perspectives and UK Policies*. London: Routledge.

Geertz, C. (1973) *The Interpretation of Culture*. New York: Basic Books.

Gov.uk. (2021) *'Right to Regenerate' To Turn Derelict Buildings into Homes and Community Assets*. Available at: https://www.gov.uk/government/news/right-to-regenerate-to-turn-derelict-buildings-into-homes-and-community-assets.

Gratton, L. and Scott, A. (2016) *The 100-Year Life: Living and Working in an Age of Longevity*. London: Bloomsbury.

Grayston, R. (2019) 'Theft or freedom? Land reform for the right as well as the left'. Available at: https://blog.shelter.org.uk/2019/06/theft-or-freedom-land-reform-for-the-right-as-well-as-the-left/.

Hatleskog, E. and Samuel, F. (2021) 'Mapping as a strategic tool for evidencing social values and supporting joined-up decision making in Reading, England', *Journal of Urban Design* [Preprint]. doi:10.1080/13574809.2021.1890555.

Hayes, N. (2020) *The Book of Trespass: Crossing the Lines that Divide Us*. London: Bloomsbury.

Howard, S. (2021) 'Is the boom in communal living really the good life?', *The Observer*. 17 January. Available at: https://www.theguardian.com/society/2021/jan/17/is-the-boom-in-communal-living-really-the-good-life.

Hughes, C. *et al.* (2020) 'Implementing a land value tax: consideration on moving from theory to practice', *Land Use Policy*, 94, pp. 104–494.

Ipsos MORI. (2020) *Ipsos MORI Veracity Index 2020*. Available at: https://www.ipsos.com/ipsos-mori/en-uk/ipsos-mori-veracity-index-2020-trust-in-professions.

Jarvis, H. (2019) 'Age-friendly community resilience', in Trogal, K., Bauman, I., Lawrence, R., and Petrescu, D. (eds.) *Architecture and Resilience*. London: Routledge, pp. 61–73.

Jeffrey, S. (2020) *Levelling Up Local Government in England*. Centre for Cities. Available at: https://www.centreforcities.org/wp-content/uploads/2020/09/Levelling-up-local-government-in-England.pdf.

Krznaric, R. (2020) *The Good Ancestor: How to Think Long Term in a Short Term World*. London: WH Allen.

Lawson, V. *et al.* (2022) *Public Participation in Planning in the UK: A Review of the Literature*. CaCHE. https://housingevidence.ac.uk/publications/public-participation-in-planning-in-the-uk-a-review-of-the-literature/

Lunde, J. and Whitehead, C. (2021) *How Taxation Varies Between Owner-Occupation, Private Renting and Other Housing Tenures in European Countries*. Available at: https://housingevidence.ac.uk/wp-content/uploads/2021/02/European-Housing-Taxation-report-final.pdf.

MHCLG. (2021) *Over £150 Million Funding to Kickstart Self Building Revolution*. Available at: https://www.gov.uk/government/news/over-150-million-funding-to-kickstart-self-building-revolution.

Monbiot, G. *et al.* (2019) *Land for the Many: Changing the Way Our Fundamental Asset Is Used, Owned and Governed*. Labour. Available at: https://landforthemany.uk/wp-content/uploads/2019/06/land-for-the-many.pdf.

NHS. (2021) *Green Social Prescribing*. Available at: https://www.england.nhs.uk/personalisedcare/social-prescribing/green-social-prescribing/.

Nicol, S. and Garrett, H. (2019) *The Full Cost of Poor Housing in Wales*. BRE/Trust/NHS Cymru. Available at: https://www.bregroup.com/bretrust/wp-content/uploads/sites/12/2019/05/The-Cost-of-Poor-Housing-in-Wales-2017..002.pdf.

Nussbaum, M. (2011) *Creating Capabilities*. Cambridge, MA: Harvard University Press.

Oxford City Council. (2019) *Oxford Citizens Assembly on Climate Change*. Available at: https://www.oxford.gov.uk/info/20011/environment/1343/oxford_citizens_assembly_on_climate_change.

Packer, I. (2001) *Lloyd George, Liberalism and the Land*. London: Royal Historical Society.

Park, A. and Ziegler, F. (2016) 'A home for life? A critical perspective on housing choice for "downsizers" in the UK', *Architecture_MPS*, 9(2), pp. 1–21. Available at: https://www.ingentaconnect.com/content/uclpress/amps/2016/00000009/00000002/art00001.

RSA. (2020) *A One Powerhouse Framework for National Convergence and Prospeciry A Vision for Britain. Planned*. London: Royal Society of Arts. Available at: https://onepowerhouseconsortium.co.uk/app/uploads/rsa_overarching_report_final.pdf.

Samuel, F. (2020) *Impact of Housing Design and Placemaking on Social Value and Wellbeing in the pandemic Interim Report*. CaCHE. Available at: https://housingevidence.ac.uk/publications/impact-of-housing-design-and-placemaking-on-social-value-and-wellbeing-in-the-pandemic-interim-report/

Scottish Land Commission. (2021a) *Land for Housing & Development*. Scottish Land Commission. Available at: https://www.landcommission.gov.scot/downloads/611ba42c46640_Land%20Focus_Land%20for%20Housing.pdf.

Scottish Land Commission. (2021b) *Land for Housing: Towards a Public Interest Led Approach to Development*. Scottish Land Commission. Available at: https://www.landcommission.gov.scot/downloads/611ba42c438c5_Land%20for%20Housing%20Review%20FINAL.pdf.

Shrubsole, G. (2019) *Who Owns England?* London: William Collins.

Simon, J. et al. (2017) *Digital Democracy: The Tools Transforming Political Engagement*. NESTA. Available at: https://media.nesta.org.uk/documents/digital_democracy.pdf.

Slade, D. (2021) 'Seizing the political moment - regulating the built environment through a healthy homes act', *Town and Country Planning*, 90(5/6), pp. 180–183. Available at: https://www.tcpa.org.uk/Handlers/Download.ashx?IDMF=a5937f73-ca71-4e3b-8f06-0b9f6a4f9fc2.

Taylor-Gooby, P. and Leruth, B. (2018) 'Why British people don't trust the government any more - and what can be done about it', *The Conversation*. Available at: https://theconversation.com/why-british-people-dont-trust-the-government-any-more-and-what-can-be-done-about-it-89627.

TfL. (2017) *Land Value Capture*. Transport for London. Available at: https://www.london.gov.uk/sites/default/files/land_value_capture_report_transport_for_london.pdf.

The Good Economy. (2021) *Scaling up Institutional Investment for Place Based Impact*. Impact Investing Institute. Available at: https://www.impactinvest.org.uk/wp-content/uploads/2021/05/Place-based-Impact-Investing-White-Paper-May-2021.pdf.

Thompson, M. (2020) 'Land commissions and municipalist strategy'. Available at: https://minim-municipalism.org/magazine/land-commissions-and-municipalist-strategy.

Tolson, S. and Rintoul, A. (2018) *The Delivery of Public Interest Led Development in Scotland: A Discussion Paper*. Scottish Land Commission. Available at: https://landcommission.gov.scot/downloads/5dd6c7fbf1d02_Land-Lines-Public-Interest-Led-Development-Steven-Tolson-March-2018.pdf.

Wanzenbock, I. and Frenken, K. (2020) 'The subsidiarity principle in innovation policy for societal challenges', *Global Transitions*, 2, pp. 51–59.

Welby, J. (2018) *Reimagining Britain*. London: Bloomsbury.

Welsh Government (2021a), *A healthier Wales*. Available at: https://gov.wales/healthier-wales-long-term-plan-health-and-social-care

Welsh Government (2021b), *Universal Basic Income*. Available at: https://gov.wales/atisn15192

Williams, C.C. and Nadin, S. (2012) 'Tackling entrepeneurship in the informal economy: evaluating policy options', *Journal of Entrepeneurship and Public Policy*, 1(1), pp. 111–124.

Chapter 11

Rethinking local authorities around 20-minute communities

Local government is able to engage with communities and is democratically accountable for their decisions; they should be the ones with responsibility for the management of social value and the creation of community.

(Welby, 2018, p. 146)

The pandemic has shown just how effective local authorities can be in rising to the occasion (Samuel, 2020). If adequately and flexibly funded, and supported by long-term policy it is very possible that local authorities could be amazing engines of holistic value generation and housing. In this chapter I will suggest some ways in which local authorities could change in order to deliver homes and neighbourhoods for hope and wellbeing. This needs to take place within the reimagining of the planning system described in Chapter 9 and the reconstitution of units of democracy into more meaningful local units than at present, potentially the 20-minute community, discussed in the last chapter. Each should have a nerve centre, the community team headquarters (HQ), sitting roughly at its centre, populated by a community team primed to co-produce social, environmental and economic value together.

Community building leadership

Hopefully the wellbeing benefits of giving people improved opportunities to develop their capabilities are, by now, starting to shine through this text. As we move towards distributed leadership it helps to have a champion that ensures that community building is at the top of the decision making tree. In London Mayor Sadiq Khan has been working with his collective of Design Advisors to implement a recovery plan for London that is holistic, with particular emphasis on diversity and inclusion. Such leaders set the tone for local authority activities and encourage those lower down the hierarchy to be brave in prioritising wellbeing. Copenhagen is an often-cited example of what happens when design has a strong champion. Here, as in many Nordic cities, they have a city architect with wide powers to champion high-quality design. The Urban Life Strategy for Copenhagen, put into place from 2009 – its aim being to promote more urban life for all, more walking and cycling and more diversity in outdoor spaces – was led by the City Architect (Saaby and Bauman, 2019). Such initiatives have contributed greatly to Copenhagen's accolade of being one of the most 'livable' cities in the world.

In the housing system described in this book people will see working for the public sector as a vocation, a badge of honour – rather like working for the National Health Service (NHS) – and they will enjoy similar levels of public support and recognition. Public Practice supports and mentors a team of remarkable architects, urban designers and planners who believe in the importance of local authority action. These people are seconded into organisations when particular forms of expertise are needed, but only on a temporary basis because of availability of funds. Committed and talented individuals like these are needed in every community team on a permanent basis.

The value maps and the environmental, social and economic codings within them will make clear what is already present and what is needed in an area in real-time, but they have to be under constant community review, building on developments and negotiations on the ground, with new layers adding to their richness and accuracy over time. The beauty of the maps is that they won't be that dictatorial about precisely by what happens in a place, their focus will be on the outcomes produced by any development. It will become increasingly easy check on outcomes, particularly with the use of the new generation of citizen science apps that are available to us (Hays, 2022). These will involve residents themselves in data gathering on their homes and neighbourhoods. Not only will the value maps provide an important method of communicating with residents about what is happening in their area, they will also close the loop on past consultations by showing what was achieved in response to what the community asked for. Shape Newham is a good example of a map that shows all the small but vitally important urban interventions that are happening across the borough (Newham Council, 2021). The value maps proposed in this book will similarly bring together small interventions into large parcels of impact, vital for both accountability and communication. A commitment to local interventions small and large is vital for a balanced community and neighbourhood ecosystem. Small interventions are good for testing ideas which can then be built on incrementally if successful.

So well-informed, digitally savvy and interdisciplinary community teams are needed to implement community-based policy both at a wide strategic level and at the hyperlocal level of neighbourhoods. Planners with excellent community design skills will work closely with residents to become curators of the built environment, ensuring that the maps are developing for the good of people. To this end there will be no pompous buildings, adversarial council chambers and impersonal call management systems that make us question the nature of 'democracy'. Community teams will work from community team headquarters (HQs) and sometimes from home, their feet in the local, but with an eye always on the wider implications of their actions.

Community team headquarters (HQs)

The community HQ will be a little like an urban room, but 'on steroids'. The community HQ will serve the 20 minute community as set out in Chapter 9, which itself will be broken down into small neighbourhoods with further dedicated

Rethinking local authorities around 20-minute communities

support. In rural or dispersed areas the community team HQ could have a peripatetic arm that travels out into dispersed homesteads bringing issues back into a physical centre. Research needs to be done on the best way to do this. This diagram of a connective social infrastructure ecosystem from the Mayor of London's *Connective Social Infrastructure* report acts as a useful prompt to think about what might be needed (Figure 11.1). It is important to stress that a community team HQ doesn't have to be one building, it is likely to be a network space that makes good use of poorly used facilities around it. It could even offer a new use for the beleaguered High Street. Wherever it is it will be easily located through maps, networks and the design of streetscapes. The impact and reach of the community team HQs will be transparent and easy to monitor continually. Members

Figure 11.1
**An illustration of a local social infrastructure system.
Source:
© Connective Social Infrastructure, GLA, 2021.**

— Hosts or runs service or activity
⋯ Referrals, sign-posting, support or information-sharing
● Hard social infrastructure (Local spaces or facilities)
● Soft social infrastructure (Groups, networks, forums or services)

163

of under-represented communities will be encouraged into the HQ to assist in the task of promoting engagement in their peers through a snowballing effect and through outreach via the peripatetic HQs. While a lot of serious information gathering will take place in the HQ it also has to be a place of connection, fun, music, food and learning with a carefully choreographed programme of events to promote sharing of every kind.

Each HQ will need careful programming to encourage fortuitous overlaps and mixes of people, for example, computer classes for the young and the very old. Connecting people will be the very heart of their mission, with the people running these places benefitting from a structured career path and training. The value maps will include visualisations of 'soft infrastructure' – care networks of meals on wheels, drop in groups, volunteering, learning and exercise opportunities. These will assist in the identification of moments in space and time to design for fruitful interaction. Local economies and local democracy will be assisted through new technologies. The HQ will also be a base for citizen science type activities involving residents in collecting data about their places. With time people of every sort will be drawn into the debate, both face to face and online.

It is however important to remember that digital exclusion is still an issue in the UK – although a shrinking figure there were still 5.3 million adult non-internet users in the UK in 2018 (ONS, 2019) so having a place for face-to-face contact will always be important. The community team HQs are likely to be mixed use facilities combining health advice with local community space and other opportunities. When we set up an urban room in Reading to discuss planning issues we were inundated by requests from health organisations to use the space to encourage healthy lifestyles, suggesting to us that these kinds of spaces are urgently needed. We also encountered a lot of people who were lonely and clearly just wanted to have a chat.

Working closely with the local authority and others, Sarah Wigglesworth Architects, have offer a vision of what they call Ebbsfleet health and wellbeing hub. This sits at the heart of the co-created spatial strategy for the town guided by a comprehensive set of 'neighbourhood principles', including the delivery of intergenerational living (Figures 11.2 and 11.3).

> Our vision illustrates a new model for community based primary care embedded in its landscape, with integral green spaces woven into the building form. This project is an exciting proposal aimed to promote mental and physical wellbeing, healthy, active lifestyles and better food choices as a form of preventative care with social prescribing at its heart.
> (SWARCH, 2021)

Like the community team HQ it offers a rich set of uses, combining residential, retail, training, community and leisure, all at close quarters.

As work gravitates towards the home more people will take up the entrepreneurial opportunities offered by the internet. Neighbourhoods will need to support small-scale manufacturing and innovation units for use by those wishing to use workshops, digital manufacturing and robots. The Sliperiet at Umea University in Sweden is an example of a community FabLab where people can freely come

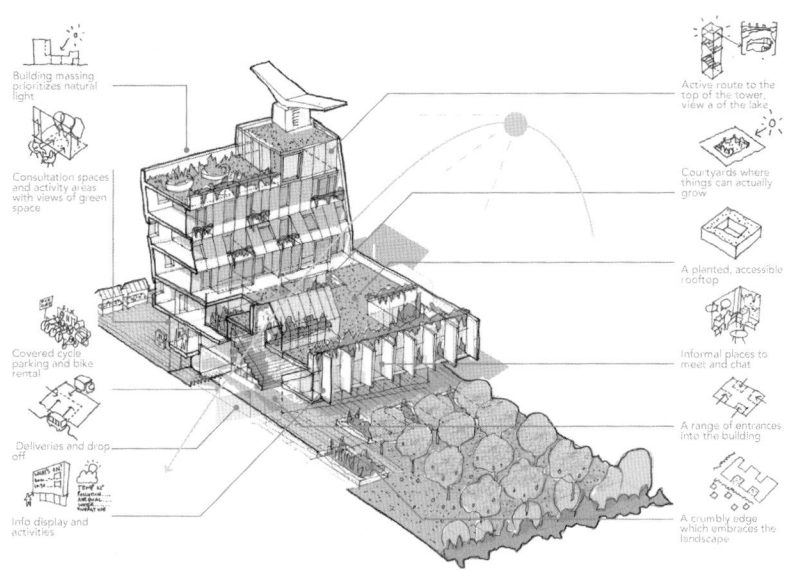

Rethinking local authorities around 20-minute communities

Figure 11.2
Concept visual of the Ebbsfleet Health and Wellbeing Hub. Source by and in memory of Toby Carr, © Sarah Wigglesworth Architects. Thanks also to Ebbsfleet Development Corporation.

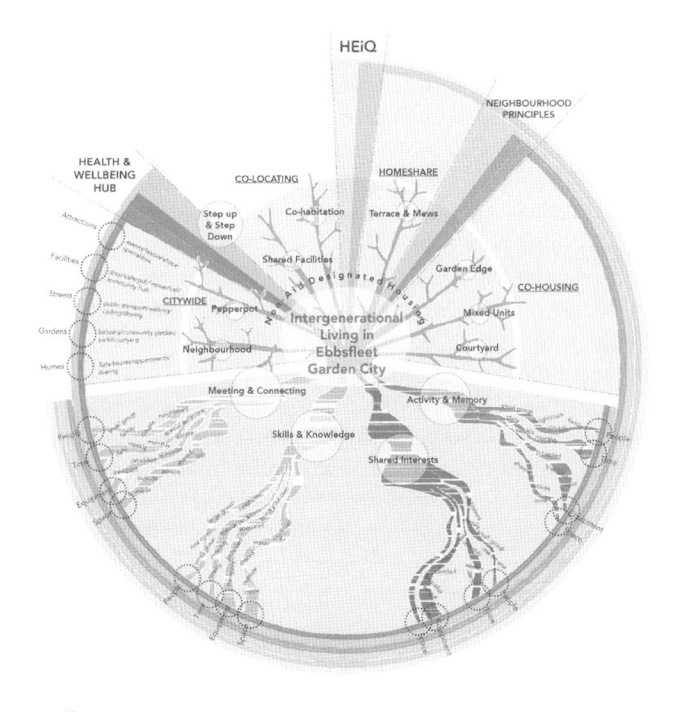

Figure 11.3
Diagram exploring the delivery of intergenerational living in Ebbsfleet. Source by and in memory of Toby Carr, © Sarah Wigglesworth Architects. Thanks also to Ebbsfleet Development Corporation.

Figure 11.4
Porters' Lodge, Sectie C, Eindhoven, Netherlands.
Source: © Flora Samuel.

and experiment with ideas using expensive kit - laser cutters, 3D printers and robots - that are also used by researchers in the institution. Universities tend to have equipment that is underutilised at certain times of the year. Cross cutting budgetary mechanisms and scheduling devices are needed to facilitate this kind of innovation. Every area needs a kind of nerve centre like the 'Porters' Lodge' in Sectie C in Eindhoven, in the Netherlands, where people go if they want to make things happen (Figure 11.4).

Ways have to be found to support the members of the public who choose to work voluntarily with the community team. I will call these people 'community team colleagues' for now. If, as discussed in the last chapter, Universal Basic Income becomes mainstream funding people for giving their time to the community should not be such an issue, as everyone will have enough income for a basic standard of living. In such a situation more people will be looking for useful and meaningful uses of their time as an alternative to work. According to recent research by the Cares Family and Power to Change 47% of UK adults say they would value being able to spend more time talking part in the community activities and connecting with their neighbours as the country gets back to normal (Cares Family & Power to Change, 2022, p. 27).

The process of working with community team colleagues needs to be carefully designed as a user experience journey, both face-to-face and digital, utilising industry best practice in this area (Nesta, 2018). Information design must be at the core of the community team's efforts as people need a baseline of clear and attractive information (with translations as necessary) upon which to base their thoughts and actions. Systems will be needed to make it simple and rewarding for a diverse sector of colleagues to find opportunities near them to contribute to suit their skills and level of commitment. When people have the ideas and enthusiasm to make good things happen themselves social investment funds need to be readily available to assist them on the journey. Community colleagues could be included in the allocation of these funds. One result will be a skilling up of the community at large.

Some members of the community team will have a strategic focus, liaising with other community teams and the wider region, some will focus on the 20 minute communities, while others will focus on the neighbourhoods within those communities. The latter team members will work across 'council' and privately owned property, the aim being to smooth the path across experiences of tenurial difference. Ideally drawn from the area itself they will need considerable on the ground knowledge and a bullish attitude to ironing out bureaucracy, facilitated by supportive managers who have a focus on wellbeing.

Building social value

The creation of connective social infrastructure at every level will be the strategic aim of the community team members responsible for social value. They will use all the tricks in the trade to do this – see, for example, the range of techniques developed by Participatory City to foster interaction (2020)- including arts, food, festival and fun. They will provide easy access to local volunteer opportunities and will have an overview of community facilities). They will have strong links to school, colleges and universities, curating opportunities for internships, work experience and other forms of volunteering and learning.

Those who have more of a social care role will check in on anyone vulnerable, connecting them to support networks a necessary. Social driven innovations will be particularly important for the delivery of care, particularly in later life (Fernandez Arrigoitia, West and Peace, 2019, p. 213). Technology Enabled Care systems that use sensors to remotely check on how people are doing will be important going forward but only in combination with other kinds of face-to-face care. Personal care will remain the most enduring of jobs in our onslaught of automation, but the people doing it need a proper career path, training and incentives.

Building environmental value

The community team with more environmental responsibilities will work closely with their 'social' colleagues to support residents in the development of more sustainable lifestyles. This will begin by helping new residents to understand how best to use the environmental systems built into their homes for the saving of resources and money. There is little point in living in a Passivhaus if you are going to wedge the door open while you have a fag. All homes will have a digital register enabling people to understand the workings and performance of their home over time. The team will support residents in the use of the home digital register and the gathering of post occupancy evaluation data, which will, in turn, feed into information gathering about the community as a whole. They will advise residents on the upgrades and changes to their home, for example, the buying of custom-build components to extend their homes. They will also offering alternative maintenance solutions to the paving over of gardens and chopping down of trees that is causing such damage to our native wildlife.

Green spaces need to be made as sustainable as possible (Thirlwall, 2020). This can be done in a low maintenance way. That each neighbourhood is an ecosystem, feeding into other ecosystems, will be at the forefront of the teams' minds. This includes managing our 1,000 square kilometres of road verges for biodiversity (Plantlife, 2019) and a cultural shift away from the tidiness epidemic that is helping to render so many species extinct and costs so much money. Rotherham Council, for example, made an 8 mile 'flower highway' for biodiversity while saving itself £25,000 on mowing (Gray, 2019). It seems that a quarter of local authorities in the UK have plans to rewild (Yeo, 2021). This has to become the norm.

In a housing system for hope and wellbeing there will be more and more parks and green spaces, pocket parks and meanwhile gardens curated with communities for maximum social value, all of this linked with active travel routes and integrated transport links for use both day and night. The Fields Inn Trust offers a useful minimum standard of green space per head of population which is currently used as an aspiration by some UK local authorities. Just imagine what might happen if we had more say in the maintenance and cultivation of our landscapes.

The community colleagues will be an integral part of the team, for example, sweeping up the leaves from trees in their streets and using them as free mulch on neighbourhood gardens. These kinds of efforts could be choreographed as enjoyable seasonal community events rather than the drain on local authority resources that they currently are. We all know places were life has been cheered by the presence of flowerpots and vegetables at the side of the pavement, as well as the activities of guerills gardeners, artists, crafters and others. One highways manager I spoke to said he'd be delighted if the local communities took up vegetable gardening on their grassy verges, all they had to do was ask, but I think it has to come as an invitation from the local authority. This too will be the responsibility of the community team.

In terms of environmental management (and value) highways, environmental services (for example, refuse collection), parks and other departments relating to 'ecosystem services' and promoting 'natural capital' (Gov.uk, 2013) must come under the umbrella of the community team which will balance a safety first attitude with the need to build social and environmental value. In the scenario that I am describing the environmental team will work closely with community colleagues to make incremental improvements to the way the built environment is managed. Community litter pickers powered by love are already commonplace. Imagine what might happen if they had more autonomy.

The value maps will capture waste production and incentivise reduction. The team will use the digital maps (and a system of human and digital 'sensors') to monitor and alleviate pollution and will have the authority to deliver fines on perpetrators which will, in turn, contribute to their income stream. More positively they will use the maps to record the revival of biodiversity, the sweetening of the air, the freshness of the water and moves towards more active and healthy lifestyles.

Guidance is needed on safely growing food in polluted urban settings, in particular on rooftop agriculture (Russo *et al.*, 2017). Edible gardens, roofs, walls and facades are all part of the mix. Creativity and imagination are needed, in other words input from the arts and humanities, to encourage people to take responsibility for their places and to treat them with care. Think about the initiative in Melbourne where trees have an email address so citizens can inform the local authority when they need help (increasingly important in climate change), one result being a flurry of love letters and eulogies to the trees (Ley, 2015).

Building economic value
In this way the community teams will be responsible for developing a diverse and rich ecosystem of employment and training opportunities, including jobs associated with housing delivery and retrofit. A recent Supplementary Planning Document by the 'Place-Shaping Team' within Strategic Planning at Tower Hamlets Council shows how 'Good Growth' can be a real possibility when community building is made into a priority (2021). There are plenty of resources on the UK government Towns Fund website for local authorities to make a business case for this (UK Gov, 2022).

In the UK there are some local authorities that are leading the way on holistic improvement through the protection and support of the local economy through their procurement practices. Preston in Lancashire in the North of England – not an affluent area – is a remarkable example. When, in 2015, a deal fell through for a large shopping centre with the usual anchor stores Preston Council set about developing improving its own economy through the development of what is known as the Preston Model (Preston City Council, 2020), in essence encouraging spending at every level to be spent locally, leading to local jobs, local identity and local pride, a process begun by asking local public institutions to use as many local suppliers as possible. In the past five years, Preston council and its partners have almost tripled their spending within the local economy, from £38 m to £111 m (Brown and Jones, 2021), at the same time creating a wealth of less well documented social value. The Preston Model has been an influence on a range of other authorities including North Ayrshire, Islington, Newham and the Welsh Assembly. Manchester City Council and Greater Manchester Combined Authority also offer inspiration in this area. The way in which procurement bids are scored can make a real difference. In Manchester 30% of the score relates to social value generation with the rest allocated to 'quality' and financial value. It doesn't seem like it will be long until we have a situation in which procurement systems are evaluated according to the triple bottom line of social, economic and environmental value. Being selected to deliver a project – whether it is rubbish collection or building – will be based on past performance. Evidence will be required of delivery in these areas, including a positive track record in community engagement.

Community team framework agreements will be carefully crafted to ensure that local small businesses are given a steady stream of employment from the placemaking team. Supply Change is an organisation that facilitates this kind of transformation (2020). One reason it will be possible to employ these small businesses is because procurement will give weight to social value and the outfit that gets the job won't always be the one that is cheapest – it will be the one that delivers the greatest holistic value and will always favour local suppliers.

Local procurement is key to delivering economic, environmental and social value. An example of the sort of thing I am talking about is offered by a recent report by the New Economics Foundation which makes a strong case for a set of comprehensive policy proposals for housing retrofit as part of 'a green recovery' which would bring 'massive benefits to the wider economy' (Brown et al., 2020, p. 4). This includes lastly an 'area- based delivery approach' which empowers local authorities to deal with local problems in a local way. Retrofit is cheaper if done on multiple homes than if done house by house. Efforts to environmentally retrofit neighbourhoods have to go in hand with efforts to socially retrofit neighbourhoods – social infrastructure needs to be built back into our places to make them better fit for purpose, particularly as we head towards enshrining the 20-minute community principle in policy. For this to happen the community team needs more control of the land and what happens on it.

The creation of a public land agency, or land commission, tasked with returning land to public ownership and the transition to a land tax system will have major implications for the community teams. Strong skills in green valuation and real estate will be needed for negotiating leases with developers that maximise community value for the local population and for the re-balancing of local economies. The way land and buildings are allocated and costed has profound impacts on the formation and sustainability of businesses, particularly small ones.

All community teams will have strategic and innovative housing delivery and retrofitting arms which aim to keep money within the local economy. Delivering more public rented housing has obvious benefits for the local economy in terms of jobs as well as for the building of community wealth for further investment. Families on the housing list will be given real choices of assured tenancies in good homes in good locations with a good mix of people. The 20-minute community mapping system will mean that there is a consistency around the kinds of facilities are available in an area. The community team will keep the homes that they deliver using rental income and government funding to deliver new homes. The money generated in this way may be augmented with local bonds and loans made by local people who want to invest in their places.

An acceleration in housing delivery across a joined up, well-funded and evidence-based public sector will transform local economies. Lessons will be learnt from the last great push on public housing during the years following the Second World War. Twenty-first-century public housing will be built utilising a growing body of increasingly sophisticated post occupancy evaluation knowledge on what really works. Residents will be involved in any process of development right from the very start through effective participation processes so there shouldn't be any nasty surprises to make people feel disempowered and defensive. NIMBYism will be on the wane. Residents will be heavily invested in the activities of the community team and confident that it will deliver on its promises. New developments will provide much needed affordable homes for their sons and daughters enabling them to stay close to family and community ties. The planners working in the background on the balancing of value maps across communities and regions will help make sure of this.

Ultimately the challenge of providing homes for the majority of the UK population will be one that the community teams approach with gusto. The government will have already invested in major off site manufacturing facilities well distributed around the UK making the use of MMC cheap and accessible, guaranteed and less risky. Because of their major contribution to social value local builders, suppliers and materials will be used for the groundworks and customisation of these modular homes in accordance with local design codes. The current trend for outsourcing to impersonal, non-local, private sector companies will be reversed as a means to save costs, regain control (Bawden, 2019). Public sector housing delivery will offer employees a proper structured career path with opportunities for learning and innovation which will, in turn, give rise to a range of new products, services and tools to be shared globally.

Conclusion

Watching investors and local authorities presenting their ideas at an impact investment event makes you start to see how hungry people are to do things better and differently. I argue that, as a necessary step towards a housing system that puts wellbeing front and centre, local authorities will need to be dissolved and reconstituted as community teams based on the 20-minute community, charged with the duty to balance social, environmental and economic value in their places, while working for the good of their wider region. Outcomes will be captured in the holistic value maps described in Chapter 9 and will be key tools for decision making with the public. If there is disagreement on the right course of action on any aspect of community development different options can be modelled and tested through the maps, with the process being as transparent as possible. In this chapter I have outlined some of the constituent skillsets and aptitudes needed within the community team if they are to deliver on social, environmental and economic value. These people are 'keyworkers' in the delivery of great homes and neighbourhoods. All of a sudden working for the council becomes a great deal more exciting.

Note

Justin Welby quotes, © Justin Welby, 2018, *Reimagining Britain*, Bloomsbury Continuum, an imprint of Bloomsbury Publishing Plc.

References

Bawden, A. (2019) 'Why councils are bringing millions of pounds worth of services back in-house'. Available at: https://www.theguardian.com/society/2019/may/29/bringing-services-back-in-house-is-good-councils.

Brown, D. et al. (2020) *A Green Stimulus for Housing: The Macroeconomics Impacts of a UK Whole Housing Retrofit Programme*. New Economics Foundation. Available at: https://neweconomics.org/uploads/files/Green-stimulus-for-housing_NEF.pdf.

Brown, M. and Jones, R.E. (2021) *Paint Your Town Red: How Preston Took Back Control and Your Town Can Too*. London: Watkins Media.

Cares Family & Power to Change. (2022) *Building Our Social Infrastructure*. The Cares Family and Power to Change. Available at: https://files.thecaresfamily.org.uk/thecaresfamily/images/Building-our-social-infrastructure-Final.pdf.

Fernandez Arrigoitia, M., West, K. and Peace, S. (2019) 'Transformation of Ageing and Meanings of the homes', *Home Cultures*, 15(3), pp. 209–221.

Gov.uk. (2013) *Ecosystems Services*. Available at: https://www.gov.uk/guidance/ecosystems-services.

Gray, B. (2019) *UK Roadside Turned into 8 Mile 'River of Flowers' to Help Support Wildlife, Adapt Environment*. Available at: https://www.adaptnetwork.com/planet/environment/rotherham-8-mile-river-of-flowers-support-wildlife/.

Hays, N. (2022) *The Trespasser's Companion*. London: Bloomsbury.

Ley, S. (2015) 'The Melbourne treemail phenomenon', *BBC News*. 16 July.

Manchester City Council. (2021) *Manchester City Council's Social Value Policy 2021*. Available at: https://democracy.manchester.gov.uk/documents/s23454/Appendix%203%20-%20Social%20Value%20Policy%202021.pdf.

Mayor of London. (2020) *Homes for Londoners: Affordable Homes Programme 2021–2026*. Available at: https://www.london.gov.uk/sites/default/files/201123_homes_for_londoners_-_affordable_homes_programme_2021-2026_-_funding_guidance_fa.pdf.

Nesta. (2018) *Playbook for Innovation Learning*. Available at: https://media.nesta.org.uk/documents/nesta_playbook_for_innovation_learning.pdf.

Newham Council. (2021) *Shape Newham*. Available at: https://shapenewham.co.uk/.

ONS. (2019) *Exploring the UK's Digital Divide*. Office for National Statistics. Available at: https://www.ons.gov.uk/peoplepopulationandcommunity/householdcharacteristics/homeinternetandsocialmediausage/articles/exploringtheuksdigitaldivide/2019-03-04.

Participatory City. (2020) *Tools to Act- Yesr 2 Report for the Every One Every Day Initiative in Barking and Dagenham*. Available at: http://www.participatory-city.org/research.

Plantlife. (2019) *Managing Grassland Road Verges*. Available at: https://www.plantlife.org.uk/uk/our-work/publications/road-verge-management-guide.

Preston City Council. (2020) *What is the Preston Model?* Available at: https://www.preston.gov.uk/article/1339/What-is-the-Preston-Model-.

Russo, A. et al. (2017) 'Edible green infrastructure: an approach and review of provisioning ecosystem services and disservices in urban environments', *Agriculture, Ecosystems and Environment*, 242, pp. 53–66.

Saaby, T. and Bauman, I. (2019) 'from city policy to the neighbourhood: an interview with Tina Saaby', in Trogal, K., Bauman, I., Lawrence, R. and Petrsecu, D. (eds.) *Architecture and Resilience: Interdisciplinary Dialogues*. London: Routledge, pp. 251–258.

Samuel, F. (2020) *Impact of Housing Design and Placemaking on Social Value and Wellbeing in the pandemic Interim Report.* CaCHE. Available at: https://housingevidence.ac.uk/publications/impact-of-housing-design-and-placemaking-on-social-value-and-wellbeing-in-the-pandemic-interim-report/

Supply Change. (2020) *Supply Change.* Available at: https://www.supplychange.co.uk/.

SWARCH. (2021) *Ebbsfleet's Neighbourhood Principles, Sarah Wigglesworth Architects.* Available at: https://www.swarch.co.uk/work/ebbsfleet-healthy-garden-city/.

Thirlwall, C. (2020) *From Idea to Site: A Project Guide to Creating Better Landscapes.* London: RIBA Books.

Tower Hamlets. (2021) *Central Area Good Growth Supplementary Planning Document Consultation Draft.* Place Shaping Team. Available at: https://www.architecture.com/awards-and-competitions-landing-page/awards/riba-presidents-awards-for-research/2020/mapping-social-values.

UK Gov (2022) *Towns Fund.* Available at: https://www.gov.uk/government/collections/towns-fund

Welby, J. (2018) *Reimagining Britain.* London: Bloomsbury.

Yeo, S. (2021) 'One quarter of English councils have planes to rewild. Does yours?', *Inkcap Journal.* Available at: https://www.inkcapjournal.co.uk/council-rewilding-england/.

Chapter 12

Professional knowledge and skills for building hope and wellbeing into housing and neighbourhoods

As long as professionals are entrusted with the curatorship of the built environment, they need an ethical, perhaps sworn, commitment to furthering hope and wellbeing through the highest calibre knowledge and skills. Only then might it be possible to regain the trust of communities that will be so necessary for the transformation of our housing system. New kinds of professionals and organisations are needed to support the development of a housing system that is a dynamic equilibrium of social, environmental and economic value. A range of new crosscutting skillsets are currently being formulated which sit very uneasily within the old and outdated Standard Industry Classification (SIC) and Standard Occupational Classification (SOC) codes that currently define our work (Samuel, 2018). How, for example, might we classify 'social activist' Hilary Cottam, trained as a social scientist, who was announced UK Designer of the Year in 2005 for her work on innovation with communities? In this chapter I will suggest some of the skills needed by built environment teams, whether in the public or private sector, to foster wellbeing in housing. The chapter encompasses data-driven digital design, valuation and finance, participation and the fostering of social value, delivery systems and organisational change. Put together these skills could also go a long way in leading the charge on sustainability (NESTA, 2017).

Data-driven digital design

We cannot make visible progress or know where best to put our efforts without creating a baseline data on what is already there. We can't however create a baseline without skills in data gathering and research. In Chapter 3 I made the case that housing professionals urgently need to develop their research capability in collaboration with universities and other disciplines in order to deliver a good evidence base for housing that fosters wellbeing.

The *Skills and Competency Framework* set out by the Centre for Digital Built Britain outlines those that are necessary to 'drive effective information management across our nations built environment'. It offers a range of choices set out in the format of a Top Trumps game (CDBB, 2021). A particularly interesting career option will be the 'ontologist', whose job is to design logical arrangements of information and collaborate with others to 'align ontologies'. In a separate piece of research by McKinsey a similar need for what they call 'platform integrators' is recognised (McKinsey, 2019, p. 17). Ontologists are urgently needed to make sure that the information flows across the different digital tools used by different professions – for example, Building Information Modelling (BIM), Computer-Aided Design (CAD), Geographic Information Systems (GIS) as well as the gaming engines that can bring these models alive in 3D (see, for example, Vu City) – align into a seamless whole. This seems to be the idea behind the National Digital Twin which isn't so much a model itself but a means to manage information. In essence digital models of buildings need to send information into digital models of places and vice versa. Only then can we promote systems thinking and link local impacts with the whole (CDBB, 2022).

In Chapter 9 I made the case for map making as a basis for transparent, inclusive, evidence-based decision making with communities. Most undergraduate geography students learn about Geographic Information Systems but GIS, QGIS and ArcGIS are less often taught to those studying the built environment. These programmes allow geographical information to be managed and analysed by pinpointing phenomena on maps which can be layered to produce holistic heatmaps of information and are central to the map based vision presented in this book.

Maps have important technical uses but also play a critical role in our connective social infrastructure, not least by making complex data simple and intelligible to others – see, for example, the Women's Safety Map (One Borough Voice, 2021) and the Metropolitan Police Crime Map (Metropolitan Police, 2022). They can also play a critical role in helping us understand the world view of others – for example, Our Stories which uses multi-layered mappings to give an account of LGBT+ experiences in Bristol tagged to certain places (Watershed, 2021). These kinds of maps, sometimes combined with digital games, can help local groupings with shared interests to coalesce. This is the idea behind Understory, a digital network map developed by the Onion Collective and Free Ice Cream (Understory, 2021). Digital groupings are particularly useful for resilience as they can be repurposed to assist with new situations. One example are the segmentation algorithms that are used by companies to cluster and rank their clients for marketing purposes. These can be reverse engineered to help develop self-help and coaching circles among community members (Strickler, 2019, p. 217).

Facilities management companies (and clients) have much to gain from the monitoring of buildings in use as the cost of running buildings for the comfort and wellbeing of inhabitants. No building or place should be delivered without a digital register, a wrapper or platform that can also be used for post occupancy evaluation, management and eventual retrofit. Building Information Modelling (BIM), if used cleverly, has extraordinary potential for collecting and sharing data both during construction and in use. I am currently working with the architecture practice Pollard Thomas and Edwards to explore ways in which BIM might be used to predict the likely social value of housing. Skills are needed in post occupancy evaluation, the collecting of quantitative data about things like energy use and more soft qualitative data about things like a sense of connection or identity (Hay et al., 2017). This data in turn can be collated across developments and estates for comparison.

The last couple of decades have seen the advance of parametric design through which the form of a building can be generated to respond to data algorithms relating to things like wind flow or footfall. Foreign Office Architects' Yokohama International Port Terminal (2002) is an early example. It is easy to imagine that social value map data will soon be built into parametric design programmes resulting, one day, in almost self generating building and place designs. If you think this is far-fetched look no further than Nicholas de Monchaux's groundbreaking book *Local Code* (2016). Ultimately codes are rules to govern action so communicating the implications of coding to the public is going to be extremely important going forward requiring a skillset of its own, perhaps 'data design and interpretation'.

Given that architecture practices like Nox have already pioneered interactive art pieces that enable the public to change its form, colour or sound, it seems quite likely that one day the public can get involved in the actual co-design of buildings which could take shape almost as a form of open-source architecture, see, for example, the Wikihouse (2021). It will however take a while for untrained people and programmes to get up to speed in delivering such co-designed environments. Professionals are needed to support such processes.

Holistic valuation, finance and procurement

Valuation skills that account for the full range of social, environmental and economic value are going to be vital for the delivery of equitable places. If predictions that 95% of the valuer's role will be automated over the next decade are correct (Thompson, 2017), it will be interesting to see how computers are programmed to make valuations that go beyond money. That we are at a critical juncture in all this cannot be overemphasised. If we fail to offer programmers a practical format for capturing social value it will not be included in the valuations of the future.

Having said this the future is looking promising for ethical investment as Environmental, Social and Governance (ESG) hurtles up the agenda of developers, investors and others, sometimes leading to preferential interest rates. Increasingly social value and green bonds are being used to drum up project finance for social rented housing (Willaims, 2021). Tideway, a project to clean up the river Thames, provides an interesting example of the use of green bonds to finance its activities (Tideway, 2018). Here the funding drove the behaviour of the client to focus on legacy outcomes.

At present, because of inertia within the system, pension funds tend to invest their money outside the UK, with very few investing outside London. This has had significant impacts on our ability to develop affordable housing. The Good Economy, working with Pensions for Purpose, is leading the agenda on Place Based Impact Investment (PBII), encouraging fund managers to invest locally by developing pilot projects across the UK. They describe the 'pillars of PBII' as: housing; SME finance; clean energy; infrastructure and regeneration with a potential extra pillar for rural situations being agriculture and forestry. They suggest that location should become part of the way funds report on their activities, including risk of negative impacts on local communities (The Good Economy, 2021). The team cite Legal and General (L & G) as pioneers in PBII, one example being affordable housing delivered within Salford Media City. There is an opportunity here for fund managers to deliver holistic value to investors and society alike, by offering a variety of local and sustainable opportunities for investment, notably in housing. This may require a return to a version of local – and therefore high social value – bank branches as a strong knowledge of the context will be needed to offer loans in a context specific way. New kinds of bank such as the 'friendly lenders', for example, Triodos, the Ecology Building Society, that offer such a personalised and understanding service to co-operative house builders are gaining ground. The Islamic bank plays a particular role in supporting Muslim communities in line with their beliefs. I anticipate a time when shares in co-operative housing are available from stockbroking Apps. An ability to translate the social value of small, high impact initiatives such as community led housing into investment mechanisms and ethical funds is going to be very important going forward.

One reason that estate agents need greater regulation is because home buyers need to be able to trust their advice (Best, 2019). Once again it comes back to offering transparent and reliable information. It is very difficult for buyers to make sense of the myriad mortgage products that are out there on the market – for example, offset mortgages, shared ownership, green mortgages, reverse mortgages in terms of equity release. Susan J. Smith suggests that new and 'radical' forms of equity finance could result in new kinds of partnerships between institutions and individuals with new forms of finance that foster a sharing of responsibility for the conception, upkeep and future of our housing stock. Excitingly such processes could be 'used to dissolve the stark binary between owners and renters that tenure-divided societies endure, creating myriad options for home occupiers to part-buy, part- share, part-rent and part-steward in housing systems comprising a thousand tiny tenures'. She calls for 'housing that is tenure neutral and profoundly diverse, harnessing the many varieties of residential capitalism to break the spell of owner occupation, without reinventing the wheel of renting' (Smith, 2015, p. 77). For this to happen skills in innovative and co-created finance systems need to be made into a priority, with insurance systems to suit. People need to be able to make trade-offs between housing, housing finance and housing infrastructure as they move through their housing pathways (Graham, 2022). Ultimately the housing sector has to be much cleverer in offering financial, fabric and capability choices to people at different points in their lives.

Lack of certainty about long-term funding impacts on the ability of community organisations to deliver on more long-term strategy. Fundraising events that tend to be our default position – quizzes, fairs and open days – all have an important role in creating social glue but increasingly communities are turning to crowdfunding for specific initiatives like buying up redundant space for community use (Gov.uk, 2021). There are a significant range of opportunities to access community funding if you have the know-how. There is a place here for a skillset that combines design research and funding nous as demonstrated amply by

Figure 12.1
Grangetown Pavilion, Cardiff.
Source: © Flora Samuel.

Mhairi McVicar who is academic lead of Community Gateway (Figure 12.1), is a pioneering organisation that links academics, design professionals, residents and businesses in the Grangetown area of Cardiff in Wales. McVicar played a key role in securing Lottery funding to rejuvenate a dilapidated bowls pavilion into what is now the Grangetown Pavilion (McVicar, 2020) and has, since then, been instrumental in developing novel methods to capture its impact. She, and its architect Dan Benham, have had an ongoing relationship with the building, its community and its manager as its fabric evolves to include new people and opportunities. Procurement systems are needed to fund this kind of ongoing social facilities management that give it the respect that it deserves.

Participation professionals and the generation of social value

'The centrality of citizens and their collective voice to civic environmentalism suggests a new role for government and experts alike' (Karvonen and Yocom, 2011, p. 9). The field of community consultation needs to be professionalised, with its own code of conduct, best practice indicators and training programmes. The International Association for Public Participation, initiated in Australia, is working in this direction (iap2, 2022). Participation professionals will play a crucial role in the inclusive masterminding of citizens assemblies and in deliberative processes, for example, in setting up representative panels of citizenry to comment on planning applications and so on. They will have particular skills in gathering data, for example, on baseline demographics, and a range of tactics at their disposal for making engagement both inclusive and engaging right across the project lifecycle and into use. Participation practices are highly interdisciplinary. Urban Symbiotics, a collaboration between an architect and a product designer, is one example.

If community team HQs are to be set up all over the nation as a nexus for discussion about the future of places, digital and face to face, expertise is needed on how to make these places as attractive and accessible as possible. As mentioned in Chapter 9 the *Community Consultation for Quality of Life* project (CCQOL, 2021) is experimenting with these issues through pilot projects across all four nations (Figure 12.1), with the aim of developing a code of conduct for participation in the UK. No consultation should happen without a 'statement of influence' that makes clear to the community exactly what can be changed as a result of the event. No consultation should happen without a feedback loop that tells the community what was achieved and why. All consultations need to report on the number and diversity of the people they consulted with. Consultation teams must make real efforts to integrate with communities, in the words of PhD community researcher Alice Mpofu-Coles: 'hard to reach are not hard to reach, you just have to come to them'. It is important to understand who the 'community gatekeepers' are and cultural traditions of allowing certain family members to be the voice. It helps if the researchers come from a similar demography to the people you want to hear from – 'use young people to reach young people', observed another community member we talked with. If this was done properly with community members trained up to undertake consultations the benefits in terms of skilling up could be immense.

The CCQOL team worked with the digital participation platform Commonplace, one of several on the market, which are growing in sophistication, capability and fun. Rather than make assumptions about how people engage with technology, digital tools can help people develop confidence in this area if people are on hand to help get through any hurdles. Mpofu-Coles observes: 'what we are lacking with technology is patience'. It was certainly our experience, particularly working with older people, that the urban room became a place to support the development of digital literacy.

Commonplace has a useful button to increase the accessibility of its site, but language remains a stumbling block – in Reading some 150 languages are spoken in city centre schools and Google Translate is not yet really sophisticated enough to be used for participation purposes. Further, according to the National Literacy Trust, 16.4% of adults in England, or 7.1 million people, can be described as having 'very poor literacy skills', also known as 'functionally illiterate'. Tactics are needed to cross language barriers including the careful use of highly visual information design as well as chains of community translators who can help bring people into the fold, but this is a labour intensive process.

Until a culture of consultation is embedded in our community incentives will be needed to get people to engage. These can take a variety of forms, for example, activities for children, art installations, games, learning activities or performance. There is a particular role for the arts and humanities in sparking people's interest. The artist Jeanne Van Heeswijk specialises in taking up residence in communities and helping things to happen, for example, on 2up2down in Anfield, her aim being to 'radicalize the local' (Homebaked, 2021). In the Reading urban room activities set up by the Museum of English Rural Life and Reading Museum brought volunteers, life and interest to our no frills empty shop (Figures 9.3 and 9.4). The physical space of consultation and the things that happen there need to be like a stage set that shifts to accommodate different demographies and interests, a free destination for all ages. In the Reading urban room Shanzina Alam experimented with making dedicated quiet times in the calendar for people on the autism spectrum to make their opinions heard. Building on what is known about designing schools for autistic pupils and our consultations with experts in the field we suggest that this requires a radical edit of the information on offer, a shift to softer lighting and softer spaces and the offering of a range of advance information to visitors so they know what to expect from the place. There is currently a deficit of knowledge among participation professionals on what communities like this might need. Ensuring that participation caters for communities with distinct needs is likely to be recognised as a specialist role in the field.

Particular skills are needed for the activation of place in a way that brings people in on the journey. Building opportunities piece by piece has to be the way forward as it allows for incremental testing and the development of trust with locals. In some ways it is a form of co-design. Carl Turner (of Turner Works) was a founder of developers Makeshift, re-envisioning the role of the architect as an enabler of short-term usage on what is commonly called 'meanwhile space'. He proposes a 'stepping stone economy' of incremental change, offering categories of intervention based on life span. An example is Pop Brixton (a Makeshift project designed by Turner Works) which is a five-year workspace project offering a range of size and types of accommodation, allowing people and organisations to move through the building as they grow and change. It now has over 200 members and has created more than 250 jobs (Figure 12.2). In these places local people take over the project enabling it to develop a life of its own. One of the criteria for getting one of the oversubscribed creative spaces in another Makeshift project, Peckham Levels, is to be local. Hackney Bridge, a third project developed by Makeshift, has been built on an empty site on the edge of the Olympic Park offering makerspace during the day and event space in the evening, including a 500 person event space (Figure 12.3). The building is open 24/7 offering series of routes through the space, 'a canvas for creativity'

Figure 12.2
Pop Farm at Pop Brixton, Turner Works.
Source: ©Tim Crocker.

Professional knowledge and skills for building hope and wellbeing

Figure 12.3
Turner Works Hackney Bridge.
Source: © Tim Crocker.

where local artists can showcase their wares while building identity. The lease for Hackney Bridge is only 12 years long so the building was conceived in circular economy terms, for re-use and recycling. Turner Works are now testing the viability of their ideas outside London with considerable success. As part of the development of a placemaking vision for Weston-super-Mare, the team were tasked with crafting a new brand identity for the place to up levels of energy, oil the wheels of investment and funding. They used this as an opportunity to get people involved in generating the vision (superweston.net) by inviting community members to send in postcards showing their wishes for Weston. Together these can be collated into something more holistic (Figure 12.4). The project, including the repurposing of a shopping centre into a cultural centre, the Weston General Store, has enabled the Council to win more funding to develop the hub and event space.

What I anticipate is that those who do work with people in the flesh will be working hard to make the experiences that they deliver that bit more magical. In *Why Architects Matter* I argued that one of the futures for the architectural profession will be in the design of 'experiences and transformations' (Gilmore and Pine II, 2007, pp. 46–47). Face-to-face consultation work will need not only to take on dimensions of pedagogy, theatre, art, performance, conviviality and food will bring the consultation into vivid 3D, the city once more used as a theatre for debates on public life. In her remarkable thesis on consultation Kate Langham has advocated the use of cake and biscuits as a modelling material that everyone can enjoy without feeling under pressure (Langham, 2020). We all need more fun in our lives. Play: Disrupt is an organisation that uses humour and a touch of the surreal to get people thinking about their places, poking fun at existing practices, for example, 'Octopus' a satirical housing agency bent on presenting 'the very worst ideas in development' (Figure 12.5). It will take a very particular kind of management, come planner come circus master, come arts administrator, come

Figure 12.4
Postcards expressing Weston wishes from the community. Turner Works, Super Weston.
Source: © Tim Crocker.

Professional knowledge and skills for building hope and wellbeing

Figure 12.5
Play: Disrupt at work.
Source: © Play Disrupt.

mediator to co-create community programmes of delights, deploying boats, barrows and bicycles to reach out to far flung communities. This is the place of art and culture in our cities in developing the economy of the imagination.

Engagement with planning has to be made a lot more appealing if we are to include young people in debates about the future of places. Engagement helps young people understand how democracy is supposed to work and how they can bring change to the system (Grant, 2020). There is a need for built environment professionals to work more closely with youth workers and teachers to develop and implement a holistic vision for a child friendly built environment (Wood *et al.*, 2019, p. 49). Cardiff Council has been doing some interesting work in using the computer game Minecraft for consulting with children on what they want from their places (Cardiff Council, 2020). The focus here is on giving children a voice which is why Cardiff is one of the six cities in the UK that has UNICEF 'child friendly city' status (UNICEF, 2021). Although Virtual Reality might still be a bit clunky, its use as a tool of participation seems undeniable. Many design practices have developing Virtual Reality offers, but these need interdisciplinary input, investment and gaming engines to make them sing. There is so much opportunity to do consultation better, developing new tools and services in the process.

Home builders

A generation brought up on SimCity and used to buying flat pack kitchens which they design at home on kitchen software will not be daunted by buying ready-made custom-built components to be plugged together into a home. For IKEA it is the logical extension of their current business offer of flat pack, affordable designerly furnishings, fitted kitchens and so on. IKEA has being building houses in Sweden and Finland through its development company BoKlok since 1997 in a joint venture with the construction arm of SKANSKSA. Such homes must be built with mending and recycling firmly in mind, leading to the development of a new breed of makers and menders. The design of the user journey through buying component parts, planning, assemblage and aftercare for these systems will take new kinds of skillsets, particularly if technology enabled care takes hold.

Many people aspire to self build and communal living but few have the time, energy or knowledge to make it happen. There is a specialist role for community development architects here in facilitating the journey towards realisation, as architect Patrick Devlin of Pollard Thomas and Edwards did for the Older Women's Co-operative Housing (OWCH) community in North London (Figures 12.6 and 12.7). The ability to keep the energy up on a project like this, sometimes over decades, is more akin to a vocation than anything else.

In a housing system that that fosters hope and wellbeing it should be easy to find local builders to work with as they will have an obvious presence within the community not only building housing, but also providing training, internships and self-build support. Changes to procurement discussed in the last chapter will mean that they will receive a steady stream of employment from the community team, but for this to happen local contractors need to skill up in terms of developing, measuring and reporting on their own social value. I've known my local builder for 30 years. I bump into him and his wife in the park. He has a good team of skilled workers that he has supported carefully for decades, carefully nurturing new talent into the team. I trust him not to overcharge me. I reckon that if we calculated the social value of Gary's business it would be extremely high but I can't imagine him doing such a thing as the processes are too abstruse and anyway he is too busy. These kinds of businesses need to get credit for what they do in the community. They need support not only to stay afloat but to thrive.

Figure 12.6
The OWCH community.
Source: © Joe Okpako.

Figure 12.7 OWCH new ground housing.
Source: © Galit Seligmann.

How to build a housing system for hope and wellbeing

Figure 12.8
Mass Bespoke housing under construction, Park Road, Doncaster.
Source: © Mass Bespoke.

Figure 12.9
Mass Bespoke housing completed in Park Road, Doncaster for Doncaster Central Development Trust.
Source: © Mass Bespoke.

One of the problems for small builders is their inability to innovate. This is what makes the Mass Bespoke project based in Leeds so remarkable (Bauman and Harker, 2020). The team here are collaborating with local builders, using a panel system to create bespoke housing solutions (Figures 12.8 and 12.9). A revamped housing delivery system will multiply opportunities for these types of company.

Making Modern Methods of Construction mainstream will require considerable upskilling of the construction team (LABC, 2020). So frustrated was TV presenter George Clark with lack of training in this area that he set up the charity the Ministry of Building, Innovation and Education (MOBIE), offering dedicated modules to learning organisations that would give students direct experience of these new kinds of facility. As MOBIE CEO Mark Southgate observes about the current lack of interest in construction careers. 'Millennials don't want to go there, they want to use those design skills, they are intrinsically digital and design, and we've got to tap into that' (LABC, 2020). It is very possible to put the pride and pleasure back into housebuilding as a skilled, largely warm, safe, offsite, manufacturing type enterprise involving the deployment of robot operatives or as a crafts based enterprise in which making and design come into focus through close knowledge of local materials, people and place with hybrid offerings in between.

In a world of robotic manufacturing laboriously hand crafted homes – sometimes involving the labour of the client, their family and friends – will have a special place in people's hearts. Architect Piers Taylor regularly undertakes projects with people who have never done any building before. This can be a very positive and empowering experience, but it sits uneasily within the rules and regulations surrounding construction. His work points to a need for forms of procurement, insurance and building control that make the risk of building with amateurs simple to negotiate. These things currently make working with contingent processes and materials (for example, wood found in a forest) very difficult to deal with. It is the very nature of many of the eco buildings that they are built by hand, slowly, often with or by non-experts. This goes against the levels of professionalism and bureaucracy that often accompany the construction process and its certification. Even if a building is hand made it still needs to be signed off by building control so they need training and encouragement to work with the local, the recycled and the hand made.

Hopeful organisations

The business models and missions of the organisations responsible for the planning and delivery of homes will also need a revamp to ensure that social, environmental and economic value are being promoted within their organisational structures. Employee ownership, for example, is known for improving productivity and wellbeing at work and at home (Wilkinson and Pickett, 2019). Accreditations like B Corp will be important to sustainably minded clients and investors – Stride Treglown is one of the first architecture practices in the UK to achieve this status. My research colleagues Stantec have been named 'fifth most sustainable company in the world' by Corporate Knights. This has resulted in a boost to their share value. I am not surprised by this as I have seen how careful they are in aligning what they do with their principles, developing knowledge systems to advance social value across the organisation. Stantec work for Grosvenor who themselves spend a great deal of energy ascertaining the sustainable credentials of their own supply chain. At the core of these organisations is a recognition of the need to reflect critically on performance over time, something that can make the job a great deal more purposeful (while enhancing the business brand). The management of data to find out how to do things better, not just in the business itself, but also in its supply chains will become a key issue for organisations who are series about improving their impact (and securing ethical and green investment).

Crucially housing organisations need to become more diverse, not just because they should, but also because diversity leads to a greater gene pool of ideas and that in turn assists with innovation and salience (Rock and Grant, 2016). A good place to start with this is a strong commitment to training up the next generation through internships, apprenticeships and other flexible and accessible modes of engagement. It is so important that organisations get involved in training and education as the experiences that they offer bring subjects alive for students while smoothing their path into jobs (Kapetaniou and McIvor, 2020). The provision of high-quality training opportunities also contributes to the social value of an organisation and needs therefore be a consideration when evaluating teams for contracts, though not as a tick box exercise. The Royal Institute of British Architects has a remarkable National Schools Programme involving over 500 'architect ambassadors' who make this contribution out of the kindness of their own hearts. These kinds of activities shouldn't be nice to haves, they need to be built into the fabric of the system.

Conclusion

There is so much opportunity to be had for built environment professionals who are pivoting into the world of hope and wellbeing. This chapter has set out some of the skillsets needed to fulfil this demand. Built environment teams will need to work closely with digital designers and programmers on the development of new tools and experiences without forgetting the importance of real-world interaction. They will need to be conversant with the delivery and evidencing of social, environmental and economic value and they will know how to embed it into their business models. A new cohort of participation professionals will work creatively and rigorously at the interface between experts and the public, fostering the sharing of knowledge, risk and responsibility (Nowotny, Scott and Gibbons, 2001). They will support communities in activating their places through green finance, incremental strategy, building and fun. As Hilary Cottam has shown so much is about leveraging the latent potential of networks. Ultimately housing needs to be reframed around the delivery of capabilities, helping people to help themselves (Foye, 2021), the subject of the next chapter.

References

Bauman, I. and Harker, K. (2020) 'New infrastructure for communities who want to build', in F. Samuel and E. Hatleskog (eds.), *Social Value in Architecture*. London: Wiley (Architectural Design, 90), pp. 38–45.

Best, R. (2019) *Regulation of Property Agents Working Group Final Report*. UK Gov. Available at: https://assets.publishing.service.gov.uk/government/uploads/system/uploads/attachment_data/file/818244/Regulation_of_Property_Agents_final_report.pdf.

Cardiff Council. (2020) *'Craft Your City' - Child Friendly Cardiff Asks Youngsters to Help Shape Cardiff*. Available at: https://www.cardiffnewsroom.co.uk/releases/c25/25659.html.

CCQOL. (2021) *Community Consultation for Quality of Life*. Available at: ccqol.org.

CDBB. (2021) *Skills and Competency Framework*. Centre for Digital Built Britain. Available at: https://www.cdbb.cam.ac.uk/files/010321cdbb_skills_capability_framework_vfinal.pdf.

CDBB. (2022) *Centre for Digital Built Britain*. Available at: https://www.cdbb.cam.ac.uk/what-we-do/national-digital-twin-programme.

Foye, C. (2021) 'Ethically -speaking, what is the most reasonable way of evaluating housing outcomes', *Housing, Theory and Society*, 38(1), pp. 115–131.

Gilmore, J.H. and Pine II, J. (2007) *Authenticity: What Consumers Want*. Boston, MA: Harvard Business School Press.

Gov.uk. (2021) *'Right to Regenerate' To Turn Derelict Buildings Into Homes and Community Assets*. Available at: https://www.gov.uk/government/news/right-to-regenerate-to-turn-derelict-buildings-into-homes-and-community-assets.

Graham, P. (2022) *Adjustable Housing*. PhD thesis University of Reading.

Grant, H. (2020) 'It isn't safe to walk": how would young people plan UK streets?', *The Guardian*. 19 Nov. Available at: https://www.theguardian.com/environment/2020/nov/19/nobody-asks-us-kids-the-youth-led-approach-to-improving-uk-streets?CMP=share_btn_tw.

Hay, R. *et al.* (2017) *Building Knowledge: Pathways to POE*. RIBA/University of Reading. Available at: https://www.architecture.com/knowledge-and-resources/resources-landing-page/post-occupancy-evaluation.

Homebaked. (2021) *Jeanne van Heeswijk*. Available at: https://homebaked.org.uk/about_us/team/jeanne_van_heeswijk_board_member/.

iap2. (2022) *International Association for Public Participation*. Available at: https://www.iap2.org/mpage/Home.

Kapetaniou, C. and McIvor (2020) *Going Green: Preparing the UK Workforce for the Transition to a Net-Zero Economy*. NESTA. Available at: https://www.nesta.org.uk/report/going-green-preparing-uk-workforce-transition-net-zero-economy/.

Karvonen, A. and Yocom, K. (2011) 'The civics of urban nature; enacting hybrid landscapes', *Environment and Planning A*, 43(6), pp. 1305–1322. Available at: http://journals.sagepub.com.idpproxy.reading.ac.uk/doi/abs/10.1068/a43382.

LABC. (2020) *Modern Methods: Where Are the Skills?*, *LABC Warranty*. Available at: https://www.labcwarranty.co.uk/blog/modern-methods-of-learning-how-are-the-builders-of-tomorrow-learning-about-offsite-construction/.

Langham, K. (2020) *Play As a Design Tool: Co-Designing Shared Community Space*. Bath Spa. Available at: https://core.ac.uk/display/327986749.

McKinsey. (2019) *Scaling Modulor Construction*. Global Infrastructure Initiative. Available at: https://www.mckinsey.com/~/media/mckinsey/business%20functions/operations/our%20insights/voices%20on%20infrastructure%20scaling%20modular%20construction/gii-voices-sept-2019.pdf

McVicar, M. (2020) '"Engender the confidence to demand better" the value of architects in community asset transfer', in Samuel, F. and Hatleskog, E. (eds.) *Social Value in Architecture*. London: Wiley (Architectural Design), pp. 46–51.

Metropolitan Police. (2022) *What's Happening in Your Area?* Available at: https://maps.met.police.uk/.

de Monchaux, N. (2016) *Local Code:3659 Proposals About Data, Design and the Nature of Cities*. Princeton: Princeton Architectural Press.

NESTA. (2017) *The Future of skills: Employment in 2030*. Available at: https://www.nesta.org.uk/publications/future-skills-employment-2030 (Accessed: 23 October 2017).

Nowotny, H., Scott, P. and Gibbons, M. (2001) *Rethinking Science: Knowledge and the Public in an Age of Uncertainty*. London: Wiley.

One Borough Voice. (2021) *Women's Safety Map*. Available at: https://oneboroughvoice.lbbd.gov.uk/women-s-safety?tool=map#tool_tab.

Rock, D. and Grant, H. (2016) 'Why diverse teams are smarter', *Harvard Business Review* [Preprint]. Available at: https://hbr.org/2016/11/why-diverse-teams-are-smarter.

Samuel, F. (2018) *Why Architects Matter: Evidencing and Communicating the Value of Architects*. London: Routledge.

Smith, S.J. (2015) 'Owner occupation: at home in a spatial, financial paradox', *International Journal of Housing Policy*, 15(1), pp. 61–83.

Strickler, Y. (2019) *This Could Be our Future: A Manifesto for a More Generous World*. London: Penguin.

The Good Economy. (2021) *Scaling up institutional investment for place based impact*. Impact Investing Institute. Available at: https://www.impactinvest.org.uk/wp-content/uploads/2021/05/Place-based-Impact-Investing-White-Paper-May-2021.pdf.

Thompson, B. (2017) *Technology: Future Impact on Surveying*. RICS. Available at: https://www.isurv.com/info/390/features/11433/technology_future_impact_on_surveying.

Tideway. (2018) *Green Bond Report*. Available at: https://www.tideway.london/media/3128/a0601_green-bond-report-2018_vis8.pdf.

Understory. (2021) *Understory*. Available at: https://www.understory.community/.

UNICEF. (2021) *Make Your City Child-Friendly!* Available at: https://childfriendlycities.org/.

Watershed. (2021) *Bristol Stories*. Available at: https://www.bristolstories.org/map.

Wikihouse. (2021) *Wikihouse*. Available at: https://www.wikihouse.cc/.

Wilkinson, R. and Pickett, K. (2019) *The Inner Level: How More Equal Societies Reduce Stress, Restore Sanity and Improve Everyone's Well-Being*. Penguin.

Williams, S. (2021) *ESG Capital Markets Issuance Exceeds £4bn for Housing Associations*. Social Housing. Available at: https://www.socialhousing.co.uk/news/esg-capital-markets-issuance-exceeds-4bn-for-housing-associations-70958.

Wood, J., Bornat, D. and Bicquelet-Lock, A. (2019) *Child Friendly Planning in the UK: A Review*. RTPI. Available at: https://aplaceinchildhoodorg.files.wordpress.com/2019/12/national-planning-policy-report.pdf.

Chapter 13

Common knowledge

The challenges are with the community. The solutions are with the community.
Esther Oenga

Housing is too important to be left in the hands of professionals and many are losing hope in policy makers to deliver so we, I am talking here with my citizen hat on, have to roll up our sleeves and join the cause. A possible housing system such as the one I have described is built on a capabilities approach that will make it easy for 'lay', 'ordinary' or 'unskilled' people to get involved in housing and placemaking whatever their background or abilities. As well as being important for hope and wellbeing this matters for work and the development of the kind of team and leaderships skills that are going to be vital for bringing about the 'eco-transformation' that we need to transport us safely to the end of this century. This chapter sets out some of the things we can do, to take responsibility for housing and for ourselves, to reach 'citizen control' the culmination of Arnstein's 'Ladder of Participation' (Arnstein, 1969).

Learning for community led housing

I am learning what is possible in this area firsthand. Over the last year or so I've been working with my daughter and our friend Michelle (young women) on plans to develop a community interest development company, Recommon, to help mainstream co-operative housing. Our plan, in the first instance was to learn through doing, repurposing a farm into a place for people to live and work (online), growing food on the side and leaving the rest for nature, with open access for everyone. We believe that there is a particular need to provide homes for people with a range of different aptitudes and dispositions who want to live independently, while having but have the benefits of community, are not rich, may not be confident about taking up a hammer and chisel but want to live in a resilient way, while bringing more jobs and diversity to more rural areas. Our plan was to have different levels of membership, with Recommon providing an affordable countryside community to both permanent and transient members as well as an investment vehicle for those who support the idea but may not want to live there. In particular we see around us people who identify as women who don't want to have children because of the Climate Change Emergency, who lack familial support in these days of broken homes, but who want safety and conviviality in numbers as they grow older. There are many other types of people who would also benefit from a safe and affordable haven. This has been borne out by responses we have received from people interested in joining the cause including families racialised black and couples who identify as gay who say they wouldn't feel comfortable to live in rural areas alone without a shield of other people. Lack of diversity in community led housing whether urban or rural is a problem (Graham, 2022). Balancing collegiality with cliquiness is a challenge. Ideally these kinds of communities need to be developed by locals who would welcome the opportunities and value that they bring to the area.

A breakthrough came when we arrived at the Community Land Trust website which directed us to Co-operative Housing Wales and the team there who have been nurturing us through a carefully honed process ever since. Apparently, it takes an average of seven years for such a community to get off the ground, a leviathan amount of time for people who need somewhere to live. The first step was to decide on our decision making structure as this would be the foundation for everything else. The Wales Co-Operative Centre has a useful factsheet (based on Sociocracy for All, 2021). We had assumed it would be 'democratic', based on numbers of votes, but further investigation revealed we wanted something more fast and sensitive to need, in other words 'sociocracy' which requires a commitment to learning through the process while distributing power. Our next step was to work out what our legal structure might be. We were guinea pigs for the new Wayshaper Tool developed by the Confederation for Co-operative Housing (CCH, 2021), essentially a set of cards that pushed us to make choices about what we want from Recommon. To be a Community Benefit Society and issue community shares you have to be prepared to relinquish control over the organisation that you are building, possibly altogether. A great deal of pro bono work has to go into the whole process and this may never be paid back if you lose control or have to give up because of an inability to get planning permission. This, I think, is a disincentive for young people who lack a financial cushion to get involved in setting up a Community Benefit Society. They can't afford to do all this work for no return. This is why we proposed a Community Interest Company for Recommon, with the housing itself being a Co-Operative, our ambition being to build more than one. Our hope was to support the development of a patchwork of these farms across the landscape to provide an access corridor for people and wildlife alike, mainstreaming this way of life in the process.

Useful information has been put out by Wrigleys Solicitors who specialise in helping groups like ours to get off the ground (Wrigleys, 2018). There is a lot of practical advice out there on whether and how to put out a community share offer (for an evolving example of the documents needed see Yorspace, 2022). This may or may not be done with the help of platforms such as Crowdfunder or Ethex which can also offer assistance in the administration. Most projects come into being with a hybrid format of community shares, loans and other kinds of finance but the whole thing is difficult without personal funds, some kind of collateral and cheap access to land. A recent very successful offer was undertaken by Bridport Cohousing, a relatively large scheme (Bridport Cohousing, 2021). The ability to go for community shares is influenced on the way in which the team coalesces as a legal entity. The kinds of lenders who support these kinds of projects – the Ecology Building Society, Radical Routes and so on – make a business of working closely with community groups to make their projects happen. It is apparently never too early to get in touch with ideas.

In this way we are pushing on through the jargon towards the twin hurdles of planning and finance, facilitated by mentors along the way. The prognosis for getting planning permission in rural areas is bleak unless you are able, like volume house builders, to get sites allocated in the local plan. It seems likely that we will be forced to relocate our ambitions to the city – Cardiff where we live – as getting planning permission in rural areas is so hard, but the cost of land is likely to present a new, and perhaps insuperable, hurdle. Hearing about the experiences of Yorspace in York we know it won't be easy. If the council was prepared to lease us cheap land the situation would be very different.

Building co-operative housing requires the kind of professional knowledge, power and financial backing that is beyond most community groups. Further it is very difficult to get through the chicken and egg of land and planning. You need to be a cash buyer to buy land and you don't really want to buy land if you don't know you have some chance of getting planning permission. The whole world of buying 'options' on land feeling terrifyingly technical and risky. Hence, in part, my plea for prioritising social value in land decision making. All the difficulties faced by groups like ours could be easily addressed through a housing system as described in this book. Communities need affordable access to land to build homes.

Those in Wales are fortunate as here planning has, theoretically, been aligned to make the establishment of 'One Planet Developments' more easy, at least at the planning stage (Thorpe, 2015). Here, if you are very serious about limiting your ecological footprint, are not daunted by the dead weight of bureaucracy and have plenty of time at your disposal you have a chance to set up home on cheap agricultural land (Welsh Gov, 2020). The extreme difficulties encountered by groups attempting to work within our existing planning system are captured by Tao Wimbush in his account of setting up the Lammas Ecovillage (Wimbush, 2021). There are well-attended tours every Saturday of different smallholdings within the off-grid settlement showing a strong level of interest in the subject from all walks of life. Visiting Lammas on a summer's day is a blissful experience. The air is sweet and our wistful procession is flanked by a platoon of butterflies, but it took ten years of struggle to get to this stage (Figures 13.1 and 13.2).

Another vanguard project is LILAC, the Low Impact Living Affordable Community in Leeds, completed in 2013, home to 20 households living in a range of homes varying between four bedroom homes and studio flats (Figure 13.2) (Chatterton, 2013). The aim of LILAC was to develop an alternative form of housing supply based on economic equality between residents, 'affordable in perpetuity, demarketisation, non speculation and mutual co-ownership' (Pickerill, 2019, p. 81). To do this LILAC set up a Mutual Home Ownership Society run by residents. The system means that owners who can afford to make high investments subsidise the mortgages of less affluent owners while keeping their investment intact. It is important to note that the land was bought directly from the council which

Figure 13.1
A summer visit to Lammas Ecovillage.
Source: © Flora Samuel.

Figure 13.2
View out from home at Lammas Ecovillage.
Source: © Flora Samuel

meant that costs could be kept down. LILAC also received financial support from Triodos bank, a commonly used resource for self builders (Triodos, 2020). The more people who switch their money to these kinds of banks the more will be available for self-builders to borrow.

Networks such as the Transition Towns, Ecovillage, Cities for Change and the website Diggers and Dreamers (for communal living) provide an important first post for groups of people who want to live in community led housing. These organisations need to be able to draw on a wide range of skills including business planning, social media and fundraising as well as planning, design, building, landscape design, ecology and food production. There are hundreds of Ecovillages all over the world, some dating back to the 1960s (Liftin, 2014). Findhorn in Scotland, for example, was founded in 1962, its aim being 'to demonstrate low-carbon, place based values and practices for human settlements to thrive' (Findhorn, 2020). Findhorn has been cited by UN Habitat as an initiative that is making an outstanding contribution to improving quality of life in cities and communities around the world (East, 2018). Many Ecovillages have become tourist attractions and are likely to play a key role in offering sustainable holiday choices for those repulsed by the usual offerings. The pressure is now on to make these developments scalable and also more inclusive.

Community Land Trusts have developed into a very powerful movement across the globe (Emmeus Davis, Algoed and Hernandez-Torrales, 2020). They are not legal entities – Community Land Trust is an umbrella term that includes legal entities such as Community Benefit Societies and Community Interest Companies. 'CLTs produce and preserve affordably priced homes, community gardens, retail spaces, and a variety of neighbourhood facilities – all developed under the guidance of the people who live nearby; all stewarded to remain permanently affordable for people of modest means' (ibid). So the models are there for us all to learn from.

Education for community construction

Skills in problem solving and self-directed learning are going to be vital in an era of uncertainty (Farrelly and Samuel, 2016). In this situation the learner is a co-creator of knowledge, not an empty vessel to be filled with facts, often soon to be outdated. Such an idea dates back to the critical pedagogy of Paulo Freire who identified what he called a 'fear of freedom' in those he was teaching. 'the oppressed' (Freire, 1981 (1968), p. 28). This isn't just for people suffering from dictatorial regimes and poverty on other sides of the planet, we ourselves are suffering from a kind of mental privatisation, with all kinds of consequences for our health and for the world, but there are many signs that this is starting to recede.

The way in which sustainability is taught has to make sense for people and their personal situations. If you've never been in a British rainforest it takes a lot of imagination to want to save one. Many people are too busy surviving to feel that they have anything to offer the cause, perhaps because the challenges seem too onerous and abstract to deal with. How best to get people on board with sustainability is an under-researched area but, building on pedagogical theory, it seems that problems have to be broken down into manageable chunks, that build on what people already know. 'Project based' (also known as 'enquiry based' or 'tasked based') learning is generally recognised as a good way to help students of whatever age to build on existing knowledge, internalise and process information in a way that becomes useful to them in real life. Project based learning is a particular approach common to architectural and design schools, often in the form of 'live projects' (SSoA, 2021). This is increasingly being used in mainstream education with an extra twist of social responsibility (Gulay Tasci, 2015).

Education is perhaps the most important contributor to sustainability, hence its prioritisation in the UN Sustainable Development Goals. Major work is needed to up the level of sustainability skills in both our youth and adult populations (Kapetaniou and McIvor, 2020). This includes offering opportunities to young people who fail to fit into mainstream education to improve their capabilities. It is never too soon to get young people involved in decision making about their places as the Incubating Civic Leadership project led by the charity Glasshouse has shown (2021). Young people have to come out of school with an understanding of citizenship and ways to enact it and with an ability to evaluate information, a strong ethical compass as well as a good sense of what it takes to make great places and what they can do to contribute to those places (ZCD, 2020). The Black Mountain College in rural Powys, currently seeking university status stands out as a community site for learning, focussing in particular on the circular economy (Figure 13.3). It currently runs a variety of relevant NVQ courses including rewilding, coppicing and seasonal catering – just the thing for a local, low environmental impact, high social value economy with the fees paid by the Welsh government – at the same time bringing new kinds of learning opportunities to a place currently dominated by sheep. Places of education must themselves model what it is to be a good community if students are to learn about the merits of creative citizenship.

Of course universities have an important role to play in the development, not only of innovative places (CaSE, 2020), but also communities. A map based system will quickly reveal the social value impacts of different Universities, though we can only hope they won't be captured in yet another league table. In the UK there is a growing agenda around the importance of 'civic universities'. A recent report by the UPP Foundation makes a series of recommendations regarding the need for universities to engage with local businesses and people (UPP, 2019). They also have a particular role to play in supporting local supply chains (CaSE, 2020). One report by Leeds Social Science Institute revealed just how random the

Figure 13.3
Black Mountain College proposal by Featherstone Young.
Source:
© Featherstone Young.

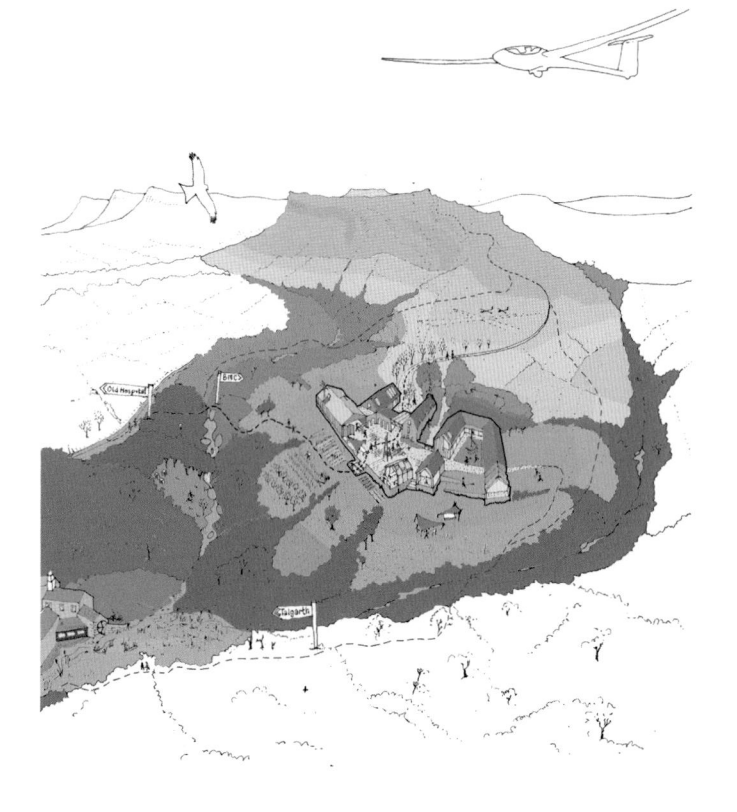

relationship was between the local authority and University of Leeds, with links between the two largely being based on individual relationships between people. Leeds has since set up a directorate that gives order to the relationship powered by designated research champions (LSSI, 2020). Adding value to the locality is likely to give middle ranking universities an edge in turbulent times.

Data literacy

In this book I have made the case for value mapping, a democratically developed and transparent means to build and share real-time information as a basis for action. As a community we have to demand better information about our places (Kapetaniou and McIvor, 2020, p. 7). An ability to understand and read data is going to be of primary importance to the next generation. 'With data having such a huge impact on our everyday choices and decisions, it is often impossible to decide whose voices are being [mis]represented and amplified online' (Pawluczuk, 2020). The Me and My Big Data Project in the University of Liverpool is an example of a 'digital humanities' project that is supporting the development of data literacy in the UK population (2021). Such initiatives need to be better connected to discussions about the built environment.

In a housing regime for hope and wellbeing citizens will be active in the collection of data that will contribute to our knowledge of how places and homes function. There are already many successful precedents of citizen science out there in which the public contributes to the creation of a body of knowledge (Sandhaus, Kaufmann and Ramirez-Andreotta, 2019)– the Big Garden Birdwatch being one. Nick Hayes' indispensable book *The Trespasser's Companion* includes detailed guidance on the multiple opportunities there are out there to get involved in citizen science (2022). The beneficial effects of citizen science – in terms of wellbeing, social inclusion and justice – on both adults and children are well known (see for a good review, Makuch and Aczel, 2019). It follows therefore that people of every age need to be enlisted in data collection about homes and neighbourhoods, not just in terms of wildlife, but also other important impacts, including the delivery of planning conditions, defects in buildings and post occupancy evaluation. 'Community led auditing', the sharing of knowledge, has an extremely important role to play in bringing forth marginalised experiences and also in bringing people together to voice their experiences (Handler, 2014, p. 32). This must be done through openness, participation and collaboration (Davies and Perini, 2016).

A housing system for hope and wellbeing won't be achieved without a discerning approach to information, whether in newspapers or online, including an awareness of the ways in which search engines, drain our attention, gather our data and feed us more of the same resulting in entrenched and extremist viewpoints (Ball, 2020). Some people use web browsers like Qwant 'the search engine that respects your privacy' – and presumably sends you a reasonably balanced diet of news – others choosing to sacrifice their data for good causes like the tree planting efforts of Ecosia. Panayotis Antoniadis offers a vision in which people take internet platforms into their own hands building up bottom-up initiatives that work at a local level and are complementary and locally competitive with currently familiar global offerings (2019, p. 204).

Choices made about major life decisions have to be based on more than the enticing aspirational allure of carefully choreographed show homes. In Chapter 9 I made the case for a home digital registers to give information to new residents on how to run their homes. In the future all new build (and retrofitted) communities need to be geotagged to websites giving a full range of intelligible information on the provenance of that development, including performance ratings and instructions on how best to use the buildings and places (including plenty of space for comments and feedback). These sites can be programmed to collect post occupancy evaluation data on the performance of these places using tools such as the Quality of Life Framework (URBED, 2021). We always look at ratings when we buy products on the internet so why not homes?

The freely available value maps will enable people to weigh up the risks of their potential new home in a highly informed way. In Wales maps have recently been published that show the places that will be flooded as Climate Change progresses, a sobering site for anyone, like my daughter, with a home facing obliteration (Hayward, 2021). Well-informed people will no longer be duped into buying homes on flood planes, meaning that they can be left to the birds and animals that love them so.

Rebuilding the commons

You only have to look at the history of the top three conservation charities – The National Trust, the Royal Society for the Protection of Birds (RSPB) and the Wildlife Trusts – to see what can happen when visionary groups of people get together (Cocker, 2018). It is worth noting that the National Trust and RSPB were started by Victorian women who ostensibly wielded little power in 19th-century Britain. These charities have done a vast amount to protect our landscapes and their inhabitants, but much more work is needed, not least in bringing forth hidden histories of slavery and displacement.

The exclusion of those racialised black and ethnic minority from enjoying our land is a serious issue (DEFRA, 2019) and is a manifestation of the wider inequalities that we see in Britain today. Significantly Emma Dabiri, at the end of her book *What White People Can Do Next* calls for a re-instatement of the commons as a key step towards equality (2021). Land in Our Name, for example, is 'working to transform the narrative around land in Britain and how it relates to intersections of race, gender and class' (LION, 2021). These kinds of organisations need our support and investment.

Community ownership, for example, Community Asset Transfer is important for increasing engaging with more people, increasing their sense of responsibility for their places. It seems that the most commonly transferred facilities are community centres, with green spaces, sports and recreation facilities and libraries coming in afterwards (Power to Change, 2016). In Scotland the formation of Community Benefit Societies have enabled tenants have been able to buy homes and land from absentee landlords. Such buy outs have support from the Scottish government (Scottish Communities Finance, 2021). In England the Community

Right to Bid (UK Gov, 2012) can be used for assets that are registered as Assets of Community Value, for example an allotment that a local authority might decide to sell off, but this requires communities to be ahead of the game in anticipating these kinds of attacks, another reason for mapping the social value of places. Models of rent subsidy, also known as social value leases, mean that assets are let subject to subsidised rents in return for local benefits like the support of local jobs. So it seems that there are many models for shared ownership of assets to build on.

We should not be daunted by the challenges of self organisation as there are plenty of resources available to guide us. Public Practice has gathered a range of existing examples of structures for community led governance on strategic sites (Public Practice, 2021). Economist Elinor Ostrom (winner of a 2009 Nobel Prize) has set out a useful list of 'design principles for governing sustainable resources' held in common-pools (Ostrom, 2008) because agreed rules are always needed for sharing. Shared ownership, while being successful in preserving local resources, also elicits the kinds of debates and co-production that are so important for the creation of resilient communities and places. Shared ownership of the Commons worked back in the Middle Ages. Is there any real reason, other than media promotion of divide and rule, to imagine that it wouldn't work now?

Using our power

All this knowledge should make us feel more empowered and to ask more from the democratic channels available to us – whether it is electing MPs, Assembly Members, Councillors or Mayors or commenting on emergent Local Plans, planning permissions or surveys. An improved planning system will give Councillors more power so we might even decide to go for election ourselves. Peter MacFadyen's book *Flatpack Democracy* gives an account of how a group of Frome residents 'swept the board' at the local elections of 2019 as independent councillors bringing a raft of change with them (MacFadyen, 2020). Citizens' Assemblies such as the one in Newham in London, including youth assemblies, provide an established format for decision making (Newham, 2021). Cllr Zulfiqar Ali speaks proudly of the work Newham has done in putting out a call for projects to the community. 194 were put forward and voted on by 11K members of the public. Ninety-two of these are now in train (CCQOL, 2021). Map based consultation platforms should make this kind of participatory budgeting easy and fair.

As individuals we have to use our spending and investment power to promote organisations that are working for high social value housing and places. Empowered by information we can impact on the way businesses work by providing feedback on their activities, voting at AGMs and pressurising them to divest from harmful investments. This includes our banks and pension funds as well as the charities we support. Charity law requires trustees to make decisions that will safeguard the financial health of charities (Law Commission Guidance, 2020). This can result in destructive decisions, for example, with charities selling land to the highest paying, but least social value, buyer. In an era when the financial value of social and environmental impacts are better understood it ought to be easier for trustees to make decisions based on a holistic view of value, not just money. Even non-environmental charities have a responsibility to take an environmental stance (Charity Commission, 2008).

Conclusion

Social change is a messy incremental thing that happens over time, a coalescence of loving action and hope. It goes against the stream of the neoliberal culture that is being pedalled to us, one of nihilism, instant gratification, individualism and inequality. This chapter has offered a range of examples of small things that can be achieved ideally with, but also without, major government intervention. I make the case for community based education, the sharing of best practice on community development, including community data gathering and the power that this can bring. Gaining societal acceptance for a possible housing system has to be done incrementally through a process of change (Kotter, 1996), bottom-up, building on the embodied experience and knowledge of people and their networks. The next, concluding, chapter provides an imaginary of what a housing system for hope and wellbeing might look like. You only need to work backwards from there to make it happen.

References

Antoniadis, P. (2019) 'The organic internet as resilient practice', in Trogal, K., Bauman, I., Lawrence, R., and Petrescu, D. (eds.) *Architecture and Resilience*. London: Routledge, pp. 204–213.

Arnstein, S. (1969) 'A ladder of citizen participation', *Journal of the American Institute of Planners*, 35(2), pp. 216–224. Available at: https://www.tandfonline.com/doi/pdf/10.1080/01944366908977225?needAccess=true.

Ball, J. (2020) *The Tangled Web We Weave: Inside the Shadow System That Shapes the Internet*. London: Melville House.

Bridport Cohousing. (2021) *Bridport Cohousing*. Available at: https://bridportcohousing.org.uk/.

CaSE. (2020) *The Power of Place: Maximising Local Economic Impacts of R & D Investment in the UK*. Campaign for Science and Engineering. Available at: https://www.sciencecampaign.org.uk/resource/placereport.html.

CCH. (2021) *Wayshaper Tool*. Available at: https://www.cch.coop/launch-of-wayshaper-the-decision-making-toolkit-for-community-led-housing-groups/.

CCQOL. (2021) *Community Consultation for Quality of Life*. Available at: ccqol.org.

Charity Commission. (2008) *Going Green: Charities and Environmental Responsibility*. Available at: https://assets.publishing.service.gov.uk/government/uploads/system/uploads/attachment_data/file/284703/rs17text.pdf.

Chatterton, P. (2013) 'Towards an agenda for post carbon cities: lessons from lilac, the UK's first ecological, affordable, cohousing community', *International Journal of Urban and Regional Research*, 37(5), pp. 1654–1674.

Cocker, M. (2018) *Our Place: Can We Save Britian's Wildlife Before It is Too Late*. London: Jonathan Cape.

Davies, T. and Perini, F. (2016) 'Researching the emerging impacts of open data: revisiting the ODDC conceptual framework', *The Journal of Community Informatics*, 12(2). doi:10.15353/joci.v12i2.3246.

DEFRA. (2019) *Landscapes Review*. Available at: https://assets.publishing.service.gov.uk/government/uploads/system/uploads/attachment_data/file/833726/landscapes-review-final-report.pdfd.

East, M. (2018) 'Current thinking on sustainable human habitat: the Findhorn Ecovillage case', *Ecocycles*, 4(1), pp. 68–72. Available at: https://www.ecocycles.eu/ojs/index.php/ecocycles/article/view/107/109.

Emmeus Davis, J., Algoed, L. and Hernandez-Torrales, M. (eds.) (2020) *On Common Ground: International Perspectives on the Community Land Trust*. Madison, WI: Terra Nostra Press.

Farrelly, L. and Samuel, F. (2016) 'Education for uncertainty', in *Research Based Education*. London: Bartlett, pp. 326–338. Available at: https://issuu.com/bartlettarchucl/docs/aae16_publication_volume2

Findhorn. (2020) *Findhorn Ecovillage: New Frontiers for Sustainability*. Available at: https://www.ecovillagefindhorn.com/.

Freire, P. (1981) *Pedagogy of the Oppressed*. London: Penguin.

Gulay Tasci, B. (2015) 'Project based learning from elementary school to college, tool: architecture', *Procedia - Social and Behavioral Sciences*, 186(13 May), pp. 770–775.

Handler, S. (2014) *An Alternative Age Friendly Handbook for the Socially Engaged Urban Practitioner*. Manchester: University of Manchester Library. Available at: www.micra.manchester.ac.uk/research/population-ageing/research-activity.

Hayes, M. (2022), *The Trespasser's Companion*. London: Bloomsbury.

Hayward, W. (2021) 'New detailed maps show the areas of Wales most at risk of sea levels rising and river flooding', *Wales Online*. 28 September. Available at: https://www.walesonline.co.uk/news/wales-news/climate-change-flooding-maps-wales-21691689.

Incubating Civic Leadership. (2021) *Incubating Civic Leadership*. Available at: https://incubatingcivicleadership.org/.

Kapetaniou, C. and McIvor. (2020) *Going Green: Preparing the UK Workforce for the Transition to a Net-Zero Economy*. NESTA. Available at: https://www.nesta.org.uk/report/going-green-preparing-uk-workforce-transition-net-zero-economy/.

Kotter, J.P. (1996) *Leading Change*. Boston, MA: Harvard Business School Press.

Law Commission Guidance. (2020) *Is It Always About the Money?* Available at: http://content.tfl.gov.uk/law-commission-guidance.pdf.

Liftin, K. (2014) *Ecovillages: Lessons for Sustainable Communities*. Cambridge: Polity Press.

LION. (2021) *Reconnecting Black Communities with Land in Britain, Land in Our Names*. Available at: landinournames.community.

LSSI. (2020) *Unlocking the Potential of Civic Collaboration*. Leeds Social Science Institute. Available at: https://lssi.leeds.ac.uk/wp-content/uploads/sites/65/2020/11/Unlocking-the-Potential-of-Civic-Collaboration-Web.pdf.

MacFadyen, P. (2020) *Flatpack Democracy 2.0*. Bath: Eco-logic Books.

Makuch, K.E. and Aczel, M.R. (2019) 'Eco-citizen science for social good: promoting child well-being, environmental justice and inclusion', *Research on Social Work Practice*, 30(2), pp. 219–232.

Me and My Big Data. (2021) *Me and My Big Data - Developing Citizens' Data Literacies*. Available at: https://www.liverpool.ac.uk/humanities-and-social-sciences/research/research-themes/centre-for-digital-humanities/projects/big-data/.

Newham. (2021) *Citizens' Assemblies*. Available at: https://www.newham.gov.uk/council/citizens-assemblies/1.

Ostrom, E. (2008) 'The Challenge of common-pool resources', *Environment*, 50(4), pp. 8–20.

Pawluczuk, A. (2020) 'From Citizens Story-Making to Citizens [Data]stories Unmaking // Data Citizenship', *alicjapayluczuk*. Available at: https://www.alicja-pawluczuk.com/post/data-citizenship-doing-thinking-participating-with-data.

Pickerill, J. (2019) 'Building eco-homes for all', in Trogal, K., Bauman, I., Lawrence, R., and Petrescu, D. (eds.) *Architecture and Resilience*. London: Routledge, pp. 76–87.

Power to Change. (2016) *A Common Interest: The Role of Asset Transfer in Developing the Community Business Market*. Available at: https://www.powertochange.org.uk/wp-content/uploads/2017/05/2016-A-common-interest-The-role-of-asset-transfer-in-developing-the-community-business-market.pdf.

Public Practice. (2021) *Setting Up Structures for Community Led Governance on Strategic Sites*. Available at: https://www.publicpractice.org.uk/resources/setting-up-structures-for-community-led-governance-on-strategic-sites.

Sandhaus, S., Kaufmann, D. and Ramirez-Andreotta, M. (2019) 'Public participation, trust and data sharing: gardens as hubs for citizen science and environmental health literacy efforts', *International Journal of Science Education*, 9(1), pp. 54–71.

Scottish Communities Finance. (2021) *Community Benefit Society*. Available at: https://scotcomfinance.scot/community-benefit-society/.

Sociocracy for All. (2021) *Comparison of Decision Making Methods*. Available at: https://www.sociocracyforall.org/comparison-of-decision-making-methods/.

SSoA. (2021) *Live Projects*. Available at: *http://www.liveprojects.org/*.

Thorpe, D. (2015) *The One Planet Life*. London: Routledge.

Triodos. (2020) *Lilac Cohousing*. Available at: https://www.triodos.co.uk/projects/lilac-cohousing/12122.

UK Gov. (2012) *Community Right to Bid: Non-Statutory Advice for Local Authorities*. Ministry of Housing Communities and Local Government. Available at: https://www.gov.uk/government/publications/community-right-to-bid-non-statutory-advice-note-for-local-authorities.

UPP. (2019) *Truly Civic: Strengtheing the Connection Between Universities and Their Places*. UPP Foundation Civic University Commission. Available at: https://upp-foundation.org/wp-content/uploads/2019/02/Civic-University-Commission-Final-Report.pdf.

URBED. (2021) *Quality of Life Framework*. Available at: https://www.qolf.org/wp-content/uploads/2021/02/PD20-0742-QOLF-Framework_v09_LR.pdf.

Welsh Gov. (2020) *One Planet Development*. Available at: https://gov.wales/one-planet-development-practice-guidance.

Wimbush, T.P. (2021) *The Lammas Ecovillage*. Southam: FeedaRead.

Wrigleys. (2018) 'Organisational forms for community led housing'. Available at: https://www.communityledhomes.org.uk/resource/organisational-forms-community-led-housing.

Yorspace. (2022) *Resources*. Available at: https://yorspace.org/resources/.

ZCD. (2020) *Voice Opportunity Power*. Available at: voiceopportunitypower.com.

Chapter 14

Housing and neighbourhoods for hope and wellbeing

Housing is 'a major part of our national reimagining' (Welby, 2018, p. 128). It therefore felt wrong to try to finish this book without trying to offer a vision of what a housing system for hope and wellbeing might actually look and feel like. There is a long tradition of utopian thinking in housing (Govers, 2018), I favour instead what Rebecca Solnit calls the 'micro utopias' of everyday acts of kindness (Solnit, 2020), a constantly evolving sequence of little actions that just might add up to something more. What I am trying to present is a reality that is within our reach, one that builds on a range of successful initiatives that have already taken place. I'm not just describing Scandinavia, I am describing something that very specifically pertains to the UK system, an ancient, multicultural society that resists homogeneity, one that has faced up to its colonialist past, a process that began with the Enclosures right here in Britain, and is intent on doing better. The declaration of the Climate Change Emergency, the Agriculture Act 2020, the Social Value Act 2012, the Wellbeing of Future Generations Act (Wales) 2015, a range of positive place-based national legislation and a potential Healthy Homes Act are going to cause a huge wave of change with a host of unanticipated consequences. With the right political breeze behind us, a new generation of ecologically minded young people working their way through the system, and some community based policies we could just get there.

A return to the commons

In a housing system for hope and wellbeing inequality will be at an all-time low, with long-term impacts on mental health and wellbeing. The implementation of Universal Basic Income offering a financial cushion for all will help to make this possible. This world will be a beautiful mixture of digital sophistication and analogue joy with robots configured as a force for good. There will be space for plants and wildlife everywhere – messy with weeds and full of life, scent, the sounds of insects and birds with, always the exciting possibility of sighting 'charismatic' creatures such as the beavers that are so desperately needed to realign our waterways, reduce flooding and create habitats for all.

Levels of community wealth will be high because of the institution of a land tax, mechanisms to ensure the public benefit from land value capture, tax on second homes, fining of neglectful landlords and the enforcement of rulings around damaging the environment. The land tax will mean that a lot of landowners will have to sell their land back to the community – for co-operative housing and other high social value activities – or do deals with conservation charities. With it our lithic class system will crumble away, revealed for what it has always been – a system based on land grabs. The aristocracy will be recognised as rentier landlords in fancy dress, their stranglehold on land ownership no longer condoned. We will have other more widespread excuses for carnival and fun.

Our infrastructure will have been brought back into public ownership in this way allowing for the creation and implementation of a proper, joined up, holistic planning system that is working to achieve clear and transparent outcomes. The transport system will largely be re-nationalised, in doing so making it more efficient and affordable, finally reducing the volume of traffic on our roads. It will be interesting to see what driverless electric vehicles mean for the organisation of space and people. Speed of transportation will no longer be such an issue as so much communication will be virtual. Reduced traffic will allow for the wholesale transformation of 20-minute communities into active travel zones with streets cleared to prioritise bicycles, wheelchairs, buggies and pedestrians.

Decentralisation of job opportunities will allow far more equal spread of homes, people and work across the fabric of the British Isles. Distributed working will mean that more people will move out to rural areas. As more land is freed up through the dismantling of animal agriculture and its facilities there will be opportunities to make new kinds of small, well connected, dense settlements in rural areas that offer high tech working environments in rewilded settings, enabling the less affluent to live out their smallholding dreams and to contribute to the healing of the land. They future will be built on small farms (Smaje, 2020). The community will have shared and equal access to a commons, not only of land, clean water and natural resources, but also to Wi-Fi, software, FabLabs and knowledge.

In a housing system for hope and wellbeing the community will use tried and trusted methods to manage and protect resources and to develop those systems that underpin them. Where practicable public space, including pavements and road verges will be recognised as part of the commons and managed by local residents to maximise food production, biodiversity and connection, all with the support of the community team. Citizens will be well informed and mobilised, enabling them to work effectively with professional colleagues. Thick networks that work for the common good will proliferate and share, like the fungi beneath our feet, breaking down the strata of division, inequality, loneliness and poor health.

A value-based planning system

Hard dividing lines between political constituencies will be dismantled meaning that good initiatives can flow freely across jurisdictional boundaries. City states will take an integrated view of the relationship between urban and rural space. More proportional representation will ensure that there are no abrupt changes in policy direction with all the wastage that this ensues. Wherever possible decisions will be made locally, but always with an eye to wider impact. In a housing system for hope and wellbeing planning will be fluid rather than fixed, informed by real-time data gathering. All systems that are put in place will be regularly reviewed and adjusted to ensure that they are fit for communal purpose.

An increasingly intelligent map matrix of Britain will be made building on and cross correlating the range of disparate mappings and datasets that currently exist across public and private sector organisations. It will include layers of environmental data, water, soil types, elevation, trees, biodiversity, pollution, agriculture and so on. It will include layers of economic data such as land values, income, ownership. It will include layers of health and social data such as mortality rates, indices of deprivation, food deserts and employment. Cultural and historical data need to be included here too not least because of their contribution to identity. These 'passive' layers of data will be augmented with 'active' social value maps that use community input to chart what people feel about their areas produced by people verified through transparent digital systems. Increasingly citizen science will enable people to feed their data into the environmental maps too. The maps will be collated together to demonstrate social, environmental and economic outcomes which will in turn feed into other wider datasets and will be an aid to evidence-based decision making. Digital mapmaking will be augmented with face-to-face debate in Community Team HQs, the physical centre of the community team. Special attention will go into making sure that participation in map making is wide, including inputs from children and young people who will be encouraged to be highly critical about the use of information.

There will be a fundamental calmness that comes with knowing things are well ordered and transparent and that we can trust those who are making decisions in our name to do the best for us. Because of the widespread online availability of data every citizen will know what is going on in their area in terms of flows of energy, money, people and so on. With time a patchwork of maps will be drawn across the whole of the UK, an alive and shimmering and multicoloured source of data, decision making and democracy intelligible to all.

Qualitative and quantitative data gathering on performance social, environmental and economic will be built into everything that we do, not in a big brother sense, but to make sure that we are getting the environment that we need. This will require a kind of systemic post occupation evaluation of buildings and places with citizen input at every level. There will be a confluence of information that starts with the digital registers in our homes and flows into the value maps which will show what is happening in real time in any area (soon in 3D), allowing planners to adjust policy to compensate for any imbalances in the maps. As technology advances the maps will be able to account for distortions of topography – the way, for example, a mountain might interfere with the ways in which communities on either side of it interact. That the value maps can never be perfect will be widely understood and they will be subject to constant improvement. This said they will be the best rule of thumb we have for transparent and holistic decision making.

The planning system will be based on these maps and the development of baggy codes that allow for the building of diverse homes and neighbourhoods that provide opportunities for individuation while ensuring that social, environmental and economic value is being kept in balance. Coding therefore needs to be built around the achievement of these outcomes. One result will be that we have a varied and interesting buildings and streets, in character with their places, that remain cohesive because of their grounding in the rules – our existing Georgian and Victorian terraces are such a beautiful example of this. Of course the codes themselves will be regularly updated based on citizen input, the archives of their activities becoming a record of community history and a tool for identity creation.

Staying local

Local authorities will be reconstituted as community teams, generators of social, environmental and economic value. Urban neighbourhoods – and rural settlements – will become 'experimental innovative sites from which new and emancipatory initiatives emerge' (Moulaert et al., 2010). Reliance on global businesses that siphon money out of the local economy will be at an end. Emphasis will instead be placed on developing circular economies in which flows of jobs, services, materials and money circulate within a small internal market building identity and possibility in the process. The watchword will be local – local government, local healthcare, local education, local culture, music and food.

The character of cities is likely to change in the wake of the pandemic as we move to distributed working. City centres will be built of smaller, club like business head quarters with most work happening from home or peppered across the country according to local need. Redundant office space is rarely fit for conversion into housing, and anyway density will be kept gentle to reduce the impact of pandemics, so these will need to be converted into centres of urban farming and other kinds of community facilities improve urban quality of life.

20-minute communities will be the norm, bringing lively civic life close to home and making out of town shopping centres redundant (the space they occupy will be reused for housing). Rent control, the reduction of business rates and codes relating to mix and social value will mean that local organisations will regain control of the High Street, making them exciting and diverse places that are representative of local identity. Shops empty for an extended period of time will be registered on a publicly available database and made available for meanwhile use by charities, artists, craftspeople, performers and others with a community mindset. Opportunities to repair and recycle will be omnipresent. On the rare occasion big things are bought they will come via the internet. The community team HQ, situated at the heart or across the 20-minute community, as defined by the value maps, will offer a range of facilities including healthcare and preventative medicine. We will see once again the return of the cottage hospital, maternity units and clinics which are easily accessible and local. These will be green places full of stress relieving plants and wildlife distractions as well as things to taste and learn from everywhere.

Neighbourhoods will be recognised as a layering of temporal sequences, not only past present and future but also a tapestry of activities across the day and into the night, a rich culture of participation attractive for a true diversity of people. Opportunities to provide service to others, so important to happiness, will be promoted on every corner. The community team will choreograph a menu of free events throughout the year to foster a culture of sharing and learning. Streets will feel alive and safe at all times of day and night throughout the year. Key moments in the calendar will be recognised through festival, decorations, dance and carnival. Local history will be taught to foster our connections with our land, our wildlife and one another, encouraging humility in the great scheme of things. New stories will be told that build on the waves of migration and colonisation that have characterised the history of the British Isles. Arts and performance will be everywhere re-enchanting our lives, filling us with wonder and making us reflect on existences beyond our own. Engagement with the community will be recognised as the health benefit that it is. People will be given opportunities to be active citizens with a sense of purpose beyond the self.

In time honoured tradition young people will test themselves and grow up in relationship with the wild. Seeking out strife to fill a void will be recognised as an addictive behaviour like any other. Mental health and support will be very widely and freely available with extensive input by the community. Self help groups for addiction and a range of traumas will be widely available to people wherever they live supported by community colleagues. It will be widely understood that responsibility for these ills is shared.

Children will be out and about, playing in the streets, exploring and learning under the watchful eye of neighbours. The nuclear family will no longer be under so much pressure to deliver everything for its members. It will develop tendrils out into the community through the making of trusted new friends and acquaintances in a network of care and sharing that will transcend race, class and religion or sexuality, extending its invitation to all those in precarious situations. People will no longer derive their meaning and status from their jobs or cars as there will be so many other visible outlets and places within neighbourhoods for self development and purposeful connection.

It won't just be about connecting with people, it will also about connecting with nature. Landscaping will be carefully planned to maximise biodiversity and organic food production, reduce flooding and increase fun and activity. This will result in a swathe of new jobs, services and tools in the design and delivery of sustainable places, as well as the promotion of ecotourism. Regulation will be used to ensure space for wildlife – bee hotels, bat boxes, green roofs and so on – will be incorporated into every home and garden. Even when out of sight we can watch and enjoy their activities through strategically placed cameras around the home, sharing our observations with nature lovers near and far.

Building homes for wellbeing

The housing supply system will be characterised by choice, with connected homes and well-distributed jobs across the nation, in this way allowing people to live the lives they want to lead. At last it might just be possible to have the kind of home you have always dreamed of but it won't be big. You wouldn't want it big as it will be well-understood that the most excessive homes are generally owned by the most parasitical people and don't actually add to anyone's happiness in any significant way. Excess will appear as a vivid blot on the landscape of the maps which will capture home ownership and land value in clearly visible ways.

At last people will have some real choice about where and how to live out their days. There will be a wealth of different types of home on offer in a wealth of different settings and places from hobbit holes to high tech inner city flats, new or retrofit. The size of developments will be limited by residents' ability to govern them in a consensual way. Housing options will be communicated in simple, and transparent formats that give people confidence that they are choosing the right one.

A very large proportion of housing will be truly 'social', public rented housing with assured tenancies that make the development of roots a realistic proposition. While community teams should be the major providers, institutions such as pension funds will assist in the provision of good quality, long term rental homes. They will acknowledge the benefits of helping older people age at home within the community and therefore build homes to make this easy, including a range of exciting choices for downsizing. Crucially homes will be cleverly planned and flexible, combining sociability with seclusion and silence, providing the opportunities for the sharing, learning, connection, care and food production that are so important for hope and wellbeing.

The construction industry will bifurcate in terms of robotic construction and the extremely hand made, with fruitful digital craft based synergies between them. Some may opt for Smart homes in which walls, floors and ceilings become screens and monitors offering a variety of experiences and assistive technologies, all governed by strict and intelligible ethical controls. Some may opt for the radically hand made, optimising environmental performance through orientation, materials and design. All this has to be underpinned by renewable energy sources made affordable through government innovation and intervention. It goes without saying that all housing will be built to be zero carbon with circular economy in mind – they must, as much as possible, be demountable and recyclable. A programme of sensitive social retrofit will result in a wave of new homes and jobs. That buildings have been retrofitted will be celebrated through the appearance of green plaques by each door, as well as tax incentives. Retrofit, both environmental and social will result in the creation of a range of rewarding new occupations.

Governments will take a lead on modular production and modern methods of construction with facilities spread across our land mass. These must be readily available to SME and microbusinesses. Agreed module sizes, standardised fixings and transportation methods will mean that the industry can confidently develop spin off services and products around the standardised modules in the knowledge that there will be a market for them. The use of value based procurement will foster innovation across the sector resulting in a range of new products tools and services. New legislation relating to procurement and frameworks will favour the small, diverse and the local as generators of the local economy and skills. The training and development of their workforce and the development of apprentices will be a strong part of their offer. The social value that they generate will be acknowledged in the project bidding process. At the same time increasing numbers of professionals will specialise in assisting amateur builders to construct their own homes and places on sites with Local Development Orders that make planning simple and quick. Getting access to land for building will be so much easier when it is community owned and allocated through the value maps.

A sense of community endeavour will return to the act of home building. At the gate of every new development the names of those that designed and built it (including community members) will be put on display as a matter of pride. Every development and indeed house will be monitored through post occupancy evaluation with a web-based kite mark system to ensure that standards are being met. The long-term curatorship of every development must be seen as an opportunity for creative facilities management. Legislation requiring that all homes be built in a truly sustainable way will make speculative development an unattractive proposition for money maximisers leaving space open for those who want to make communities properly.

Even the most basic of inner city homes will be small but well designed, full of sunlight and possibility. Housing will be low rise (no bigger than five stories), allowing for connection with the land below, timber construction and the promotion of a gentle density. Each home will have access to a balcony, at the very least, with shared green space at ground level where food can be grown. Space will be provided for a dining table where people can do their homework or talk to one another and see the birds, sky and trees while appreciating their food. A rebalancing of income will mean that it is no longer necessary to take multiple jobs to make ends meet. People who want to dedicate themselves to their caring responsibilities or work within the home will have the financial support to do so. High-quality affordable childcare will also be available for all those who want to work. People will have the time to cook and eat well together, abilities that may have been relearnt. The home, the neighbourhood, the street and the turtle dove in the tree across the way will be topics of conversation and social glue.

In a housing system for hope and wellbeing life will be slow in pace allowing gratefulness to come to the fore. The tide of mental health problems and isolation will start to ebb away. This will be a place that you can move around without being afraid of cars or people, a place that offers interesting distractions around every corner, a place where you can make a meaningful contribution to the world, a place where you can move around without fear of getting sick from the air, a place where you can swim without fear of getting sick from the water, a place where you know your children have a fair chance of a good life, a place where people can grow old at home, a place where both you and your mind are free to roam. These communities won't be full of slick shiny buildings, weedless tarmac and tidy verges. They will largely be something we can mend and alter without reliance on too much technology, something that we understand, something that will hold up in the face of extreme events. They will be verdant, flawed, diverse and exciting, offering a synaesthesia of response. Lessons learnt and changes made will be built into the identities of communities like upcycled clothes and visible mends. These are all part of the palimpsest of our land and ourselves, to be celebrated and loved. Only then might we feel truly feel at home.

Conclusion

A housing system for hope and wellbeing will feel like a place of abundance where people trust that there will be support in difficult circumstances, held together by mutual respect and an ethos of love that encompasses future generations. This book has unravelled our grey and scratchy housing system, knitting it back together into a light and protective multicoloured blanket for all. Housing touches on every aspect of our lives. If we can change housing we might just be able to change everything.

Note

Justin Welby quotes, © Justin Welby, 2018, *Reimagining Britain*, Bloomsbury Continuum, an imprint of Bloomsbury Publishing Plc.

References

Govers, R. (2018) *Imaginative Communities: Admired Cities, Regions and Countries*. Antwerp: Reputo Press.

Moulaert, F. et al. (eds.) (2010) *Can neighbourhoods Save the City? Community Development and Social Innovation*. Abingdon: Routledge.

Smaje, C. (2020) *Small Farm Future*. London: Chelsea Green.

Solnit, R. (2020) *Recollections of My Non-Existence*. London: Granta.

Welby, J. (2018) *Reimagining Britain*. London: Bloomsbury.

Index

Note: *Italic* page numbers refer to figures.

Aalto, A. 114
Abbot, A. 2
absenteeism 98
accessibility 90, 100, 101, 102, 103, 138, 146, 205, 206
accountability 73
active ageing 90, 108, 120, 152, 164, 192, 209, 210
active data 77, 141, 206
active lifestyles 164, 208
active travel 19, 76, 98–100, 164, 168, 205
activism 61, 83, 120, 128, 174
Adam Architecture 125
Adams, M. 155
addiction 23, 208
Administrative Data 53
adoption (of space) 20, 100
Adverse Childhood Experience (ACE) 19
aesthetics 34, 59, 116, 129, 206
ageing 23, 115, 119, 120, 152; in place 22, 152; population 6, 22, 120
agribusinesses 21, 141
agriculture 58, 88, 169, 176, 204–206
Agriculture Act 2020 204
agroecology 107
Airbnb 18
air quality 19, 22, 99, 103, 168
Ai Wei Wei 127
Alam, S. 179
Alexa 93
algorithms 57, 144, 146, 175, 176
alienation 162
A Life on Our Planet 5
Ali, Z. 199
Allen, C. 61
All in the Best Possible Taste 116
allotments 105, 199
amateurs 187
Amsterdam 61, 120

An Alternative Age Friendly Handbook 103
analytical psychology 114
Anfield 179
Anthropocene 79
anthropology 18, 58
Antoniadis, P. 197
app 162, 177
apprenticeships 75, 167, 188, 209
Archadia 90
archaeology 141
architect ambassadors 188
architectural expertise 34, 37, 40, 42, 51, 56, 57, 58, 60, 87, 105, 115, 161, 162, 176, 178, 180, 182, 184, 195
aristocracy 30, 205
Arnstein, S. 62, 191
Array Collective 128
art 51, 57, 58, 61, 62, 114, 116, 126, 127, 128, 131, 167, 176, 179, 207; activism 61, 126, 127; festival 128, 167,208
artefacts of knowing 60
artistic quality 128
arts and humanities 6, 52, 61, 62, 113, 127, 128, 154, 169, 179, 208
Arts and Humanities Research Council 141
assembling sites 32
Assembly Members 199
Assets of Community Value 199
Atkins 56
atmosphere 87, 93, 98, 102, 115, 118, 119, 180
Atmos Totnes 41
Attenborough, A. 5
audit culture 73, 74
Australia 178
autistic spectrum 86, 180
automation 146, 167, 176
autonomy 7, 76, 101, 120

213

Index

balconies 104, 210
banks 36, 38, 176, 177, 199
baseline 174
Beacon Hill, Boston 120
beavers 204
Bed and Breakfast accommodation 17, 18
The Bed and Breakfast Star 17
behavioural economics 60
Belfast 128
Bellway 38
belonging 120, 123–131
benefits 17
Benham, D. 178
Bentley, A. 75
Better Neighbourhoods 144
Better Reykjavik 143, 144
Big Garden Birdwatch 197
big society 130
bins 34
biodiversity 20, 31, 74, 102, 115, 123, 141, 168, 205, 208
biodynamic food growing 115
biology 4
biomedicine 57
Bitcoin 144
Black Forest farmhouse 114
Black Lives Matter 61
Black Mountain College 196, *196*
Blair, T. 74
Blitz Team 118
blockchain 144
blue infrastructure 141
blue zones 108
Blythe, W. 62
body 4, 94, 98, 102, 103, 104, 116
Bohn & Viljoen 105, *106*
BoKlok 183
Bollingen (tower) 114, *114*
bonds: green 176; local 170
bonuses 39
borrowed landscapes 115
boundaries 4, 113, 139, 151
Boundary Commission 151
boundary objects 60
Boyer, E. 2
Bozen's Cottage 130
branding 126, 182, 187
brandscape 125, 126
Brexit 37, 52, 76
Bricks 124
Bridgend 19
Bridport Cohousing 192
Bristol 99, 128, 175
British Household Panel Survey 53
Buccleuch family 30

Buglife 141
building contractors 37
Building Information Modelling (BIM) 57, 175
building regulations 125, 187
Building Research Establishment (BRE) 19
build life 36, 180
built environment 63, 73, 78, 98, 139, 145, 174, 183, 188
bureaucracy 38, 56, 127, 167, 187, 193
Burnside, J. 115
Burra Charter 129
business benefits 101
business models 187
Byfleet 90
Byker Wall 123, *123*

cabinets of curiosities 116
cafes 84
cake 182
Camborne, Cornwall 40, *41, 42*
Cambridge 59, 62, 91; University 154
camping 101
Canal and River Trust 76
capabilities approach 1, 78, 113, 152, 156, 177, 188
capital 30
carbon 74, 107, 124; low 194
Cardiff 35, 38, 105, 129, 178, 193; Council 183; Salad Garden 105; University 41
care 22, 39, 85, 90, 93, 98, 116, 118, 153, 164, 167, 204, 210; homes 152; networks 164, 167; technology enabled 167, 183
career path 164, 167, 171, 174, 187
Cares Family 166
cars 34, 99, 205
Castlemaine Court 90
CCTV 85
cemeteries 120
Census data 54, 138, 141; geography 139
Centre for Cities 151
Centre for Digital Built Britain 57, 174
The Centre for Studies of British Slavery 30
Chancellor of the Exchequer 151
change 60, 174, 200
character 145
charities 198, 199, 205, 207
charity law 199
Chartered Institute of Housing qualification 55
Chatbench 85
Chernobyl 5
Chesney, R. 143
childbirth 98

Index

childcare 90
child friendly city 183
children 15, 21, 22, 77, 91, 100, 101, 102, 105, 114, 115, 146, 206, 208, 210
China 37, 52
choice 15, 22, 42, 58, 78, 113, 119, 207, 208, 209
churn 29, 37
circadian rhythms 104
Cities for Change 194
citizens 61, 62, 63, 87, 101, 144, 178, 191–200, 205, 206; assemblies 144, 150, 178, 199; control 191; science 63, 162, 164, 197
city architect 161
city-regional land commission 150
city states 150, 151, 205
civic environmentalism 178
civic pride 128
Clapham, D. 149
Clark, G. 187
class 2, 61, 116 198, 205, 208
classifications 73, 79, 145
cleaners 118
cleaning 113, 118
client teams 29, 36, 37, 75, 175, 187
climate 145
climate change awareness 101, 149, 150, 169
climate change emergency 4, 22, 61, 123, 150, 191, 204
club (social) 84
coaching 175
Cobb, E. 114
Cocker, M. 30
Co-Creation Copenhagen 101
co-creation, co-production and co-design 7, 87, 123, 137, 164, 176, 180
code of conduct for consultation 36, 143, 178, 179
codes 59, 145, 162, 171, 206, 207
cohousing 31, 91
collaboration 56, 59, 73, 75, 197
collecting 113, 115–117, 120
collective good 7
Colombes 87
colonialism 30, 116, 131, 204, 208
comfort 19, 76, 103, 104, 152, 175
commensality 86, 210
Commission for Architecture and the Built Environment (CABE) 3, 74, 116
Committee on Climate Change 16
commodification 5, 127
Commonplace 141, 143, 179
commons 6, 30, 87, 170, 198, 199, 204, 205

communal value 76, 170
communication devices 93, 205
community 3, 22, 32, 33, 35, 40, 42, 58, 62, 63, 77, 78, 83, 84, 87, 99, 100, 105, 106, 108, 124, 125, 126, 128, 129, 130, 137, 141, 145, 154, 156, 161–171, 174, 175, 178, 191, 194, 200, 204, 205, 207, 208; gardening 87, 98, 105–107, 195; identity 79; map making 138; space 84, 86, 87, 195, 198, 207; under-represented 163; wealth 6, 52, 150, 155, 156, 169, 204
Community and Conflict 61
Community Asset Transfer 198
Community Benefit Society 192, 195, 198
Community Consultation for Quality of Life 141, 142, 143, *143, 178*
Community Infrastructure Levies (CIL) 32
Community Interest Company 192, 195
community land contribution 154
Community Land Trusts (CLT) 31, 41, 192, 195
community led: auditing 197; developments 40, 41, 42, 90, 177, 191–195; governance 199
Community Right to Bid 199
Community Right to Build 42
Community Shares 192
community team 161–171, 183, 207, 208, 209
community team colleagues 166
community team headquarters (HQs) 162–167, 206
Computer Aided Design (CAD) 57, 175
computer science 57
Confederation for Co-operative Housing 192
connection 23, 76, 77, 79, 83–94, 100, 104–107, 164, 175, 205, 210
connective social infrastructure 83, 84, 85, *85, 163*, 164, 175
consciousness 52
conservation 130, 141, 198, 205
Conservative Home 16
conservatives 6, 16, 17, 74, 149
construction 36, 37, 38, 57, 59, 60, 61, 74, 209; career 187; improvement agenda 37; material costs 37; research 55; workforce 8, 42
Construction Innovation Hub Value Tool 75
consultation 35, 60, 61, 62, 141, 142, 143, 152, 162, 170, 178, 179, 182, 183
consumerism 22, 117
continuing professional development 33
Continuous Productive Landscapes (CPUL) 105, *106*, 207
contracts (building) 37

215

Convention on the Protection of World
    Culture and Natural Heritage 129
cooking 86, 117, 210
co-operative housing 41, 177, 192, 193, 205
Co-Operative Housing Wales 192
Copenhagen *100*, 101, 127, 161
coppicing 196
Cornwall 18, 40, 125
Corporate Knights 187
corruption 31
cost 40
cost of living 19
Cottam, H. 7, 61, 152, 174
Council for the Protection of Rural
    England 32
councillors 36, 199
council tax 155
countryside 30
Countryside and Rights of Way Act
    (CROW) 101
COVID 19 Community Fund Mapping
    Tool 139
COVID 19 pandemic 1, 4, 20, 37, 83, 86, 88,
    98, 105, 128, 207
cradle to cradle 153
craft 187, 209; beer 125
Creative Industries 57, 180
creativity 51, 114, 116, 156, 169, 180, 182
Criado Perez, C. 78
crime 23, 90, 105
crisis 22
cross correlation of data 53, 54
Crowdfunder 192
crowdsourcing 144, 177
cultural capital 127
cultural heritage values 129
culture 115. 116, 123, 124, 128, 129, 131,
    182, 206, 207
custom build 40, *41, 156*, 168, 183
cycle lanes 100
cycling 19, 22, 98, 99, 100, 101, 161, 205

Dabiri, E. 198
dance 62, 208
danger 99, 100
Darke, J. 60
data 31, 33, 53–54, 56, 63, 78, 93, 138,
    141, 162, 164, 174, 175, 178, 197, 198,
    200, 206
data design and interpretation 176
data driven digital design 174–176
data literacy 197, 198
data management 139
data mining 144
data science 139

datasets 138
David Chipperfield Architects 103
Davidson, D. 39
death 115, 116, 118
The Death and Life of Great American
    Cities 83
deathscapes 120
decentralising 205
decluttering 113, 117–118
decoration 118, 208
Default man 2
defensible space 89
defensible space on the move 2
degrowth 79
delegated responsibility 35
Delivering Design Value (CaCHE) 34
delivery (supply) 29–43, 113, 152, 169, 170,
    174, 208, 209
Dementia 21
democracy 21, 34, 62, 64, 137, 143, 145,
    162, 164, 171, 199, 206; deep 150
De Monchaux, N. 176
Denmark 21, 101
density 19, 53, 83, 84, 207, 210
Department for the Environment Food and
    Rural Affairs 139, 151
Department of Business, Energy and
    Industrial Strategy (BEIS) 151
Department of Culture Media and Sport 51
Department of Levelling Up, Housing and
    Communities 56, 138, 146, 150
deprivation 99, 151, 206
design 3, 5, 19, 34, 57, 59, 60, 61, 73, 74,
    75, 85, 90, 92, 98, 99, 100, 102, 103,
    104, 113, 115, 123, 127, 145, 162, 174,
    187, 194, 199, 209
design advisors 161
design and build contracts 37
design code 145
designing buildings wiki 36
design review 34
design studio 60
destinations 101
determinism 59
developers 29, 32, 35, 36, 40, 61, 64, 126,
    170, 176, 180, 210
development 33, 34, 153, 182
Devlin, P. 184
devolution of power 4, 150
diagrams 60
Diggers and Dreamers 194
Digimap 53
Digital Built Britain 57
digital communities 175; connectivity
    21, 23, 83, 93, 94, 138, 143, 164;

216

construction 37, 187; exclusion 53, 143, 164; guardians 138; humanities 197; literacy 178; register (for buildings) 167, 175, 198, 206; skills 162; transformation 22, 56, 138, 206; voting 144
Digital Democracy 144
Digital Planning Manifesto 137
Digital Twin (National) 57, 175
dining table 22, 210
Directorate of Building Materials 55
Directorate of Post War Building 55
disability 16, 21, 102, 146
discounted cash flow 31
discrimination 16
disease 107
displacement 198
distributed working 139, 162
distribution 17
diversity 42, 52, 83, 84, 123, 150, 161, 188, 192, 206, 207
doctor's surgeries 152
Doncaster 186
Doughnut Economics 73
downsizing 117, 120, 209
dowsing 119
drawing 60, 77
dreams 114
drugs 22
Duchy of Cornwall 125
dwelling (lived experience) 15, 58, 61, 63
Dyson, J. 54

early career researchers 55
Earthshot Prize 86
East Quay 126, *126*
eating 22, 125, 130, 164, 210
Ebbsfleet 164, *165*
ecologists 33
Ecology Building Society 177, 193
Ecology of the Imagination in Childhood 114
economic: assessment 35, 53; growth 78; man 60; monetary value 1, 2, 3, 29, 35, 52, 74, 76, 78, 101, 125, 139, 145, 151, 161, 169. 170, 171, 176, 187, 188, 199, 206, 207; units 151
economics and economists 3, 5, 58, 60, 63, 73, 149
economies (circular and closed loop) 153, 182, 196, 207, 209
economies of scale 39
economy of the imagination 183
Ecosia 197
ecosystems 123, 168
ecosystem services 76, 168

eco-transformation 191
Ecovillage 193, 194, 195
Edinburgh University 141
education 6, 29, 55, 56, 60, 63, 76, 98, 102, 105, 138, 149, 150, 152, 188; community learning 163, 164, 168, 191–200, 207; digital 178; sustainability 195
Egan Report 37
Eindhoven 166
electrical engineering 57
Eliana, J. 117
emergency 18
emotional self 62
employee ownership 187
employment *see* jobs
empowerment 1, 6, 35, 62, 87, 88, 93, 103, 113, 123, 199, 207
Empty Dwelling Management Orders (EDMO) 18
empty homes 18; tax 155
empty shop 179
enclosures 30, 204
energy 57, 93, 103, 116, 162, 175, 176, 206
engagement (community) 35. 101, 103
engineering 61
England 4, 5, 18, 35
enlightenment 52
enough 6, 117, 208
entrepreneurs 154
environment 4
environmental: performance 19, 38; psychologists 59; value 1, 3. 29, 30, 42, 74, 78, 139, 145, 161, 169, 170, 171, 176, 187, 188, 206, 207
environmentalism 5
Environmental, Social and Governance (ESG) 176
equality 84, 100, 107, 198, 199, 205; *see also* inclusion
equity finance 58, 177
Erskine, R. 123
estate agents 177
estates: (private) 30, 54, 139
Ethex 192
ethics 195; practice 74, 138, 174, 209
ethnicity 2, 6, 16, 61, 87, 150, 192, 198, 208
eudaimonic wellbeing 1, 113, 156
Europe 116
European models 40, 53
European Research Council 52
evidence based decision making 53, 55, 59, 60, 62, 74, 206
evolutionary biology 83
exclusion 35, 145, 198

217

exercise 22, 76, 98–103, 145, 152, 164
existing housing 155
extinction 20, 168

FabLab 164, 166, 205
face to face contact 83, 164, 167, 182, 188, 206
facilities management 175, 178, 210
faith groups 86
The Fall of the House of Usher 118
families 16, 113, 191, 208
farmers 21
farming and farms 20, 30, 39; subsidy 30, 54, 139, 192
Farrell Centre 143
FAT Architecture 116
Featherstone Young Architects 196
Federation of Cambridge Residents' Associations 62
Felix project 86
feminism 3, 6, 59, 117
Feng shui 119
festival 167, 208
Fields Inn Trust 168
film 62, 113
financial 31, 38, 174, 188, 192, 193; crash 144; cuts 20, 33, 54
financial services 57
Finch, D. 39
Findhorn 120, 194
fitness 98
Five Ways to Wellbeing 76
Fixing Our Broken Housing Market 29
flat pack 183
Flatpack Democracy 199
flats 16, 22, 34
flexibility 76, 88, 102, 209
flipping of land 32
flooding 198, 204, 208
flower highway 168
food 22, 23, 54, 57, 86, 93, 105–107, 123, 125, 152, 163, 167, 168, 182, 205, 207, 208, 210; desert 22, 206; redistribution 86; security 21, 57; solidarity 86
footpaths 19, 20, 101
forecasting 34, 60
Foreign Office Architects 176
forestry 139, 176
Fortress Farm 20
framework agreements 37, 169, 209
Freire, P. 195
Freud, S. 115
frictionless experience 57, 94
friendship groups 94
Frome 199

fuel poverty 162
fun 164, 167, 182, *183*, 205, 208
funders and funding 36, 38, 39, 52, 127, 128, 168, 171, 178, 182
fundraising 176, 177, 191–194
future 5, 34, 51, 57, 59, 60, 126, 138, 150, 176, 183; generations 5, 129, 138, 150, 211

gaming (computer) 57, 102, 183; engines 175
gangs 22
gardens and gardening 20, 90, 93, 101, 105–107, 115, 167, 168, 169, 210
Geertz, C. 155
gender 2, 6, 18, 22, 36, 42, 57, 102, 116, 117, 150, 192, 198, 208
General Practitioners (GP) 152
genius loci 123
gentrification 18
geographers and geography 57, 63, 105, 175
Geographic Information Systems (GIS) 57, 138, 175
George, L. 154
Geospatial Commission 54, 56, 138
geotagging 138, 141, 198
Germany 52, 100
gerontology 57
gig economy 5
Girls (space for) 102
Glasshouse 195
global businesses 35, 207
globalisation 4, 125, 127, 131
Global Village 4
Goldsmiths Street, Norwich 40
Goodbye Things 117
The Good Economy 176
Good growth 169
Google Translate 178
Gorman, A. 127
governance 91; units of 150, 151
government 3, 5, 17, 29, 31, 32, 33, 39, 40, 52, 53, 54, 57, 60, 61, 63, 74, 144, 149–156, 199, 200, 209
grand tour 116
Grangetown Pavilion 178, *178*
Greater Manchester Infrastructure Framework 139
green: recovery 170; space 19, 31, 33, 84, 93, 101, 102, 103, 104–107, 115, 141, 145, 164, 168, 198, 210; valuation 170
green belt 31, 141
Green Book 74
greenery 52, 76, 98, 102, 104–107, 114, 115

Index

greenfield sites 141
green infrastructure 139, 141
Greenspace Demonstration Project 101
Grenfell Tragedy 29, 37, 86
grey literature 76
Griffiths, J. 6
Gross Domestic Happiness 73
Gross Domestic Product (GDP) 57, 73
Gross Domestic Value 73
Grosvenor Estate 30, 36, 187
Grosvenor, Hugh 30
grounding 104
growing food 86, 105–107, 168, 169, *180*, 205, 208
Growing Villages Differently 141
guerilla gardening 88, 105

Hackney 84, 87; Hackney Bridge 180, *181*
HACT 75
Halligan, L. 17
Hamilton-Baillie, B. 100
Hampstead 115
Handler, S. 103
hand made 187, 209
HAPPI 90, 104
happiness 1, 4, 22, 86, 120, 209
hard to reach 178
Hatleskog, E. 77
haunting 118
Hawkins Brown 84
Hays, N. 197
health 3, 6, 19, 21, 22, 23, 29, 33, 54, 57, 76, 86, 93, 98–108, 126 138, 145, 149, 165, 195, 205, 206, 208
health and safety 105, 168
health and wellbeing hub 164, *165*
health capabilities 152
healthcare 57, 149, 150, 152, 153, 165, 207; buildings 75, 98, 165; decentralising 152, 207
Healthy Homes Act 149, 204
Heartache 21
Heidegger, M. 114
Help to Buy 17
Henderson, J 61
HerCity 102
heritage 31, 41, 76, 105, 123, 124, 125, 128–130; intangible 129
Heritage Counts 129
heritage value 76
Hertzberger, H. 88
high rise housing 16
High Street 163, 207
highways 33, 34, 38, 99, 100, 101, 105, 125, 168

The Hill We Climb 127
Hinch, Mrs 118
Hinch Yourself Happy 118
Hiraeth 113
Historic England 76, 129
Historic Scotland 76
history 58, 124, 129, 130, 131, 206, 207, 208
holistic value 43, 145, 161, 170, 171, 177
hollowing out 37
home 3, 29, 113–120
homebuyers 116, 177
home décor 116
homelessness 18, 19, 23, 58
homeless shelters 18
homemaking 18, 58, 113, 115, 187
home ownership 16–18, 177
Homerton 86
Homes England 32, 156
Homes (Fitness for Human Inhabitation) Act 149
homesickness 113
Home Truths 17
homogeneity 38, 101
hope 1, 15, 168, 174, 191, 197, 200 204, 210
hospitals 98, 152; cottage 152
hostels 18
House 61
housebuilders 22, 29, 32, 38, 153, 171, 177, 183, 186, 187
housebuilding 29, 32, 38, 39, 210
House for Essex 116
households 16, 34, 113; growth projections 34
House of Lords 150, 154
houses 15, 16, 34
Houses in Multiple Occupation (HMOs) 2, 16
housework 117–120
housing: adequate 4; affordable 5, 17, 29, 31, 34, 39, 41, 76, 90, 91, 154, 170, 176, 177, 192, 193, 195; associations 38, 39, 40; construction levels 16; co-operative 2; dimensions of 2; distribution 15; education 51–64; knowledge 7; list 17; management 16, 39, 88, 90; ministers 29; need 34, 42; owner occupied 15, 16; pathways 1; precarity 84; private rental 15, 16, 17, 167; quota 32; regime 18, 149; single occupancy 16; social rented (public) 17, 18, 39, 40, 58, 153, 170, 209; studies 51, 58, 61; supply 153
Housing and Economic Needs Assessment 34

219

Index

Housing Fit for Purpose 60
Housing Revenue Accounts 40
Hull 126
Humanitas Deventer 120
human rights 19
human scale 83
hunting 30

Iceland 144
ICOMOS 129
identity 18, 105, 123–131, 169, 175, 182, 206, 207
Igloo 40
IKEA 103, 118, 183
imaginaries 60, 78, 138, 200, 204
immigration 34, 123
impact agenda 54, 61, 77, 162
incentivising engagement 178
inclusion 35, 73, 101, 102, 103, 123, 131, 150, 175, 192, 195. 197
Incredible Edible 105, 106, *107*
Incubating Civic Leadership 195
individuation 113–116
industrial revolution 116
inequality 5, 15, 42, 52, 118, 138, 200, 204, 205
inflation 17, 18
influencer 117
informality 73
information design 62, 63, 77, 100, 150, 163, 166, 177, 197, 206, 209
information technology 57
infrastructure 19, 32, 55, 56, 75, 145, 176, 205
inheritance tax loopholes 30, 155
injustice 5, 18, 118
innovation 37, 39, 42, 51, 75, 83, 138, 144, 153, 154, 164, 166, 167, 170, 171, 174, 186, 188, 196, 209
insecure accommodation 18
instructions 198
insurance 37, 187
intangible outcomes 57, 61, 129
intensive agriculture 20
intentional communities 90, 120
interactive 176
interdisciplinarity 55, 58, 59, 60, 61, 63, 162, 178, 183
intergenerational: living strategy 164, *165*; space 86, 88, *89*, 90, *90*, 102, 103, 105, 106, 120
Intergen project 87
Interior design 117
International Association for Public Participation 178

Internet 128, 143, 164, 197, 198, 205, 207
Internships 167, 184, 188
intrinsic value 73, 75
investment 18, 32, 36, 56, 125, 153, 171, 176, 177, 182, 187, 188, 191, 193, 199, ethical 188
Invisible Studio 187
Invisible Women 78
Involve Foundation 144
Ireland 115
Islamic Bank 177
Islington 169

Jacobs, J. 83, 84
Japan 117
Jarvis, H. 90
Jeffrey, S. 151
jobs 55, 75, 83, 84, 105, 127, 138, 139, 167, 169, 180, 199, 205, 206, 208–210
Jones, A. 119
Jordan, B. 60
Journal of Happiness Studies 1
Juniper, A. 93
justice 150, 197

Kahn, S. 161
Karn, V. 61
Kent 18
keywords 145
keyworkers 171; housing 77
Kier Living 38
King, P. 58
kitchen 118
Knepp Estate 139
knowledge 37, 51–64, 138, 174–188, 205; community 128
Kondo, Mari 117
Korea (South) 52
KPMG 156
Krasnostein, S. 118
Krznaric, R. 150

labour: party 154
Ladder of Participation 62, 191
Lammas Ecovillage 193, *194*
land 30, 123, 131, 154, 155, 156, 170, 208; access 20, 38, 42, 192, 210; acquisition 30; agricultural 31; banking 32, 39; blindness 30; brownfield 31, 141; ownership 29, 30, 31, 39, 54, 170, 205, 206; promoters 32, 35; secrecy 30; supply 34, 155; unimproved 155; value uplift 32, 33
land commission 150, 170
Land for the Many 154

220

Land In Our Name 198
landlords 17, 30, 155, 198, 204, 205
Land Promoters and Developers Federation 32
Land Registry 31, 39, 54
landscape 115
land tax 155, 170, 204
land use planning 141
land value capture 156, 204
Langham, K. 182
language 62, 76, 79, 145. 166, 179
Lares and penates 116
Lawson, V. 34
leadership 63, 106, 161, 167, 191
learning 63, 84, 94, 102, 128, 152, 154, 164, 167, 171, 179, 187, 191, 192, 195, 207, 208
lease 155, 170
Le Corbusier 114, 116, 118
LEED 76
Leeds 37, 91, 186, 196, 197; University of 196
Leeds Social Science Institute 196
Lees, L. 2
legacy 176
Legal and General 37, 177
leisure activities 102, 113, 138, 164
levelling up 138, 139, 154
LGBTQ+ 18, 87, 175, 192
libraries 128, 150, 198
life expectancy 113
lifestyle 115
light 83, 87, 93, 104, 115
light pollution 104
LILAC 91, *91*, 193, 194
literacy 179
litter pickers 168
Little Mermaid 127
livability 101, 161
live projects 195
Liverpool 150; University 197
Liverpool Land Commission 150
Liverpool One 34
liveworks 143
Living Streets 101
Llewelyn Davis, R. 59
local 4, 139, 154, 164, 169, 177, 187, 196, 197, 199, 205, 207, 208; economy 84, 131, 164, 169, 170, 207; materials 124, 125, 131, 169, 207, 209; suppliers 37, 38, 84, 123, 124, 125, 131, 164, 169, 170, 207, 209
local authorities 3, 7, 17, 19, 29, 31–37, 39, 40, 54, 56, 62, 64, 74, 75, 78, 86, 105, 118, 125, 141, 145, 161–171, 193, 196, 199, 207; combined 150; financial reform 156. 161; housing construction 40
Local Code 176
Local Development Order 40, 210
Local (Development) Plan: 34, 35, 193, 199
Local Enterprise Partnership (LEP) 150
location 3
Lock Down Library 128, *129*
London 18, 52, 59, 60, 84, 85, 86, 87, 100, 103, 116, 123, 127, 141, 156, 161, 162, 169, 176, 180, 184, 199
loneliness 15, 21, 33, 83, 86, 90, 98. 164, 205
longevity 108
long term impacts 74, 75
Lottery Funding 105, 178
low impact 196
low income groups 16
low use domestic properties 17

MacFadyen, P. 199
Made in Roath 128
maintenance 168
Makeshift, 180
Make Space for Girls 102
making 116, 187
Manchester 87, 169
manufacturing 37, 126, 187; small 164
mapping 7, 53, 56, 60, 62, 75, 76. 78. 137–146, 162, 170, 175, 176, 196, 197, 199, 206
Mapping Eco Social Assets (MESA) 76, 77, *77*, 79, 141, 151
March, L. 59
marginalisation 86, 197
market 29; overheating 31
marketing 175
Marmalade Lane 91, *92*
Married Women's Property Act 30
Martin, L. 59
Mass Bespoke 186, *186*
mass production 116
materials 115, 118, 124
Matter Architecture 88, *89*
Mayor of London 84, 100, 103, 161, 163
Mazzucato, M. 3
McDonald, B. 139
McKinsey 174
McLuhan, M. 4
McVicar, M. 177
Me and My Big Data 197
meanwhile space 180, 181, 182, 207
measurements 57, 61, 73–79, 101
media 18, 62, 128, 197, 199

221

Megaregions 151
Melbourne 169
memorials 120
memory 105, 117, 124, *125, 128*
mending 183
Menin, S. 114
Men's Sheds 87
mental health 2, 15, 16, 19, 20, 21, 22, 87, 98, 105, 113–120, 164, 204, 208
mergers 39
methodology 2, 55, 58, 78
metrics 3, 77, 78
Metropolitan Police Crime Map 175
Midlands Engine 151
migration 123, 208
Mikhail Riches 40
Milan 86
mindfulness 104, 118
minecraft 183
Mini-Hollands 100
Minimalism 117
Minister of Works 55
Ministers of Parliament (MPs) 199
Ministry of Building, Innovation and Education (MOBIE) 187
Ministry of Housing, Communities and Local Government 3, 29, 138, 139, 145, 150, 153
Minorities 16, 42, 87
MISERY 87
mixed development 39, 83, 100, 104
mobile homes 117
mobile phones 94
models 60; cake 182; digital 145, 175
modernism 51, 52
Modern Methods of Construction (MMC) 37, 153, 171, 186, 187, 209
modular construction 37, 171, 209
Monbiot, G. 30, 42
monetising 75
money laundering 31, 155
mood boards 115
Moore, R. 61
Morris, W. 116, 130
mortality 34
mortgages 17, 177, 193
mowing 168
Mpofu-Coles, A. 179
Multi-Agency Geographic Information for the Countryside (MAGIC) 139
multigenerational housing 90
multinational companies 93
Museum of English Rural Life 179
Museums 57, 116, 128
music 62, 164, 207

Mutual Home Ownership Society 192
myths 113, 119, 208

Nansledan 125
National Building Specification (NBS) 59
national curriculum 63
National Custom and Self Build Association 40
National Health Service (NHS) 19, 22, 33, 101, 152, 162
nationalisation 205
nationalism 123
National Literacy Trust 178
National Model Design Code 145
National Park City 141
National Parks 104, 139
National Planning Policy Framework 34, 145
National TOMS Framework 75
National Travel Survey 98
National Trust 92, 130, 198
natural capital 75, 168
Natural England 139
Natural Health Service 101
Natural Language Processing 145
nature 7, 76, 83, 92, 98, 101, 103, 105, 114, 115, 139, 208
nature reserves 92
neighbourhood 2, 7, 58, 63, 75, 83, 84, 85, 86, 87, 93, 98, 99, 100, 104, 113, 120, 123, 130, 144, 151, 161–171, 174, 195, 207, 208
Neighbourhood Planning 153
neoliberalism 3, 4, 5, 17, 23, 29, 38, 61, 63, 73, 74, 200
NESTA 144
Netherlands 100, 120, 166
networks 4, 60, 83, 84, 85, 126, 152, 163, 175, 188, 200
Newcastle upon Tyne 123, 143
New Economics Foundation 32, 76, 127, 170
Newham 162, 169, 199
New Labour 3, 74
Newman, O. 90
nightclubs 87
night shelters 17
night shifts 103
NIMBY 170
noise 83, 209
Nomadland 117
North Ayrshire 169
Northern Ireland 4, 128
Northern Powerhouse 151
North Kensington 85

Nostalgia 61
Nottingham 40, 62
Nox 176
nutrition 105, 152
Nvivo 144

obesity 22, 103, 105
objects 116, 117, 129, 130
occupational therapy 114
OECD 21
off-grid 193
Office of National Statistics (ONS) 53
office space 207
office to residential converted accommodation 20
off site construction 37, 171
Off Site Homes Alliance 37
older people 21, 23, 42, 86, 87, 103, 104, 108, 120, 164
Older Women's Co-Operative Housing (OWCH) 184, *184*, *185*
Olio 86
Olympic Park 180
One Planet Development 193
One Powerhouse Consortium 150
Onion Collective 126
Ontologist 174, 175
open: access 53, 54; source 145
Open Data Institute 54
Open Government Data 54
optional agreements 193; register of 155
ordinary people 61, 191
Osgerby, B. 117
Ostrom, E. 199
Our Stories 175
outcomes base procurement 75
outdoor activities 22
outsourcing 171
over crowding 20
owner occupation 15, 16
Oxford and Cambridge arc 154
Oxford Citizens Assembly on Climate Change 150
Oxford Conference on Education 59

pain 98, 105
palimpsest 130, 210
panel systems 37
parametric design 59, 176
Parc Derwen 19, *20*
Paris 87
parkour 102
parks 20, 168
participation 62, 76, 84, 127, 150. 170, 174, 177–183, 188, 191, 197, 206

participatory budgeting 144, 199
Participatory City 167
passive data 77, 141, 143, 206
Passivhaus 103, 167
Peckham 127; Peckham Levels 180
pedagogy 182, 195
pension funds 176, 199, 209
pensions 150
Pensions for Purpose 176
People's Budget 154
perception of safety and walkability 85, 98, 99
performance 62, 87
Perriand, C. 117
Perry, G. 116
Persimmon 38, 39
personalising of homes 60
pesticides 20
pets 93, 102
philosophy 58, 113
physical experience 94
physical health 16, 22, 79, 98–108, 164
Pickerill, J. 40
Pinker, S. 6
place 3, 5
place based impact investment 153, 176, 177
place based values 194
place branding 125
placemaking 88, 100, 138, 182
place marketing 126
place shaping team 169
places of worship 84, 86
Place Standard 5
planetisation 4
planners 33, 34, 74
planning 6, 7, 31, 33, 34, 35, 38, 51, 56, 57, 58, 59, 60, 62, 101, 103, 137–146, 149, 152, 161–171, 183, 197, 199, 205; Aid 36; appeal 33; code 145; consultant 3, 36; gain 32; violations 145
Planning for a Better Future 137
Planning Policy Wales 5
plant based (vegan) diet 107, 108
plants 204
platform integrators 175
play 88, 91, 101–103, 108, 114, 115, 182, 183
playboy pad 117
Play: Disrupt 182, 183, *183*
playing Out 88
Poe, E.A. 118
police 29, 175
policy 7, 15, 30, 58, 60, 149–156, 204
policy thinking 58
politicians 149

Index

politics 5, 6, 52, 74, 127, 130, 137
Pollard, Thomas and Edwards 175, 184
pollution 99, 168, 206
Pop Brixton 180, *180*
population projections 15
pop-ups 103, 143, 180
postmodernism 52
Post Occupancy Evaluation (POE) 56, 76, 90, 153, 167, 170, 175, 197, 198, 206, 210
potential space 114
poverty 23, 103, 105
Power to Change 166
practice base research 56, 75
practices 130
Prescott, J. 74
present (being) 94
preservation 31
Preston Model 169
preventative medicine 152, 207
primitive 116, 119
primogeniture 3
privacy 83
private sector 34, 39, 42, 52, 55, 56, 153, 167, 171, 174
privatisation 5, 19, 31, 33, 58, 125, 171; of the mind 195
processes 60, 61
procurement 6, 37, 75, 78, 169, 170, 183
Procuring for Value 75
product design 61, 178
productivity 187
professionals and professionalism 3, 55, 56, 64, 127, 174–188
programmers 176
programming of community space 87, 164, 207
project based learning 195
project management 60
property ownership 32, 42, 43
property rights 30
proportional representation 150, 205
Proptech Engagement Fund 56
psychoanalysis 114
psychology 58
public: good 30, 161; land 32; sector 29, 31, 32, 34, 39, 42, 55, 56, 73; space 18, 33, 205; spending 17
public footpaths 20
Public Health England 22
Public Limited Companies 38
Public Practice 162, 199
Public Service Board 33
public (the) 62, 63, 64
pubs 84

qualitative data 73, 144, 145, 175, 206
quality 29, 31, 34, 37, 74, 85, 86, 90, 154, 169
quality of life 1, 53, 59, 99, 101, 108, 141, 143, 152, 194, 207
Quality of Life Foundation 79, 141
Quality of Life Framework 79, 198
quantitative data 3, 42, 55, 73, 78, 144, 175, 206
Queen (the) 54
Queer Eye 117
Qwant 197

rabbits 123
Race, Class and State Housing 61
Radical Help 6
Radical Routes 193
rainforest (British) 195
Reading 22, 151, 164, 179; Museum 179; University 141
real estate 60, 170
real-time 138, 162, 206
recommon 191
recovery 98; plan for London 161
recycling 87, 180, 184, 187, 207, 209
Red Book (RICS) 31
Red Line 35
Redrow 38
refereed journals 52, 55
reflexivity 52, 113
refugees 18, 105
refurbishment 130
refuse 104, 168
regeneration 31, 41, 153, 176
regions 150, 151, 152
registered providers of housing 38
regulation 7, 61
relationships 84
religion 6, 52
relocation 124
rent 15, 17
renters 16, 17, 176
rent subsidy 199
research 51–62, 187:; academic 58, 87; councils 52; funding 52, 55, 56
Research and Development (R & D) 15, 52, 125, 126; tax credits 154.
residual valuation method 31
resilience 38, 88, 105, 107, 108, 162, 175, 191
restoration 130
retail industry 35, 104
Rethinking Construction 37
retrofitting 4, 16, 169, 170, 175, 198, 209
reuse 180

224

revealed preferences 77
Revit 57
rewilding 139, 168, 196, 205
Rex, J. 61
Reynolds, M. 115
Right of Way 54
Right to Buy 17, 40
Right to Regenerate 153
risk 39, 51, 52, 99, 100, 102, 153, 188
ritual 115, 116, 119
robots and robotics 57, 93, 118, 164, 166, 204
Robson, E. 76
Rotherham Local Authority 168
Routine activities perspectives 90
Royal Institute of British Architects (RIBA) 57, 188
Royal Institute of British Architects (RIBA) Business Benchmarking 57
Royal Institute of Chartered Surveyors (RICS) 31, 42
Royal Society for the Protection of Birds (RSPB) 198
Royal Town Planning Institute (RTPI) 137
Ruonavaara, H. 58
rural 21, 30, 32, 74, 83, 101, 125, 139, 140, 141, 143, 191, 193, 196, 205, 207
R-URBAN 87, *87*

sacred 116, 117
safety 20, 83, 85, 98, 100, 101, 104, 191, 208
The Sage Handbook of Housing 60
sales 17
Salford Media City 177
Sarah Wigglesworth Architects 164, *165*
Sasaki, F. 117
satisfaction 15
Savills 156
scale 7, 88, 103, 104, 152, 162
scheduling 166
scholarship of integration 2
school 63, 77, 87, 99, 102, 167, 188
science and scientists 51, 52, 53, 58, 129
Scotland 4, 40, 101, 155; government 198
Scottish Government 138
Scottish Highlands 30
Scottish Land Commission 155, 156
Scottish National Outcomes Framework 5, 150
screens 22
sea 123
second homes 18, 155, 204
Sectie C 166
Section 106 32

security 83, 104, 115; data 138
segmentation 175
segregation 58
self actualisation 18, 79, 113–120, 123, 208
self build 29, 31, 40–42, 58, 113, 153, 156, 193, 194, 210
self-esteem 108, 208
self knowledge 115, 119
self organisation 199
Selfridges 103
self sufficiency 107
sense of purpose 1, 128
senses 125
sensors 168
Shadow City 144
Shadow Parliament 144
Shape Newham 162
shared ownership 199
shared space 100
shareholders 39
sharing 21, 73, 83, 85, 86, 87, 88, 90, 91, 100, 164, 198, 208
sheep 123
Sheffield 2, 102, 115, 143
Shinto 117
shopping centres 22, 182, 207
shops and shopping 21, 22, 83, 84, 117, 164, 195, 207
Short journeys 101
short-termism 29
show homes 198
shrines 116, 120
Shrubsole, G. 20, 39, 54, 155
signage 100
SimCity 183
Siri 93
Sites of Special Scientific Interest 141
SKANSKA 184
skills 7, 37, 56, 86, 105, 174–188, 194
Skills and Competency Framework (cdbb) 174
SKOR 61
slavery 30, 38, 60, 130, 198
sleep 103, 104
sleeping rough 18
Sliperiet 164
small businesses (SMEs) 37, 38, 154, 169, 170, 171, 176, 209
smallholdings 193, 206
smallness 162, 164
smart: city 57, 93; homes 57, 93, 94, 209; maps 141
Smith, S.J. 177
Soane Museum 116
sociability 83, 86, 99, 150, 182, 192, 209, 210

225

social: assets 76; capital 76; care 149, 152, 153; cohesion 21, 84, 151; discounting rates 60; infrastructure 15, 77, 83, 84, *85, 86*; interest 76; investment funds 167; justice 4; prescribing 128; purpose 76; sciences 58, 59, 60, 61; security 6; services 29, 167
Social Life 84
Social Return on Investment (SROI) 75
social value 1, 2, 4, 7, 22, 29. 30, 42, 73–79, 108, 120, 125, 126, 129, 137, 138, 143, 145, 156, 161, 167, 169, 170, 171, 174, 175, 176, 177, 178, 183, 187, 188, 196, 199, 205, 206, 207, 209; leases 199
Social Value Act 2012 6, 75, 149, 204
Social Value Bank 75
Social Value Toolkit for Architecture 75, 76, 77, 79
society 3, 73
Society for the Protection of Ancient Buildings (SPAB) 130
sociocracy 192
sociology 58
software development 57
Solnit, R. 204
Sortition Foundation 144
South-East England 52, 150
Southgate, M. 187
South-West England 150
space 22, 55, 102, 117, 129, 164
speed 99, 100
spending power 199
spiritual experience 1, 52, 117, 119
spiritual value 129
sport 117, 130; facilities 198
squatting 58
stamp duty 155
standard house types 39
Standard Industry Classification (SIC) 174
standardisation 55, 59, 209; data 138, 139
Standard Occupational Classification (SOC) 174
Stantec 141, 187
stated preferences 77
Statement of Influence 178
Statements of Community Involvement 35
Steiner, R. 115
STEM 52
stepping stone economy 180
stereotypes 43, 59, 85, 87
Stevenson, F. 60
Stirling Prize 40
Stock Orchard Street 118, *119*
Storror 102
story 208

strategy 60, 138, 169
street closure 102
Street Vote 144
stress 98, 108
Stride Treglown 187
student accommodation 55
subcontracting 37
subjectivity 34, 52
subsidiarity 151
Supplementary Planning Document 169
supply chains 37, 75, 125, 153, 169, 187, 188, 196
Supply Change 169
surveillance 83, 85, 90, 93
surveyors 155
sustainability 16, 76, 78, 83, 90, 103, 105, 107, 145, 162, 168, 174, 193, 198, 210
sustainability assessment 35
Sustainable Outcomes Guide (RIBA) 76
swales 102
Sweden 21, 164, 184
systems thinking 59, 139, 175

talent (attracting) 42, 154
targets 31, 35, 74
Tasmania 130, 131
taste 61, 115–117
tastescapes 125
tax 16, 54, 55, 56, 209; inheritance 30
Taylor and Hind 130
Taylor, P. 187
Taylor Wimpey 39
technological change 35, 93, 164
teenagers 22
Teilhard de Chardin, P. 4, 116
temperature 103, 104
temporary accommodation 17
tenants (council) 59, 60
tenure 16, 167, 208; neutral 177
terminology 2, 3
terrace house 124, 207
text mining 144, 145
Thames Valley 150
Thames Water 103
Thatcher, Margaret 3, 17
theatre 182
therapy 114, 115
thresholds and in-between spaces 88, 89, 90, 114
Tideway 176
tilted balance 34
time 115 118, 164, 209; lack of 21, 23
Todmorden 105, 106, *107*
toilets 103

Tomlinson, B. 99
Tomlinson, I. 107
topography 137, 141
Totnes 41, 42
tourism 125, 195, 208
Tower Hamlets 169
Towns Fund 169
trade deficit 37
traffic 98, 99, 100, 104, 205
traffic noise 99
transformations 182
transitional phenomena 114, 115
Transition Towns 194
translation 166
transnational elites 127
transparency 137, 155 163, 175, 177, 197, 206, 209
transport 19, 83, 99, 100, 101, 104, 138, 141, 168
Transport for London 156
Trauma 114, 208
The Trauma Cleaner 118
Tree, I. 139, 210
trees 104, 115, 168, 169, 206
The Trespasser's Companion 197
Triodos Bank 177, 194
triple bottom line of sustainability 1, 3, 21, 29, 74, 76, 79, 145 146, 170, 171, 176
trust 36, 62, 64, 98, 137, 138, 149, 150, 170, 174, 177, 180, 206, 210
Tunäker, C. 18
Turner Prize 61, 128
Turner Works 180, *180*, *181*, 182, *182*
Twedwr Jones, M. 35, 138
twenty minute community 146, 152, 161–171, 205, 207
twenty minute neighbourhood 145, 146
2up2down 179

UK Green Building Council 3, *4*
UK Research and Innovation 54
UK Spatial Framework 138
UK Statistics Authority 53, 139
Ulster University 141
Umea University 164
uncanny 118
uncertainty 195
Understory 175
UN Habitat 102, 194
UNICEF 21, 183
United Nations 107
United States of America 21
Unité, Marseilles 118
Universal Basic Income (UBI) 153, 166, 204

Universities 51, 53, 54, 55, 56, 59, 60, 61, 144, 166, 167, 174, 196, 197; civic 196; rankings 197
unpaid work 86
UN Sustainable Development Goals 195
UPP Foundation 196
urban agriculture 58, 88
urban design 6, 84, 99, 126, 162, 163
urban land use 58
Urban Life Strategy Copenhagen 101, 161
Urban Metabolism 139
urban roam 143, 163
urban room 143, 165
Urban Symbiotics 178
Urban Transport Group 99
URBED 79
user experience 166, 182, 184
Utopian thinking 204

vacant land 32
valuation 31, 36, 170, 174, 176, 177
value 29, 43, 73, 87, 146, 151, 152
value analysis 74
value based procurement 75, 209
value engineering 74
Value Handbook 74
value management 73, 74
value maps 145, 146, 151, 154, 162, 164, 168, 170, 171, 197, 198, 199, 206, 209, 210
The Value of Everything 3
values 6, 73
value uplift 32, 155
van 117
Van Beek, N. 61
Van Heeswijk, J. 179
VeloCity *140*, 141
verges (road) 168, 205
viability assessment 31
vibe 119
Victorians 36, 116, 198
views 115
village makers 99
village movement 120
villages 141
virtual reality 183
visioning 61, 126, 127, 182
visually impaired 100
volume house builders 17, 19, 38, 193
voluntary sector 86
volunteering 84, 85, 86, 152 164, 166, 167, 179, 208
voting 16, 144, 145
Vu City 145, 175
vulnerability 18, 19, 23

227

Index

waiting lists 17
Wales 4, 5, 17, 18, 32, 40, 102, 152, 153, 169, 193, 196, 198
walking 19, 20, 98, 99, 100, 101, 102, 146, 161, 205
Warwick, E. 2
waste 29, 33, 205
Watchet 126
water 100, 102, 103, 104, 139, 206
Waterways and Wellbeing 75
Watson, K. 75
Wayshaper Tool 192
wealth (monetary) 127
weather 19, 115
Welby, J. 6, 39, 73
welfare state 6, 33
WELL 76
wellbeing 1, 2, 3, 7, 15, 17, 18, 19, 21, 29, 37, 38, 57, 59, 73–79, 87, 93, 98–108, 123, 126, 144, 149, 152, 153, 156, 164, 167, 174, 175, 191, 197, 204, 208, 210; eudaimonic 1, 137
Wellbeing and the Historic Environment 129
Wellbeing of Future Generations Act (Wales) 2015 5, 204
Welsh Baccalaureate 63
Welsh Government 128, 151, 152
Wessendorf, S. 84
Westminster 149
Weston General Store 182
Weston Super Mare 182, *182*
What White People Can Do Next 198
Whitehead, C. 63
White Heat of Technology Speech 55
White Paper 29
Whiteread, R. 61

Who Owns England 54
Why Architects Matter 51, 182
Wigglesworth, S. 118
Wikihouse 176
Wilderness Therapy 114
wildlife 20, 31, 32, 52, 88, 93, 100, 141, 168, 192, 197, 198, 204, 206, 207, 208
Wildlife Trusts 198
William the Conqueror 30
Wilson, H. 55
Wilson, J. 17
Wimbush, T. 193
Winnicott, D. 114, 115
Wintles 99, *100*
women 18, 30, 42, 52, 59, 85, 103, 116, 118, 191
Women's Safety Map 175
work: unpaid 22
work 22, 113, 166, 187, 207
work experience 167
working from home 162, 164, 205
workspace 180, 205
world building 113
World War II 55, 170
worry 15
Wrigleys Solicitors 192

Yarmouth 77
Yes Men 61
Yokohama International Port Terminal 176
Yorspace 192
young people 16, 21, 23, 34, 86, 87, 105, 120, 150, 164, 178, 183, 188, 195, 206
Your Priorities 144

zero carbon 153, 209
zero hours contracts 5, 23, 55